A Rainbow Book

Also by these authors:
Exploring New Mexico Wine Country

THE LION IN THE MOON
TWO AGAINST THE SAHARA

BABS SUZANNE HARRISON • STAEFAN EDUARD RADA

RAINBOW BOOKS

Copyright ©1994 by Babs Suzanne Harrison and Staefan Eduard Rada
Printed in the United States of America
All rights reserved. No part of this book may be reproduced or
transmitted in any form or by any means, electronic or mechanical,
including photocopy, recording, or any information storage and
retrieval system, without permission in writing from the
publisher. All inquiries should be addressed to Rainbow Books, Inc.
P. O. Box 430, Highland City, FL 33846-0430.

THE LION IN THE MOON
Two Against the Sahara
by Babs Suzanne Harrison and Staefan Eduard Rada
Design by Marilyn Ratzlaff
$19.95
ISBN: 1-56825-006-1
Library of Congress Card Catalog Number: To Follow

Library of Congress Cataloging in-Publication Data

Harrison, Babs Suzanne, 1956-
   The lion in the moon : two against the Sahara / Babs
Suzanne Harrison & Staefan Eduard Rada.
     p.   cm.
   ISBN 1-56825-006-1 : $19.95
   1. Sahara—Description and travel. 2. Harrison, Babs
Suzanne, 1956-   —Journeys—Sahara. 3. Rada, Stephen
Edward, 1943- —Journeys—Sahara. I. Rada, Stephen
Edward, 1943- .II. Title.
DT333.H185 1944   93-375415
916.604'329—dc20   CIP

CONTENTS

Snapshot: Expectations — 9

Chapter 1: Solitude — 17

Chapter 2: Facing the Dream — 24

    Snapshot: First Encounters of the Third World — 30

Chapter 3: Sliding into Africa — 37

    Snapshot: The Woman Behind the Blue Door — 45

Chapter 4: Sweet Money and Bitter — 50

    Snapshot: The Magic Rug Palace — 59

Chapter 5: Algeria on the Horizon — 66

    Snapshot: Wonderfully Lost — 77

Chapter 6: Playing the Black Market — 81

Chapter 7: The Sandman Brings Nightmares — 88

    Snapshot: Good Guys Wear Black — 96

Chapter 8: Blue Skies and More — 99

    Snapshot: The Oasis of my Discontent — 106

Chapter 9: An Evening on the Town — 112

    Snapshot: My Dinner with Moulay — 122

Chapter 10: A Little Detour in the Desert — 132

    Snapshot: Desert Trekkers — 138

Chapter 11: Saharan Crossroads — 145

Chapter 12: Crossing the Line — 153

Snapshot: Into the Black — 162

Chapter 13: The Bowls of Poverty — 167

Snapshot: Tea in the Sahara — 174

Chapter 14: Face to Face with Rambo — 182

Snapshot: Still Looking in Tahoua — 188

Chapter 15: Where Religions Collide — 193

Snapshot: The African Laundromat — 200

Chapter 16: The Great Oil Spill — 204

Snapshot: Do I Have a Deal for You! — 210

Chapter 17: Another Park, Another Dollar — 214

Chapter 18: Sign Painters and Foreign Aid — 222

Chapter 19: Art and Development — 230

Snapshot: Victim of Circumstance — 236

Chapter 20: To Go To Togo — 239

Snapshot: CP's Village — 247

Chapter 21: Unanswered Questions — 253

Snapshot: Fufu and the Marlboro Man — 262

Snapshot: The Curse — 268

Chapter 22: World Class Scams — 273

Snapshot: Visiting a Voodoo Pharmacy — 279

Chapter 23: Goodbye with Regrets — 286

Snapshot:The Lion in the Moon — 290

Postscript: 293

About the Authors — 295

Staefan's material is presented
as, "Chapters."
Babs' is distinguished by
the heading, "Snapshots."

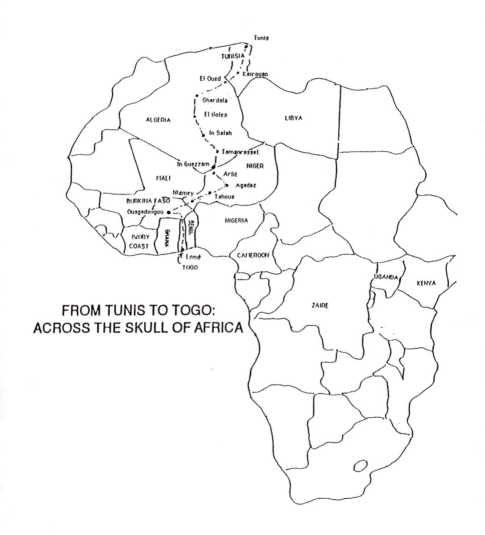

Snapshot

EXPECTATIONS

"So, are you still friends?" everyone wanted to know when I miraculously returned from our two-month odyssey across the Sahara. No one really expected us to be talking to each other.

I had met Staefan on a blind date four months before embarking on our African adventure. I had sworn I would never go on a blind date.

He invited me to breakfast. I accepted.

At dinner the next evening, he brought up Africa. His idea, he related to me with an overabundance of enthusiasm, was to cross the Sahara — the skull of Africa, from Tunis to Togo — and encapsulate the experience in a book. He was looking for a travel partner and writer.

"I'll go," I said.

What was I doing?

I had never even thought about Africa. Yet, I had just volunteered for a two-month trip across the greatest desert on earth, with heat and thirst, and into black Africa with more heat and mosquitoes, with a man I had just met. What must I have been thinking?

But he had beautiful blue eyes and an unguarded sense of adventure I admired.

"Are you crazy?" a girlfriend asked.

I had considered the possibility. I had also read that a writer was supposed to 'experience' life. Alright, so I was a food writer and this wasn't exactly the gastronomic tour of the century. But it did smack of experience.

"Have you told your mother you're going? Do your parents know?" asked the others.

"Haven't told them yet, not all the details anyway," I replied. "I thought I'd tell them when I go home Thanksgiving."

"When are you leaving for Africa?"

"Not 'til January seventh," I said.

"Tell them Christmas."

Yes, maybe I would wait for Christmas. No use giving them too much time to think about it.

The day after Christmas, the Associated Press reported from one of our destinations, Ouagadougou, Burkina Faso: "As of Dec. 25, more than 50 people have been arrested, and their number is likely to double in the days to come, according to disquieting information coming from Burkina Faso," it (the Burkinabé League of Human Rights) said. I read on.

"Earlier Monday, the French news agency *Agence France-Presse* quoted what it called well-informed sources in Ouagadougou as saying seven people were executed Sunday night and Monday morning, and about 30 others, mostly soldiers, were arrested."

My mother's tears were not for joy.

"Don't ever do this to me again," she warned, adding she would be praying for me every night. "I don't know where you get this from," she said, talking about my need for putting myself in dangerous places (i.e. leaving home).

"What will you wear?"

"Where will you take a shower?"

"You are bringing a gun, aren't you, or at least a sharp knife?"

These questions, and many more, spilled from my mother's mouth and in short order were echoed by every family member and friend.

Having recovered from the initial shock, my mother's only parting advice was to wear a wide-brimmed hat with a chiffon scarf to shield the face.

"It's very glamorous, you know. Besides, you have to protect your skin," she cautioned, brushing aside a tear.

SNAPSHOT: EXPECTATIONS

My father, a retired doctor, was worried about my skin as well. He packed a first aid kit that included sutures, pain killers, gauze bandages and a copy of the U.S. Armed Forces Survival Manual. A bottle of Jack Daniels was tucked into my suitcase.

Miss Yana, my facialist, packed me off with moisturizer, eye cream, and sun block along with other jars and tubes for a weekly facial, "for whenever you find water," she joked. "Then come see me as soon as you get back." She especially wanted to see a photo of me with "one of those funny things wrapped around your head," she said.

Even my ex-fiancé had an opinion. A lawyer, and Major in the Marines, he rounded up a jury of his fellow Marines who had been assigned duty in Africa. Together, they tried to persuade me not to go. Finally, blue in the face from arguing, they accepted the verdict that I was "hellbent on destruction." Everyone expected the worst to happen.

As for myself, I didn't know quite what to expect. I instructed my hair stylist to shorten my hair and file my nails to a sensible length. No point in breaking a nail over this silly trip, was there? I made a point of catching the re-released film "Lawrence of Arabia" and read all sorts of books trying to imagine what it would be like in former French West Africa.

Would it be wild and primitive? Exotic bush country? A sinister desert that punished trespassers with mirages, quicksand and broiling heat? Would we encounter headhunters and become involved in a violent coup? My imagination worked overtime.

I decided to keep an open mind and remember the phrase of André Gide: "The less intelligent the white man is, the more stupid he thinks the African."

So while my friends and family anticipated the worst, I became an optimist, though one soaked in SPF 25 sunscreen.

I even expected (hoped? prayed?) that Staefan and I would remain friends throughout the trip. After all, we were going to spend two months together in a desolate place, living under trying conditions with only each other as a constant companion 24 hours a day.

But, more important than remaining friends, however, was the question: What to wear?

Planning a wardrobe would not be easy. If I had any romantic notions about Africa, they were that the weather was interminably hot and sunny.

"What are you going to wear?" the girls wanted to know.

"Oh, just pants and T-shirts, nothing fancy," I replied.

After all, this wasn't "Out of Africa" and I wasn't going to concern myself with something as vain as personal appearance on an adventure trip. I was going to rough it and prove I could, although a little lipstick wouldn't hurt, plus some moisturizer and, what the heck, maybe even a little mascara (smudge-proof, of course).

I had started a pile weeks before of what I would take: two pairs of long pants with zippered pockets, several T-shirts, two long-sleeved shirts, a sweatshirt and jacket. I'd wear one pair of shoes and one belt that coordinated with everything. I would travel light and fast.

My packing became complicated when my Marine ex-fiancé volunteered his services. A military issue duffel bag was hauled out and we made a tour of his house. As I held the bag open, he threw in the appropriate desert props from various closets and shelves crammed with exotic tools of the trade. Unfortunately, everything was drab olive, not my best color.

Staefan had warned me not to bring anything remotely military looking. African security police and border guards were paranoid about foreign mercenaries and political coups. Equipment that sniffed of the military, including canteens and hunting knives, was suspect. They were intriguing, none the less, and hard to resist. Surely no one would take me for a mercenary.

Into the bag went an emergency signal mirror in case we became stranded, a bush hat with netting that tied at the neck to keep out deadly mosquitoes, a military rain poncho for killer downpours, fatigues, and other bits of must-have equipment. I did, however, nix the machete.

Standing on a ladder in the last closet, the Major reached into the dark recesses of the top shelf and hauled down military

SNAPSHOT: EXPECTATIONS

13

issue wool shirts, a down vest and heavy gloves.

"I won't need all this, we're going to the Sahara," I explained. "It's going to be hotter than hell."

"It gets cold in Africa, take it," he ordered.

His admonition would come back to haunt me as, wet and shivering cold, I would sit out an intense tropical rain storm in El Golea, an oasis in the Algerian Sahara.

I had been certain it would never be this cold, nor rain this much. So certain, I had thrown out all the warm clothes provided by my mentor in a last minute packing frenzy before rushing to the airport. It would not be "hotter than hell" until we were a thousand miles into the Sahara, several weeks later.

Thanks to friends and relatives, I had everything I needed. Or so I thought.

What if something happened to my shoes? Being a size 10 AAA, I'd be doomed. In went a second pair of Reeboks. Who knows when we'd do laundry or take a shower? Seven sets of socks and lingerie seemed the absolute minimum, along with additional body powder and *eau de toilette*. Wouldn't shorts be splendid for riding in the truck, plus tank tops? In they went. Perhaps a long skirt and blouse in case we were invited someplace formal? With sandals and another belt, just for a change, the pile took on new proportions.

Still, something was missing. I called L.L. Bean.

In the predawn hours, I was suffering mild writer's block as I attempted to finish two months' worth of assignments before I left — three days from now. Shopping would help me relax. Bean was the only store open at this hour. I flipped through the winter catalogue and found several items necessary for the trip. Why hadn't I thought of this before?

I would charge it on my new Visa card issued through the Junior League. A small percentage of each purchase went toward the League's projects. If I couldn't volunteer my time the least I could do was shop. Every member was expected to do her part.

I picked up the receiver and punched in the toll-free number. A recording put me on hold. Must be a lot of writer's block out there tonight, I thought to myself. Or other insomniacs heading for Africa.

A perky voice came on the line. "What item number do you wish?" The process was not unlike a game show.

I dutifully read the number.

"That is the Bollé mountaineering glasses?" she asked.

"Right!" I thought these would be perfect for those Saharan sandstorms.

"We have that one in stock. I have reserved one for you. May I have the next item number please?"

I repeated the number for the Chinese silk long underwear, a must for driving our Mercedes UNIMOG through Europe. Again, she reserved me a pair in off-white.

The game went on, the tension building until I lost on the Australian crushable hat.

"We will have to back order the hat. It's a very popular item," she assured me.

Pity, I had no time to back order. With a large package due to arrive by Federal Express, I experienced that natural high known to successful shoppers who, mistakenly, think they have finally achieved the perfect wardrobe.

Once again I believed I was prepared for the trip. The right clothes, and plenty of them, neon orange hiking shoes to accessorize all that drab olive, sixty rolls of film, even cloth napkins and tableware that coordinated with our folding table and chairs. What else could I possibly need?

Plenty, as it turned out. But I had no idea at the time.

My first visit to Africa — my first visit to a Third World country — would reveal I had sorely mis-packed. Cosmetics became a luxury I had neither the time nor desire to use. As for all the changes of clothes, they remained packed in a duffel bag. A favorite pair of pants, T-shirt and denim shirt became a uniform I wore and even slept in on cold nights.

Taking a daily shower proved to be an ordeal of ice cold water and undressing in the dark and dirty stalls while men lurked in the corners. Vanity and pretense quickly fell to the wayside.

SNAPSHOT: EXPECTATIONS

What I needed much more than cute shoes and sexy sunglasses were the intangibles: a sense of humor, perspective, resourcefulness and determination. These would prove far more valuable than anything L.L. Bean could hope to provide.

If only I had known.

1

SOLITUDE

When the sun rises in the Sahara it makes nary a sound.

This may seem an all-too-obvious observation, but all my life I had associated the rising of the sun with certain noises: the cry of a baby, the distant bark of a dog, a bird's song, rooster's crow, engines and horns, radios, the muted tick of a clock—those small reminders of the churn of civilization—until in my mind they had become inseparable.

But deep in the Sahara, there is no sound. The sun rises an orphan accompanied by nothing more than the pall of silence, a silence so deep and profound it absorbs all matter, including your thoughts; even before they occur, it seems. Not only is sound absent, but so are disturbances of any kind—the skitter of an ant, the spurt of a jackrabbit, the dance of a leaf. In this great vacuum there is no visible life; no sense of time, of distance, of past, present or future.

Black holes are supposed to exist in space where gravity is so strong all matter, light included, is thought to collapse and disappear. Scientists, intent on their heavenly observations, have overlooked the black hole that is the Sahara.

It is a prehistoric place, moon-like, alien and inhospitable. Nature exists in its raw, primordial state. Soil and life have been peeled back by hundreds of years of drought and eroding wind to reveal the underearth—piles of naked volcanic rock, powdery sand, alkaline dust, and crusted salt flats left from ancient lakes.

One moment the sky is blue, the next the wind bursts forth from absolute stillness driving the sand before it in sheets obliterating the sun and shifting great dunes. A few hours later the sun burns through the vail and shines brightly.

There exists a profound sense of trespass when crossing the Sahara; that the footprints and tire tracks left behind don't belong; that intruders aren't welcome. Nature has its private places, too. It could be the Sahara, like the polar ice caps, are God's inner sanctum, intended only for his or her private use and kept severe on purpose.

The very inhospitableness of the place, the absence of water, of life, the intense heat, the wind and blowing sand are nature's 'keep out' signs that mankind has misinterpreted as an invitation and challenge. If that is true, then for several weeks the Princess and I violated the sanctity of one of nature's most stunning and memorable secrets.

A thousand miles deep into the Algerian Sahara, at the first hint of dawn, I would tumble out of the MOG, our four-wheel-drive African cruiser, and scale a small mountain of yellowish-brown sand to face the east and patiently await the sun's appearance. Not a whisper arose from the deadness around me.

Huddled in my leather coat, my hands stuffed deep in the pockets trying to beat off the chill of a forty-degree January morning, I searched the horizon thinking of the Tuaregs, the Berbers and Fulani, those tough, resilient nomads who roamed these desolate spaces with their camel-skin tents searching for water and a few blades of grass.

They called the Sahara home, at least part of it. There were still vast stretches that even these seasoned desert dwellers avoided. Sadly, the frequent droughts of the last decade and expanding desert have forced many of these people into settlements to become shop keepers or farmers. To see nomads now is a rare treat. Even camel caravans have become little more than a romantic notion.

Folklore tells of eighteenth-century Arab traders snaking across the desert from oasis to oasis with a train of twenty thousand camels that stretched for miles. They carried cloth, tools, knives and beads to the south returning a year or two later loaded with ivory, gold and slaves. It's an image worthy

SOLITUDE

Vast seas of sand with their wind-sculpted dunes remain the classic image of the Sahara.

of Hollywood.

Behind the scenes thousands died of thirst and exhaustion. Water holes dried up; dunes shifted; whole camel trains were swallowed never to be seen again. It was a killing kind of life. Three Saharan crossings were considered a lifetime's work; five were phenomenal. It was easier for us in our motorized cocoon, but still not without risk.

Sitting on that dune my mind moved ahead to when our gear would be stowed and I would climb into the cab of the Mog ready for the day's journey. I would always pause before pressing the starter button for a short prayer. What if nothing happened? What if the batteries were dead; if sand had choked the carburetor; if a cracked radiator hose had leaked away our coolant during the night; if a fan belt snapped, a water pump froze or a transmission bearing burned out?

A thousand 'what ifs' raced through my mind as I reached for that button. At that moment the future was frozen. I braced for that hollow, dead 'click' that signaled disaster. Fortunately, we never had to confront the *'what ifs?'*

When the sun came, it rose swiftly, freezing my presence on the dune like the torch of a night watchman suddenly switched on to catch a trespasser in the act. Freeing itself from the earth's curvature, the sun cast the desert in hues of oranges and yellows before pausing above the horizon to throw it's warm glow across my cold face. In that instant, I knew I was looking into the face of God.

The Princess and I were three weeks into our two-month African odyssey. We had set out to cross the sandy skull of West Africa from the Mediterranean city of Tunis to the port city of Lomé, Togo, on the Gulf of Benin, a distance of 3500 miles. It was the equivalent of driving from Vancouver, British Columbia, to Key West, Florida, through some of the poorest and most desolate stretches on earth.

I had met her a few short months earlier on a blind date in Dallas. Both of us had nearly cancelled; she had a sick cat and I was madly trying to cram a week's worth of business into three days before returning to my home in Santa Fe. We finally managed an early Saturday morning breakfast at a greasy spoon ham 'n' eggs joint on lower Greenville Avenue. I was late.

As I opened the door a tall woman with black hair cut in a chic French style and wearing round, steel-rimmed John Lennon dark glasses brushed past me, a newspaper tucked under her arm. She slid into a booth next to the window and buried herself in the paper.

I surveyed the crowd for an expectant face. I had no idea who to look for. We had not identified ourselves. There were single men and couples. She was the only single woman. I approached her table.

"Are you the person I'm looking for?" I asked, hesitantly. Blind dates were always hard to confront.

She looked over the top of her glasses. "I think so," she responded without a smile. "Are you who I'm waiting for?"

I nodded and slid into the opposite booth while she pushed the paper off the table. She really wasn't my type, I concluded in an instant. Fashionably dressed, even at this hour, she contrasted sharply with my worn Levis and tennis shoes.

SOLITUDE

21

"You didn't have any trouble finding this place?" I asked, looking for an opening gambit.

"No. I know it well. I reviewed this restaurant a couple of years ago."

She nodded toward a framed article on the wall across the room. I took a closer look. It was from a Dallas magazine, yellow-brown from age. Her lengthy name was displayed in prominent letters under the headline. I had never dated anyone who used all their names. I was doubly on guard.

Breakfast progressed well. The small talk flowed. She was a freelance writer for the Dallas paper and specialized in food, wine, and travel. I, too, was a writer of sorts, I admitted, although with me it was more a hobby than a livelihood. We found a few other threads in common. She invited me for dinner the next night at one of the 'in' restaurants downtown.

The next evening I responded to the challenge by pulling out my best pair of jeans, freshly washed and ironed, and black loafers. She, as feared, was dressed to the nines.

Dinner went even better than breakfast. She had studied art history and French; traveled a bit, the Caribbean, Europe, all the usual places; lived in Paris a year and had worked in the Paris showroom of a French designer. Truly a Princess, I thought.

Talk drifted to the subject of places we would like to visit. She told me her's—Thailand, Singapore, Malaysia. I wanted to cross the Sahara, I volunteered. It had long been a dream of mine. I had lived a year in west-central Africa in Cameroon on a Fulbright three years earlier and Africa was in my blood. I wanted to go back. The States were too predictable, too commercial, too boring. Only Africa offered the unpredictability of true adventure. I have this idea for a book, I explained, but haven't found the right person. I could see her eyes light up.

"I want to go with you," she blurted out, leaning across the table.

It was a response I had not expected particularly as I hadn't even said I was actually going.

I had often traded travel fantasies with dates on a casual basis, never expecting much more than token interest, which was usually what I got. Mental travels could be bantered about without posing a threat to either side. In one short sentence, though, the Princess had called my bluff. Was she really serious? I had my doubts.

Most people, I had discovered, were passable tourists but uncomfortable travelers as they lacked the ability to empathize with alternative cultures and lifestyles. They were content in the safety of their small routines.

There is little in the American experience that prepares one to cope with the physical, emotional and psychological hardships of Africa. I am not referring to the well orchestrated tourist routes through the game parks of Kenya where most Americans venture, but to the vast remains of the continent, where there is no tourist industry; where infant mortality reaches forty percent; where people sleep in mud huts, wash clothes in muddy streams and drink from buckets drawn from open wells; where toilets are smelly pits and the dust blows and the flies swarm and the mosquitos bite. That is the reality of most Africans; it is not the reality of Americans. By all appearances, it was not the reality of this woman across the table.

I promised little more than to consider it. We would keep in touch. Even if she were serious, was I? We need our dreams— they offer escape from life's tedium. But when you live them, you tame them, destroy them and must fabricate new ones. Was this dream important enough to destroy it? With what would I replace it?

Later that night, as I thought through the evening, I concluded she couldn't be serious, not with a name like Babs. She had never been to Africa; she knew nothing about it. It would be a tough trip. I doubted her suitability. Yet, it might be worth the risk. She was a fascinating woman and gutsy in a naive way.

Her maternal grandfather was a California doctor who went to the Philippines in 1900, married a socially prominent Filipino woman, and stayed. His daughter, Babs' mother, was born in Manila and whisked off to boarding school in England at fourteen for her high school years, returning only occasionally for brief summer visits.

SOLITUDE

At nineteen, upon graduation, she returned to the Philippines in the summer of 1941. Only a month remained before the Japanese invasion.

Holding both Filipino and American passports, Babs' mother and grandmother were interned in a Japanese POW camp for three-and-a-half years until MacArthur liberated the country. They were transported by Army troop ship to San Francisco. Babs' father, an Army doctor, was also on the ship. Her parents were married two years later in San Francisco.

The Princess was born in Texas, but not raised there. In her mother's tradition, she was sent to a private girl's boarding school in Virginia, then on to Hollins, a women's college before returning to Dallas to study journalism at SMU. She wrote for a Dallas home and garden magazine and later for the Dallas paper. Somewhere along the route, she had been engaged to a Dallas attorney, but had canceled the engagement three days before her wedding. A few years later we met over breakfast.

The question continued to roll around my mind: Could a woman like this survive Africa? Equally to the point, could we survive each other?

I had often thought during my year in Cameroon I had not known a single woman who would have been comfortable with the experience. Would the Princess be the exception?

My uncertainty was underlined a few weeks later when planning was well along. She called from Dallas.

"I just bought my sleeping bag," she gushed. "I rolled it out on the floor and crawled in. It's wonderful. It's so cute. I've never been in a sleeping bag before."

Quietly, I beat my head against the wall.

2

FACING THE DREAM

It was August when we met. We decided to leave in January and return in March. Not only would it be winter in the Sahara with temperatures ranging from the mid-forties at night to the high eighties during the day, it was the slowest time of year for my business. In the next few months, other than documents and shots, we would have two major problems to surmount: transportation and supplies.

As for transportation, renting a car would be impossible. We would have to buy. But what and where?

I had met a rancher in southwestern New Mexico who owned a unique Mercedes off-road vehicle known as a UNIMOG, a civilian version of a small German Army truck. It featured a six-cylinder gas engine, six gears forward, two in reverse, two-wheel drive, four-wheel drive and a special lever, which when engaged, would lock the transmission enabling all four wheels to drive.

In normal 4 X 4 configuration only two wheels actually drive: one in the rear and one in the front. If the drive wheels slip, power is transferred through a differential to the opposite wheels. The MOG, with the differential locked and all four wheels driving, was, in effect, a rolling tank, capable of fording a three-foot river or climbing a 45-degree embankment. It was virtually impossible to get stuck, in mud or sand, as we learned to our immense relief later on.

The MOG had numerous backup systems — three fuel strainers, a necessity for the dirty gas sold in Africa; dual batteries;

Our African cruiser rests under a thorn tree in the Sahara desert.

mechanical and electric fuel pumps and 35-gallon internal gas tanks, which we were to supplement with five, 5-gallon jerry cans giving us a range of about 600 miles, sufficient, we hoped, to cross the most desolate stretches.

In the cab, dual bucket seats straddled the engine compartment. Between the seats was a maze of gear levers and knobs. Above the passenger seat was a turret manhole enabling the passenger to stand on the seat and poke through the roof—a great camera nest. Behind the front cab was a second compartment, about four-by-six, where we had bunks installed creating a comfortable and secure sleeping compartment. Immediately behind the sleeping quarters were lockable storage compartments, one on each side, and a large one at the rear, which became our kitchen.

With the rancher's help I was able to locate a MOG in Germany, which in spite of its 1963 vintage had low miles and was in excellent mechanical condition. This particular MOG had been used as a rescue truck by a municipal fire station. Although the emergency lights and siren had been dismantled, it was still fire engine red, the perfect disguise for a knock-off

Army truck. We could cross the continent self-contained, like a steel shelled turtle.

Due to the constant threat of political coups, military equipment is barred from most African countries, even down to canteens and knives. An olive drab paint job, or any dark color, would have aroused immediate suspicion and certainly jeopardized the trip. We might possibly have made it through but only at the expense of exhaustive explanations and continuous and thorough searches.

The only other item that would have placed us in greater jeopardy was a gun.

Both of us were asked during our days of preparation if we weren't going to take a gun 'to protect ourselves.'

It's an unfortunate tribute to the ignorance of Americans about Africa that the subject of guns would even be raised. True, there is unrest in different parts of the continent, in the extreme east, for example, in Ethiopia and Somalia, or in the southern African country of Angola or to the extreme west where the Spanish Sahara borders Morocco.

Distances are so great, however, that what happens in one part of Africa has little bearing on the rest of the continent. Envision a European couple planning a trip to Dallas being warned to bring a gun because, 'there's trouble in San Francisco.'

The kind of protection that's needed—from malaria, dysentery and the psychological stress brought on by culture shock — a gun won't provide. The best defense for any African traveler is soap, a water filter, shots, common sense and a healthy sense of humor.

Africans, by and large, are relaxed about most everything except internal security. If a gun happened to be uncovered at one of the many security checks experienced on a daily basis in most African countries, it would probably result in some mean-spirited interrogation at the least, and most likely deportation accompanied by a few days in jail in the meantime. As a reminder, African jails don't have television, flush toilets, fresh water, or food. If your relatives are preoccupied and fail to bring your supper, you starve.

FACING THE DREAM

We had read every book we could find on North and West Africa and those on crossing the Sahara. Still, planning for supplies proved to be a shot in the dark. How much water would we need? Was it available? Where? Would it need filtering? How about cooking? What could we buy fresh? What should we bring?

What about medicine? Would aspirin be sufficient, or should we load up on antibiotics? What if we got sick or lost? Broke a leg?

How long would it take to cross the Sahara? How many miles could we cover in an hour; a day; a week? We had five borders to cross. What were they like? How long would each take? Were there roads? The Michelin map said yes. What were they like? A red line on a piece of paper could mean a paved highway, a mud track or a dream. (All three proved correct.) We only had two months. What if we ran out of time? Of money?

We planned to pick up the MOG in Hamburg and drive south through Frankfurt, Zurich and Milan to Genova to link up with the Mediterranean ferry to Tunis. But it was winter. How long would it take to get through Switzerland? What day did the ferry leave? How much did it cost? An old steamship guide said once a week on Fridays but didn't give a price; a recent guide listed times and cost as 'unavailable.' The Italian tourist office in New York didn't know, neither did travel agents.

We decided to arrive in Genova on Thursday gambling the ferry left on Friday or Saturday. If we guessed wrong and missed it by a day we would lose a valuable week. As it turned out, we guessed right. The ship left every Saturday evening for the twenty-five hour crossing to Tunis but we needed to register two days early to guarantee passage.

Planning trips at home is based on an implicit understanding of certain constants. Interstate driving requires so many hours to go a given distance. Motels and restaurants saturate the landscape at known prices. Phones dot every corner and credit cards are available for emergencies. State boundaries are curiosities, not impediments. We are able to plan, because life is reasonable, logical and predictable.

There is little that is reasonable, logical or predictable in

Africa. Distance is measured in days, not kilometers. Time is of little consequence. Border crossings are obstacles that consume a few hours or entire days. One security post would wave us through while the next, quite arbitrarily it seemed, would subject us to an hour-long search. Motels do not exist and most restaurants are convincing arguments to diet.

If God wills it is a comment heard all too frequently. It means just that. If something is accomplished it was only by the 'Will of God.' It is also an expression that pardons a multitude of sins. It is God's Will, not ineptness or lack of motivation that delays the shipment, or accounts for your car not being fixed when promised, or for the appointment never kept.

As Americans, we believe in free will; most Africans, in a captive will. The chasm between these two concepts is so wide it cannot be simply understood. It means we don't share the same thought patterns, the same values or visions, or the same sense of the purpose and destiny of humans on this earth. We approach each other as aliens from different planets.

As frustrating as this philosophy is to those of us who live in industrialized societies, it is very much in tune with primitive, agricultural societies. Fatalism is a natural philosophy of a people victimized by the overpowering forces of nature. Generations have seen their crops wither from heat, their homes washed away by swollen rivers and their children mysteriously sicken and die. The vagaries of life are so mysterious and so beyond their feeble powers to influence that taking refuge in God's Will seems the sensible recourse.

We began this trip with the smugness of those raised in the American culture where science is religion and all things are probable, if not possible. Natural disasters, while inconvenient, are often viewed as opportunities to rebuild, to make the old better. Society as a whole scarcely skips a beat. Disasters are not a source of fatalism that reinforces feelings of impotence.

It didn't take long, however, before the philosophy of fatalism began to influence our behavior and decisions. The concept of planning, for instance, implies a command of the future. It is the most outrageous of conceits. Since, as Africans

FACING THE DREAM

believe, only God can read the future, it is much wiser to content oneself with the present.

The Princess and I, being of the other persuasion, had our crafted plan for the day, for the week and for the entire trip. By the end of our first week on African soil we had junked it all and learned to just live. Time spent in Africa has a way of reordering one's perspective, of setting one straight with nature. To an African mother who has just lost her third child out of five, there is no question who's boss.

Snapshot

FIRST ENCOUNTERS OF THE THIRD WORLD

Without makeup and wearing the same clothes I left Dallas in four days earlier, I had hoped to remain inconspicuous. Impossible.

I was one of the few women aboard the Habib, a Tunisian car ferry, bound from Genova to Tunis where our adventure would officially begin.

Within moments of boarding the ship, a steward in a crisp white jacket took my hand and grandly offered to be of assistance.

"You could help us find our cabin," I suggested in French.

He led us into the bowels of the ship, down one flight of stairs after another, until we were in a long, low and very narrow corridor. He chatted at me all the way.

He was excited I would be visiting his homeland, Tunisia, and promised to bring literature on his country to my cabin. He went on to offer all his male services, which I politely refused. Staefan, who did not understand much French, was obviously not following the gist of this conversation.

The steward pointed down a corridor. "Your cabin is at the end," he smiled.

Sliding open the miniature door, I was sure the pea-green closet with four thin bunks could not possibly be ours. What had happened to the cabin for two with private bath the ticket agent had promised?

"This is not ours," I complained to the steward. "We were supposed to be alone."

SNAPSHOT: FIRST ENCOUNTERS

"Please, your tickets." He compared them against the number on the door. "Yes, this is it," he confirmed. He still had that smile. Was he smiling with us or at us?

"Two months in Africa, you will be very black," he assured me, kissing my hand as he said goodbye. I wondered if he meant my attitude or my skin.

We entered our closet to a standing-room-only crowd. Luckily, our roommates for the crossing were a quiet and mannerly Swiss couple, who were taking a year to travel through Africa. They had been planning their trip for over a year and were amazed we had begun to plan only a few months ago. More than anything, I envied her clean, shiny hair.

Staefan and I occupied the lower bunks across from each other so we could talk. A Naugahyde mattress, tubular pillow and thin blanket were the only amenities. The Swiss had brought their sleeping bags and chocolate chip cookies. The Swiss are always prepared.

One women's bathroom served second class. It was down a long smoke-filled corridor lined with staring men. A sign on the door indicated 'Dames,' but men were going in and out. Each time the door opened, a horrendous odor escaped the room. I desperately didn't want to go in but nature was forcing the issue.

I opened the door to the yellow-tiled room. It had not been cleaned in months. A few men were using the facilities; others had different thoughts in mind. They leaned against the wall and watched as I entered. There were toilet paper holders, but no paper. I had none with me.

This was not the picture of an overnight ferry with a first-class cabin Staefan had painted on the phone. It wasn't even the second-class cabin the ticket agent had promised. I remembered telling a friend how romantic it would be taking a ferry to Tunis.

"Don't be so sure," he had warned me.

"No, really. They have first-class cabins, dining rooms, everything," I said.

"Don't get your hopes up," he replied.

My friend had a talent for being on the mark. Perhaps

sensing my naiveté, he had presented me with a scarab on a silk cord before I left for the Dallas-Fort Worth airport. He had acquired it on his last adventure overseas and thought it might help me on this one. I would finger it continuously throughout the trip only to lose it at the very end on a beach in Togo. Perhaps by then I didn't need it anymore.

As I made my way back to our cabin, I fingered the talisman and thought it best to lower my expectations. Not that I was depressed, by any means. Italian wine was still in good supply and I was drinking it all the time now. I would have to visit the bathroom again, soon.

As the ferry departed from Genova, birthplace of the famous and infamous explorer, Christopher Columbus, I ran up on deck to watch the sun cast a golden haze on the ancient pastel-hued city that spilled into the sea. The engine rumbled beneath my feet. As we slipped from the dock, I said farewell to Europe and the familiar. For the next two months, life would be very different.

Tunis was twenty-five hours south. The time would pass quickly, I hoped. For the moment I was content to study my shipmates: a handful of wild-looking European adventurers, a few Australians and hundreds of intense Tunisian men with dark piercing eyes, deeply lined, olive-skinned faces and coarse, black, wiry hair cropped close to the head. They would look directly into my eyes as I passed, not at my body as other men would.

The Tunisian men were as I had remembered them from my college days in Paris: dark and brooding with impossibly mismatched clothes. But the Tunisians on the ship, still motley-dressed, displayed a different attitude. They kept a respectable distance.

College days were in 1976 when I had decided to celebrate my country's bicentennial by spending the year in Marquis de Lafayette's mother country, France. Happily ensconced in the 16th *arrondissement*, an elegant neighborhood in Paris, I played with friends in the more colorful parts of the city knowing I had a cushy home base to which I could retreat.

There were many North Africans (Tunisians and Algerians) who had come to 'The City of Light' in hope of finding work.

SNAPSHOT: FIRST ENCOUNTERS

They would congregate in the seedier sections of the city around the cheap bars of Montmartre where the WCs were not unlike the ones on this ferry, except in Paris they had indentations in the tile floor for your feet.

The North Africans of Paris would chase me down the street. They were persistent and extremely bold in their attempts. My protestations served only to entice them. In Paris, away from their home and culture, they exercised all their suppressed desires. But once headed for home, as the Tunisians on this ship were, their strict Arab culture and mannerisms returned.

Remembrances of things past haunted me as I stood in line in the Habib's dimly-lit cafeteria. Surrounded by hordes of Tunisian men, I was squeezed in so tightly I could not move. A wave of claustrophobia washed over me. I desperately wanted to run, anywhere, just to be away from all these men. It was impossible. There was no where to hide. I concentrated on the *plat du jour* that was being dished out.

The choice was fish or chicken with ratatouille. Since we were at sea, I chose fish. A salad of sardines, beets and carrots was served along with fresh fruit and yogurt for dessert. Bottles of mineral water and red or white wine completed the meal. It was filling and in some respects better than cafeteria food back home.

The next day's breakfast was similar, and so was lunch, except we did not have enough Tunisian money for both of us to eat. Staefan had not bought enough dinars in Genova and the ship's bank would not open until mid-afternoon, after the dining room had closed. The cafeteria cashier was totally unsympathetic. He didn't want dollars: no dinars, no dinner.

We shared one plate of food with two forks. All around us, Tunisian workers each had a multi-course meal complete with a bottle of wine. It was an odd feeling to be a 'wealthy' American yet without the resources to buy one's own food, especially when mealtime was the only diversion on board.

Meals did little to eat up the time, however. I prolonged small pleasures to fill the evening hours. Relaxing in the pea-green closet was not one of them. I would walk the deck, slowly peeling oranges as if they were Fabergé eggs and eating the

34 THE LION IN THE MOON

sections as if they were the first I had ever tasted. Or I would dissect a chocolate cream-filled cookie piece by piece and think of the things I should have brought: a Walkman and lots of tapes, a few good paperbacks, perhaps the entire set of Will and Ariel Durant's, "The Story of Civilization" I had been meaning to read. I could certainly get a jump on it, at least make it through the Renaissance.

I had ruthlessly eliminated such excesses from my duffel bags at three in the morning on the day of departure thinking they took up too much space. I had wanted to totally absorb the experience of Africa and its people. No books for this traveler. I was going to soak up atmosphere and write copious notes. After a couple of hours on the Habib, I had seen and written everything I could think of importance. Only twenty hours to go: wine supply still good, humor in check.

I set out again to explore the ship from stern to bow. First class had its own bar and lounge decorated in serene shades of blue complete with swivel chairs. Large windows overlooked the ocean and music was piped in from somewhere unseen. Their bathrooms, from what my olfactory sense could pick up, were no better than Second Class.

Through a narrow passage and down a floor was the Second Class lounge, a large rec room crammed with second-hand sofas, chairs and card tables. No decorating scheme was apparent. It was crowded with men smoking, playing cards, and huddling in groups. The music was live, provided by the passengers. As the hours dragged by, the Arabic singing slowly degenerated into an off-key melody, then disappeared altogether as the passengers slumped over the chairs and tables, drunk and asleep.

I spied an espresso machine I had missed earlier and felt instantly revived. I sat alone at a tiny table and sipped the strong brew from a small china cup. The room was crowded with the same drinking, smoking, singing men aimlessly sprawled across tables, on the floor and leaning against walls.

At midnight, thoroughly exhausted, I retired to our miniscule closet. An overhead vent shot cold air into the room chilling the Naugahyde mattress. My thin blanket was not warm

SNAPSHOT: FIRST ENCOUNTERS

enough. I curled up in a ball and covered my arms and body with clothes from my duffel bag.

Strangers, searching for an empty bunk, constantly slid open our door flooding the compartment with fluorescent light. Faint singing drifted in from somewhere down the corridor. I slept fitfully shaking from the cold. After a few hours, I was wide awake.

I decided topside was the place to be. The sea air blew away all disagreeable odors. It would be quiet. There would not be many people on deck, I hoped, since it was night with nothing to see. I leaned against the rail and stared at the white wake cut by the bow against the blackness of the ocean. Below a door opened and the crew began to dump the ship's garbage overboard. For ten minutes, bag after bag was thrown into the sea. Shocked, I watched as the procession of bags rode the ocean swells into the curtain of blackness.

What good would it do to recycle at home when these ships, these Third World countries, dumped their untreated sewage and garbage directly into the ocean? The Mediterranean must be a swirl of garbage. Soon, returning Tunisians will be able to walk home from Genova to Tunis from one bag of garbage to the next.

We docked at seven the next night and the Habib regurgitated her load of passengers and cargo as a whining Arabic tune played over the loudspeaker. Half-dazed from a sleepless ferry ride, I floated down the gangway among a sea of strange faces. Like gentle waves, they pushed me along until I washed up at customs.

Gun-toting officials in important-looking uniforms were yelling at me. I did not understand and simply stared at them.

"Ouvrir, Ouvrir!" they finally demanded in French, grabbing one of my bags and shaking it.

I unzipped it for inspection. Another customs man ordered me to remove the lens cap from my camera so he could look inside it. Satisfied, he nodded his head and motioned for me to move on. No one returned my smile. I lost it quickly and headed out into the unknown.

I felt already as if my familiar self had ceased to exist. It wasn't me, really, that huddles of Tunisian men looked at and surrounded. I had crawled deep inside my body and was looking out, detached, a mere android observing life.

As we descended deeper into Africa, I would withdraw deeper and deeper into myself. My body and mind would acquire a protective shield, unadorned and impenetrable.

Many months later, I would pull out two photographs of myself: one taken in Tunisia at the beginning of our trans-Saharan trek, the other in Togo at the end. The difference would amaze me, not only in my physical appearance but in the mind-sets I can read in my two faces.

I did not realize it when I stepped foot on North African soil, but as the steward had predicted, I was already beginning to turn 'quite black.'

3

SLIDING INTO AFRICA

Our descent down the southern slopes of the Alps into Italy was the beginning of our slide into the chaos of Africa.

The first hint was the craziness of Genova with its ant-like mini Fiats skitting here and there, climbing onto sidewalks and even sides of hills to park, criss-crossing the road in front and behind the MOG like insects. I felt as if I had poked a stick into an anthill.

The second warning was our ferry, the Habib. Tunisian registered, it was similar in appearance to the cruise ships that ply the Carribbean, except the stern opened to reveal a lower deck able to accommodate a hundred or so cars, vans and campers.

I shoved my way through the crowd of short, olive skinned men toward the ticket window to purchase our passage. Being a foot taller than the others I was spotted by the agent who yelled the price over the heads of three men vying with each other to shove their money through a small window. I edged closer, pulled out a roll of money, peeled off several fifty dollar bills and pushed them through the small window.

The crowd became quiet. Someone behind me whispered: "Dollars. He has dollars."

Only dollars could subdue this crowd. They represented something to these men that went beyond money. It was a promise, an ideal, a vision. Ultimately, dollars represented access to the American dream.

I hastily shoved the bills back into my pocket. This was a

tough crowd.

Tickets in hand, I backed off and stood next to the Princess at the far end of the room and watched the shoving match at the window. These were Tunisian workers, short, tough, and muscular, who after months, perhaps years abroad, were heading home with pockets full of liras, francs or marks.

Many were bringing back cars, small beat-up Fiats and Peugeots, their tires flattened from enormous loads. Stacked on the roofs were small refrigerators, washing machines, tires, furniture, food, spare parts — the consumer goods unavailable in their own country.

There are millions like them — Algerians, Turks, Tunisians, Egyptians, Mexicans, Guatemalans — tough, hard-working men who drift from one country to another providing cheap fodder for the furnaces of the industrialized societies. The French use them, so do the Germans, the Italians, the Spanish, Saudis and Americans.

They are the world's permanent underclass of raw labor — uneducated, nameless, faceless, expendable — born into their own social cast system that gives them nothing other than the opportunity to break their backs for a foreign master. They may drift across Europe searching for work but they are rarely allowed to rise above what they were at home. These men are a microcosm of the world's semi-slaves itching for a crack at economic freedom and the opportunity to excell. No wonder they dream of America.

Historically, we have welcomed the rejects of the earth with open arms. We reward effort and ask few questions about the past. Religion and politics bow to opportunity and money. We will not long tolerate an ideology that shackles a person's initiative or interferes with their quest for a buck, legal or otherwise.

America is still the golden lamp that beckons from afar. These people may resent our wealth, but want to be part of it. They may detest our politics but would immigrate in a minute. They are willing to work hard to earn citizenship but are rarely given the chance. Frustrated, they become bitter with despair. Despair turns to jealousy, and jealousy to contempt and hatred for America. But still they would come.

SLIDING INTO AFRICA

Outside the terminal two long rows of cars had formed waiting to roll into the ship's belly. The cars that didn't belong to the Tunisians were owned by Europeans — Germans, Swiss, Dutch, French — bound for vacations in North Africa.

A few were headed for the Sahara with elaborately outfitted Land Rovers, four-wheel-drive Toyotas and various sizes and shapes of German and French trucks with balloon sand tires and oversized gas tanks. Strapped to the sides were sand ladders, jacks and shovels. Jerry cans were mounted in special locking racks. Compartments were full of spare parts, food and five-gallon white plastic containers of water.

I had a funny feeling, as my eyes swept these professionaly outfitted rigs, that in spite of our preparations we were babes in the woods, woefully ignorant, under-equipped and ill-prepared. The vastness and desolation of the Sahara suddenly became a reality. This was not going to be a Sunday drive.

A knot formed in the bottom of my stomach. I had gotten myself, not to mention the Princess, into something I knew little about. But then, I reasoned, there are occasions in life when naiveté is a priceless possession.

I had learned after I left the window that the MOG was being sent on a different ship, one reserved for commercial trucks, and not with us in the hold of the ferry. It would arrive in a different section of the port of Tunis reserved for commercial shipments.

I had made the mistake of refering to the MOG as a truck instead of a camper. That little slip, in addition to our having to pay a higher commercial rate, would cause us considerable grief when we reached Tunis.

The Princess and I climbed aboard the Habib and tried to make ourselves comfortable but it was an impossible situation. We had been assured a private cabin but instead found ourselves packed into a third-class closet with another couple from Switzerland. The bunks were hard, narrow and coated in plastic with no bedding.

We sought refuge in the lounge, but it was crowded with Tunisian workers. They swarmed over the ship filling it with cigarette smoke and empty beer cans: their final binge, no doubt, before returning to the relative austerity of Islamic North Africa. There were few places for us to retreat.

It was after dark the next evening when we stepped from the ferry onto North African soil. We were to stay with friends who were with the Canadian Embassy. I had known them several years earlier in Cameroon and they were expecting us, although I had been unable to provide specifics. Now that we had arrived, I had to let them know. But it wasn't that simple. There were no public phones in sight.

I knocked on an office door. A tired looking man answered.

"Are there public phones in the terminal?" I asked.

"Yes, but they are broken."

"All of them?" He nodded. "Is it possible to use your phone?"

"My phone is broken. I cannot help you."

"Is there a phone that works, anywhere?"

He shook his head. "Try the police station down the road. Maybe their phone works."

It was very dark outside. There were no street lights. I thought of a cab but didn't know where our hosts lived. With bags in tow, we began to walk cautiously down the dark, waterfront road toward town. We had gone only a short distance when a figure approached from the shadows. The Princess moved a bit closer. It was a good place to stay close.

In the faint light I could decipher a uniform with a German cut. He was a policeman, he announced. We explained our situation. He would let us use his phone, if it worked.

We followed him to a small, spooky building off the road. He unlocked the front door and flipped on the single light. In the bare, concrete room was a small wood desk, a chair and a telephone. He toyed with it for a few moments trying to get a dial tone, then handed the receiver to me. Fortunately, our friends were home. Forty minutes later we were sipping Tunisian wine with Max and Frederique in comfortable surroundings, our nerves still frayed from our introduction to North Africa.

I would have to return to the port the next morning before eight to get the MOG, I explained to Max, who was shaking his

SLIDING INTO AFRICA

41

head slowly.

"If you are very lucky it might take only one day," he warned. "But, I would count on several. It might take even a week."

"A week?" My heart sank.

"This is Tunisia. They're better organized than other Arabs, but this isn't Europe. If you had driven the car off the ferry it would've taken only a few hours. But since you didn't." He let the sentence dangle. "It has probably been classified as commercial. Good luck is all I can say."

The next morning Max graciously took the day off and drove us back to the port where we began our frustrating battle to liberate the MOG from Tunisian bureaucracy.

We started at eight sharp and crunched away the hours running from one bureau to another, standing in lines, pleading for attention, criss-crossing the port from building to building, creating a domino effect of paper work as we progressed.

Forms were needed for every conceivable, and often unexplicable, reason: to exit the port, to transit the country, for payment of road taxes, insurance coverage, for police authorization to enter the country, customs inspections, for exemption of commerical duty, to verify personal use. The bundle of documents in my hand grew at every turn.

Each bureau required a special form, each form a signature and each signature a stamp, all from persons located somewhere else who also required a special form before they could sign or stamp the original form. One copy of each rarely proved sufficient. Duplicates were needed but the forms were never provided in duplicate. They had to be Xeroxed at our expense at the only copy machine in the port, which was secured behind locked doors in a separate building located outside the port. Only one man had the key and he was always somewhere else.

By four that afternoon, after running hard for eight hours, I had collected fifteen separate documents, each with two or more stamps and several signatures. My nerves were frazzled; my sense of humor had been dumped by late morning. Only one last signature stood in the way: the chief of the port.

After a twenty-minute wait in line, I laid the bundle of

papers on his desk. He carefully thumbed through the pile asking questions as he progressed. Finally, he pulled a new form from his desk, filled it in and seemed about to sign it, then handed it across the table.

"You must go to the cashier and get a fiscal stamp," he explained. I glanced at the form—it was permission to leave the port, the precise document I had spent all day trying to obtain. I was one form away from being a free man. I glanced at the clock on his desk. It was already four-thirty. In half-an-hour the port would close for the night. We would have to start again in the morning. The thought made me nauseous. It was now a race against time.

I grabbed the form and sprinted to the cashier's window. Five dollars in Tunisian dinars produced a small, blue fiscal stamp at the bottom of the form just below where the chief would sign. When I returned another line had formed in front of his door. I cut to the front and boldly charged in. The chief eyed me with irritation, scratched his signature on the bottom and handed it back.

Twenty minutes later I handed the same form to port security and drove the MOG out the gate. It had been an unbelievably exhausting and frustrating experience. Six months later when I flew to Houston to process the MOG through U.S. Customs, I completed all the paperwork — three simple forms — and drove out of the port in less than ninety minutes.

There seemed no purpose for most of the hurdles other than to test my desire. In fact, there was a purpose behind all the forms, stamps and signatures, and that was the over-riding need of the Tunisian government to create jobs. In most developing societies, where there are few meaningful jobs available, the government becomes the employer of last resort.

In deflating the bureaucracy, which has now become one of the preconditions of the World Bank and the International Monetary Fund for making loans to developing countries, thousands are thrown out of work creating political instability and paranoia in the upper circles of government.

The educated are precisely the people you want to keep

SLIDING INTO AFRICA

43

employed, even if they do nothing meaningful. It is better to have a bloated bureaucracy where nothing happens than to have thousands of educated young people loitering in the streets plotting against the government.

Americans typically approach bureaucracies with the assumption they are user-friendly. Living in a consumer society, we expect our social institutions to be service oriented. As I was to learn and relearn, this is not an attitude widely shared by the world.

A small incident at a bank in Nigér (pronounced Nee-gér and not to be confused with Nigeria, which it borders to the south. People from Nigér are Nigerienes and speak French, while those from Nigeria speak English and are known as Nigerians.) later in the trip nicely illustrates this point.

I had just signed several traveler's checks and passed them through the window with my passport when, for no apparent reason, the clerk, a rotund woman wrapped in bright African cloth with a shiny face, suddenly hung a closed sign in the window, dropped a blind and departed. My checks and passport were still in her possession. I had no idea what to do. She hadn't said a word. Would she be back? When? Had she left for lunch? I had no idea.

After fifteen minutes of pacing the lobby, the blind was suddenly raised, the sign removed and the clerk resumed her seat. She smiled at me as if nothing had happened, and said, "I had to talk to a friend."

I nodded that I understood, but in truth, I didn't. I assumed since I was the customer her job was to serve me. That's not how it works.

Her personal business was more important than bank business and much more important than my business. It never occurred to her that I might need money immediately, that I might be in a hurry or have an emergency.

My sense of urgency about changing money — about doing business, in general — was imported from my own culture and had nothing to do with this woman's priorities. If I had commented to her that she had kept me waiting, she most likely would have been astonished at the thought and would have replied, "waiting for what?" She might also have added, "you're lucky I was only gone fifteen minutes. This was a good friend."

She could have easily just shut the window and told me to come back tomorrow. It's happened to me before. In her culture there isn't much difference between today, tomorrow or sometime next week. They are all pretty much the same. Life goes on. If I choose to operate under a self-imposed sense of urgency, that is my cross to bear, not hers.

Africans die from an assortment of causes. Stress isn't one of them.

Snapshot

THE WOMAN BEHIND
THE BLUE DOOR

Habiba lived behind a blue door in the narrow streets of La Marsa Cubes, a whitewashed neighborhood in the posh section of Tunis. She was employed as a domestic by a diplomatic family who were also our hosts. Working for foreigners, she enjoyed certain advantages which, had she been more modern, would have resulted in a far easier life.

Habiba was not a liberated woman. She did not wear Western clothes and would only appear in public with her head covered. Thanks to Habib Bourguiba, Tunisia's past president and a man intent on dragging his country into the 20th century, women enjoyed many of the rights of men, including the right to vote and attend school. Somehow, many of these privileges were lost on Habiba.

In spite of living in one of North Africa's most modern and progressive cities – only miles from Italy — Habiba continued to wear long, gray, ankle-length skirts and buttoned-up, conservative, monochromatic blouses. The only hint of an inner sparkle was the head scarf of petite yellow and red flowers she knotted tightly under her chin. Several times a day she would kneel on her small prayer rug in the kitchen, face the east towards Mecca, and recite her prayers.

Habiba was thirty years old and proud to be a virgin. She was saving herself, she confided in me, for the right man. How would she know? Allah would send him to her when the time was right. In the meantime, she would practice chastity, recite her prayers five times a day and be a decent Muslim woman.

As housekeeper and cook, Habiba was entitled to a small, private apartment at the rear of the main house. Her employers had tried in vain to convince her to move into these private quarters but she refused. Habiba had a consuming obsession: She feared being raped in the night and losing her chance at marriage and happiness.

It was all very simple, she explained. Happiness was children. There could be no children without a husband, and no husband without virginity. She could not chance losing her passport to marital bliss. To secure her safety, Habiba preferred instead to live in one of the guest bedrooms of the main house.

Unfortunately, there were no male prospects in sight and Habiba was becoming more and more desperate. In her mind, Allah was punishing her for something, although she hadn't the slightest clue what. She retreated further into her religion, exercising greater self-discipline and locking out more of the world as atonement.

Habiba would fade away when Staefen appeared, perhaps a result of her rigid self-discipline in not wanting to expose herself to other men. She and I developed an immediate, if not superficial, relationship. At least she felt comfortable enough to ask questions.

"Doesn't Madame want children?" she would ask me in French more than once.

I found the children issue difficult to confront. She obviously assumed Staefen and I were married. I doubt it occurred to her otherwise. The fact I was unmarried yet a cohabitant with a man might have traumatized her. As a result, I wished to limit her knowledge of my personal situation and any mental anguish it might cause.

"Not just yet," I would answer. "There is plenty of time."

She nodded her head in understanding. Had I told her I was four years older then she and still did not have children, she would have been less sanguine; it might have raised serious doubts in her mind as to my womanhood and generated further probing questions.

SNAPSHOT: THE WOMAN BEHIND THE BLUE DOOR

Classic Tunisian architecture: white to combat the heat, domes to help circulate cool air and a simple, inscrutable facade to belie inner wealth.

Habiba became concerned one evening after eating a chocolate from a Whitman's Sampler box we had brought as a hostess gift. Obviously agitated, she pulled me aside and in a conspiratorial whisper, asked: "Does this chocolate have alcohol? Alcohol is forbidden to me."

Even though I assured her the candy was non-alcoholic, I

could see she was only partially relieved. The sugar may have given her a rush, which she may have mistaken for alcohol even though she wouldn't have the faintest idea what an alcoholic high might feel like.

Habiba loved watching Troy Donahue movies on TV and would discuss the day's activities at length with her friends on the phone. Yet she still did all the laundry by hand in the bathtub and ignored the modern washer and dryer in the laundry room. A reluctance to learn how to operate modern equipment was only part of her problem. The other part was a nagging feeling that cleanliness was commensurate with work. Loading a washing machine was not work, therefore, she was suspicious of the results. In the bathtub she could feel beads of perspiration and watch the dirt float away.

I would join Habiba in the kitchen where we would share minor culinary secrets although I soon discovered she was not an adventurous cook. Her specialty was *breik* or eggs in a package, Tunisia's national dish: Break an egg over a square of phyllo dough, sprinkle with chopped onions and parsley, fold one corner over to form a triangle, and fry the package in hot oil until crisp. Voilá! *Breik* seemed to keep her going.

I demonstrated several variations on the egg theme (soufflés, omelettes and plain old American scrambled eggs), but Habiba was not captivated by my flexibility. There seemed a strong impulse in her toward the conservative, the tried-and-true way of life. Even when she changed clothes, they were consistently bland to the point where I began to see her as a permanently gray figure, like a colorless-vase topped with a sprig of yellow and red flowers

I wondered of her self-perception. Were the words exciting or interesting in her vocabulary? Or was I a creature of Madison Avenue expectations?

I did become fond of Habiba and her shy, diffident smile. We had so little in common: I, a seemingly reckless Western woman who pretty much did what I pleased and she, an Eastern women trapped in the comfortable but frustratingly rigid rules of Islam. Even in her wildest dreams, she didn't dare approximate my life style.

SNAPSHOT: THE WOMAN BEHIND THE BLUE DOOR

Habiba would be the only Muslim woman I would meet on our trip. As we distanced ourselves from Tunis, women were only seen scurrying by in the shadows, their heads and bodies draped in shades of white and gray. In the future, my contact with North Africans would be with men who had no trouble accommodating themselves to a Western woman.

As we drove away from the blue door in La Marsa Cubes to begin our journey, I glanced back and caught a fleeting view of Habiba watching from behind the lattice of a second-story window. She was wearing her scarf of red and yellow flowers tightly knotted under her chin. Was she watching us leave, or was this her daily vigil for the man of her dreams?

4

SWEET MONEY AND BITTER

Tunisia is a small, sunny Mediterranean country that clings to the North African coast for sustenance and protection like moss to a tree. About the size of Missouri, it is wedged between its two huge and religiously conservative neighbors, Algeria and Libya.

Only eighty-five miles separates the capital city of Tunis from the island of Sicily, which is the closest point of contact between North Africa and Europe besides Morocco and Spain.

It is no surprise that Tunis and Morocco also seem the most open and willing to absorb ideas and lifestyles from their European neighbors. Everywhere in Tunisia are reminders of Europe, Italy and the early Romans. The people, though Arab and Muslim, are handsome, open and friendly without the reserve or religious orthodoxy of their more isolated neighbors.

Tunis is a modern city that bustles with energy and a sense of prosperity. The streets are palm lined, the coffee bars full of men in Western business suits and traditional garb. Women, though less conspicuous, are still very much a presence in their modified Western dress, unlike their obscure sisters in other Arab countries who, covered head to foot, seem to slide unnoticed through your mind.

Shops offer a reasonable variety of consumer goods. Tunisian wine is plentiful and inexpensive. Gasoline, at $2.50 a gallon, is reasonable by African standards and a new trolly system speeds Tunisians and tourists alike about the city.

Running south of Tunis is a new *Autostrad*, a sleek four-lane freeway that has the look, feel, name and even the same road signs

Five times a day, speakers atop the minarets of the holy Tunisian city of Kairouan call the faithful to prayer.

as those found in Italy.

Tunisian beaches are favorites of Europeans who flock south in the winter to warm their bodies at Sfax, Gabes or at the Club Med on the Island of Djerba. There are at least four airports that offer international flights to several European cities and Tunisia is one of only a handful of North and West African countries that do not require a visa of Americans (the others: Egypt, Morocco, Togo and Liberia).

On the outskirts of Tunis lies one of the most famous of all Roman ruins—Carthage. Unfortunately, Carthage remains little more than an idea. The great artifacts were carried off to French and British museums years ago leaving behind mounds of green grass, a few broken columns and the deep blue of the Mediterranean as a backdrop.

At the entrance gate is a small sign: Photography Permit Required, and the price. Once inside, photography proved difficult. The site was contiguous to the grounds of the Presidential Palace but separated by a high white wall, rolls of barbed wire, guards, closed circuit TV and signs everywhere that cautioned: No Photography Permitted. With the sun in the southern hemi-

52   THE LION IN THE MOON

sphere it was impossible to photograph Carthage without including the Presidential Palace.

After our mad winter's dash from Hamburg and the overnight ferry trip from Genova in less than comfortable circumstances, Tunis was a pleasant respite. We shopped the *suk* (open market), filled our water jugs from chlorinated city water and stocked our rolling kitchen with last-minute provisions—local sardines, olive oil, condiments, wine, and crackers.

A couple of days later we fired up the MOG and headed out of Tunis in a southwesterly direction toward the Algerian border town of El-Oued, about four hundred miles inland. En route we would pass through the Tunisian towns of Kairouan, Gafsa and Tozeur.

From El-Oued our plan (we had to have our "plan") was to proceed west another three hundred miles to Ghardaïa in central Algeria where we would join the main trans-Saharan route, which ran south from Algiers through the oases towns of Ghardaïa, In Salah and Tamanrasset. In three weeks we hoped to arrive at the southern border outpost of En Guezzam, about 1500 miles into the Sahara.

The agricultural belt along the entire North African coast varies from fifty to a hundred miles wide. In some sections along the Libyan coast sand rolls right to the sea, while in other places, date and olive orchards exist in profusion.

As we headed inland away from the Tunisian coast, the massive eucalyptus trees that shaded the road and sheltered crops from the wind, the fertile fields of millet, the geometric orchards of date palms and the olive trees gradually gave way to the realities of desert life.

The irrigation projects ceased. The eucalyptus, once trunk to trunk, thinned and disappeared. There were fewer orchards with greater separation between trees. Grain fields were replaced with vistas of wild, brown grass that bent before the wind, and this to singular clumps that strained through the rocky soil.

We arrived in Kairouan, a center for fine, hand-woven Tunisian rugs about mid-day and parked outside the massive mud and

SWEET MONEY AND BITTER

rock walls of the old city in a place reserved for tour buses.

As I was locking up a young Tunisian approached. He was mid-height, with a handsome olive face wearing a tan collegiate windbreaker with an upturned collar. A cigarette dangled from his lips.

He said something in German, assuming our nationality from the German license plates on the front of the MOG.

"We speak English," I replied, which would be our first words in most every conversation we would have for the next two months.

"Ah, English." He quickly switched languages. "British?" I shook my head. "American?"

Yes, I nodded.

"I have a brother in New Jersey," he began, acting very much like a hip college student. "He is married to an American girl. I have been to New Jersey. I like Americans."

It was amazing how many people we would encounter who claimed to have relatives or 'good friends' in one American city or another. Although it might be true — most of us do herald from some other country — I always had the feeling it was a prelude to a hard sell.

"I'd like to show you around," he continued. "No obligation. No money. I know Americans like to be left alone. I will show you some special places where only the finest Kairouan rugs are sold. Someone will explain them to you. No obligation."

Reluctantly, we followed as he led us through the gated walls of the old city into a maze of serpentine passageways. I quickly lost my bearings. Abruptly, he stopped before a nondescript arched door and knocked gently.

Once inside, our guide faded away and another appeared to conduct the tour. This had been the home of a wealthy sheik, he explained, as he led us through a dozen cool pastel rooms ornamented with hand-painted tiles.

The tour ended in a large central room lined with plush cushions. Intricately carved panels of cedar and olive wood shielded the arched balconies above from the commerce below.

Another man appeared holding a brass tray and distributed

54　　　　　　　　　　　THE LION IN THE MOON

small glasses of syrupy mint tea.

"I will explain to you about our rugs," our guide began. The tone of his voice changed to business. "If you find something you like, we accept credit cards — Visa, American Express. No problem." He reeled off a list of other acceptable cards, mostly European.

For close to an hour we sifted through a pile of rugs of different sizes and designs finally narrowing the selection to a handful of Berber rugs with particularly colorful and intricate patterns.

"How much are these?" I asked casually.

"You have chosen well," the salesman began. "These are exceptionally high quality with very tight weave."

"They are fine rugs," I agreed. "How much are you asking?"

"For one or two?"

"Two," I replied, indicating which ones.

He thought for a few moments as if he really had something to decide and quoted a figure, which even to my untrained eye was exorbitant. I responded with a figure forty percent of the original price. The man smiled, not the warm smile of greeting, but the cold smile of combat.

"Impossible. These are the highest quality. That is even below our cost."

Unshaken, I asked if he had a better price. He suggested a figure about ten percent less than the original. I complimented him on the quality of his merchandise, then reminded him we were negotiating for two fine rugs not one, and we deserved special consideration.

"Yes, of course," he responded. He waved his hand and our tea glasses were refilled. The bargaining was about to get serious. The young Tunisian who had escorted us from the MOG was slouched in a corner chain smoking cigarettes. He never looked at us.

We sparred back and forth suggesting various prices, countering offers, inspecting the rugs carefully, making small talk, drinking tea, alternating between showing a great deal of interest and feigning boredom, until a second hour had passed. I had

SWEET MONEY AND BITTER

come up to about fifty-five percent of the original price; he had come down to seventy percent. A gulf of fifteen percent still separated us. I was starting to get tired.

"I am afraid that was our last offer," I said standing, casually helping the Princess with her coat.

"Wait," the man responded. "I will ask." He disappeared behind a door. I sat back down. He returned shaking his head gravely. "I have already offered the best price. But I will go down another five percent. That is the best I can do. It is my last offer."

We were now only ten percent apart. Our tea glasses were filled again. The Princess and I put our heads together. Did we really want these rugs? Yes, we decided, for the adventure, if nothing else.

"I will offer five percent more," I announced. "That is my last price." I rose very slowly and began an overly elaborate process of slipping into my jacket.

"I will ask the boss." With a dramatic sigh as if to announce that it would do no good, the man disappeared once again returning promptly with a sad look.

Before he could speak, the boss, a handsome man in his mid-thirties sporting a finely tailored suit, stormed into the room, planted himself before us and shook his finger vigorously at the salesman admonishing him in Arabic.

It was impossible to translate but the jist was obvious: "Why do you insult me by bringing me these low prices? Why do you waste my time?" At the end of the lecture, the boss man disappeared in three quick strides. It was carefully orchestrated theater.

"My boss says I have already gone too low with my price. He was very angry with me."

"I can go no higher," I announced gravely glancing at the Princess and shrugging, as if we had reached an intractable impasse. "That is all we can afford."

We rose to leave thanking our hosts for the tour and tea and were walking across the room toward the open door when from behind us a voice called: "Wait! The boss says OK. He will accept your price."

I pulled out my Visa.

The salesman frowned. "That is a problem. The charge on Visa is very high. I would prefer cash. We take dollars, francs, marks, liras." He went through a list of every hard currency in the world adding yen and sterling.

"We are buying two rugs because you said you would accept Visa," I reminded him.

"Oh, yes. We do accept Visa. We prefer cash. Can you give part of it in money?"

For the next five minutes we negotiated how much of the price would be in cash; how much credit. We finally settled on twenty percent cash, half of what he wanted.

"You have made an excellent price," the salesman whispered as he led us to the front steps, as if whispering were the proof.

Perhaps we did. But I would have been happier if I had shaved another ten percent from the price. I had not been sufficiently clever as a negotiator. That meant as much to me as the money.

We left under the wings of our young guide who had miraculously appeared at our side. He led us back to the MOG in a more direct route than the one he had taken earlier. I knew he expected something for his services despite his claim to the contrary, but I also knew he would get a kickback from the rug sale. I handed him a pack of cigarettes.

"Oh, American," he mumbled as he stripped off the cellophane and stuck a cig in his mouth. Adjusting the collar of his khaki windbreaker, he wandered off in search of new prey without a further word. So much for friendship, his brother in New Jersey and his love of Americans.

The negotiations had taken nearly two-and-a-half hours. As we drove out of Kairouan it was turning dusk. The MOG ate the desolate miles while I reflected on the whole process of bargaining.

Americans are generally loath to participate in such a process. Our retail system is built around absentee owners; prices have a built-in margin of profit and clerks are not allowed bargaining discretion and would likely lose their jobs if they tried.

SWEET MONEY AND BITTER

Posted prices are also advantageous to the consumer as they offer a certain psychological security — a shopper can make up his mind in private without having to involve a salesperson or subject herself to the hassle of arriving at the true market value, which is the lowest possible price the seller will accept.

American culture places a high value on non-confrontational behavior. The process of negotiating a price means confronting the seller in an adversarial relationship. To bargain is to suggest the price is high to begin with and is tantamount to calling the seller a liar, or suggesting consumer fraud, something we might do behind a seller's back, but never to his face.

To an Arab or an African, however, bargaining is part of life and serves a distinct social purpose. It is embraced as a game of wits that ultimately establishes mutual respect and even admiration between parties.

An African buyer assumes from the outset that the asking price is inflated. He takes up the challenge not only to obtain a better price but to demonstrate both skill and cleverness — traits that are greatly admired—and to show he is also a man of the world. Nothing is more humiliating than paying too high a price. On the other hand, nothing is sweeter than driving a hard bargain and gaining the respect of the seller in the process.

For the seller there is sweet money and bitter money. Sweet money is what is accepted after a full session of negotiation and conversation, even if it is less. Bitter money is that derived from an unsuspecting buyer who, because of ignorance or lack of cleverness, fails to participate in the bargaining, even though in the end, the seller emerges with greater profit. Sweet money is preferred over bitter.

For those who are nervous at the thought of bargaining, here are a few tips:

First, understand bargaining is a verbal game of chess. It is a social exercise and a battle of wits normally carried on with light-hearted banter in an unhurried fashion. Money is often less the object than the process, which builds mutual respect.

Second, do not initiate bargaining at any level just for kicks. It is alright to ask the price but do not counter unless you are prepared to go all the way, and ultimately, to cough up some cash.

Many tourists begin to bargain as a joke only to walk away when it turns serious. The seller feels a fool and resentment towards all foreigners mounts. Remember, you are toying with another's pride. If you reach an impasse, however, it's acceptable to walk away as long as you have bargained in good faith.

Third, when the seller quotes a price, you can usually assume he will settle for much less, often half. If cutting his price by fifty percent is your goal, counter with an offer about thirty-five percent of the seller's. Your strategy is to grudgingly give up another fifteen percent as leverage to get the seller's price down by fifty. It can be done.

Lastly, if the seller finally accepts your price, it is good form to offer a small tip in addition to the agreed price. This leaves the negotiations in psychological balance. You have won the battle but the seller is compensated in some extra way for ceding to your price. You both win.

Rug bargaining on a grander scale is diplomacy. Our country's often futile attempts at negotiating political solutions to world crises, particularly those in the Middle and Far East, and our quick reversion to a military solution, stems, in great part, from our lack of patience and understanding how to bargain for a rug.

Snapshot

THE MAGIC RUG PALACE

I thought we were hopelessly lost by the time we reached the rug palace.

Staefan and I had been following our guide for twenty long minutes through a maze of dusty, blind passages. At each turn I expected to break out of the labyrinth, but one passage led to another, and that to still another. I kept glancing at the slice of blue sky above us for reassurance. It was the only visual escape from this narrow vacuum of dead ends and solid walls.

Mary Howitt's fable came to mind: "Will you walk into my parlor?" said the spider to the fly." Wasn't this something my mother had warned me not to do? "'Tis the prettiest little parlor that ever you did spy."

Our young Tunisian guide had promised to take us to the best rug market in Kairouan, the fourth holiest city of Islam after Mecca, Medina and Jerusalem. Tunisians believe seven visits to Kairouan is the equal to one pilgrimage to Mecca. It was also a shopper's shrine for fine rugs.

"But you are not obligated to buy," he had assured me numerous times, as if reading my mind.

I would have walked right by the rug palace without giving it a second thought if our guide had not stopped before a small door. It was just like all the others we had passed, painted blue and set in a high, dusty white wall. In the center of this door, however, was nailed a female hand, its brass fingers pointing downward. It was the hand of Fatima, the Prophet's daughter, immortalized as a door knocker.

Kairouan rugs are displayed everywhere, even on the drab walls that line the serpentine passageways at the heart of the city.

Our guide pounded once and the door opened. A doorman in a flowing white robe greeted us as if we had been expected. Behind him, several men reclined on cushions in a corner taking slow puffs from their glass hookahs. The sweet scent of their smoke curled upwards in playful arabesques, disappearing in the sparkling gold mosaics of the domed ceiling. The men did

SNAPSHOT: THE MAGIC RUG PALACE

not speak as we passed. The only sound was the sweet melody of tiny songbirds captured in lacy white cages suspended from the ceiling.

"I will give you a tour of the palace," our new guide announced. "This once belonged to a prince. Now, it has the most beautiful rugs in the world. Of course," he added, "there is no obligation."

Great white arches carved from stone and rimmed in gold led us from one room into the next. Blue and white ceramic-tiled walls echoed the designs of the elaborate silk carpets that cushioned our steps across the marble floors. The domed ceilings were encrusted with sparkling mosaics forming fanciful geometric patterns.

Stepping through another gilded arch revealed a room filled with rugs. Some were stacked two and three feet high; others were tightly rolled and shoved into corners. I had never seen so many rugs and was fascinated by the range of colors and intricate patterns. There were small prayer rugs, pomegranate red rugs with Persian designs, saffron rugs bordered by emerald green and enormous palatial rugs of multicolored geometric shapes edged in black.

I knelt beside a pile of silk rugs and watched the nap change color as I ran my hand over the surface. Our guide made a noise. He was motioning to me in a fit of impatience. "I will show you many fine rugs in a moment. Please, follow me."

Staefan and I followed him up a dark stairway to a partially enclosed room on the roof. "This is how the rugs are made," our guide explained.

In one corner, an older woman with a shawl over her head worked quietly at a large foot loom. The naked walls were painted a shade of green long since bleached pastel from the harsh rays of the sun that splashed through the open arches. The woman did not look at us, but continued weaving a colorful pattern from memory.

I wondered if she had woven all the rugs I had just seen downstairs. My imagination pictured her as a young Arab princess grieving for her one true love. A tragic twist of fate had taken her prince from her. In mourning, she had exiled herself to this rooftop where she wove her tales of woe into beautiful rugs. I kept hoping she would turn around so I could see if her face mirrored my fantasy. She continued, oblivious to my presence.

At the edge of the roof was a terrace overlooking the city. Minarets and palm trees broke the flat horizon; the sun created a study in shadows among the rooftops. I took a photo that would later appear on the front page of a newspaper travel section.

On the second floor our guide paused before a carved filigreed screen.

"When this was a palace," he began, "the women could look through the screen to see the entertainment in the room below without themselves being seen. Of course, that is no longer the case. We no longer have princes and our women are very Western."

I peeked through the holes. Directly across, a second carved screen shielded another room. There were screens to my right and left. All overlooked a great salon one floor below. Even today, to be an Arab woman would be to live forever in a world of screens.

Our tour ended in the grand salon downstairs where we were invited to sit on beautiful banquettes scattered with pillows and offered *thé a la menthe*, "courtesy of the house."

High overhead, a dome laced with stained glass windows offered inspiration. The filigreed screens shielding the women's rooms were below the dome. Our guide had been right. There was no way to tell what might lay behind those screens.

A young boy appeared with two tall shot glasses filled with sweet, hot tea on a brass tray. He bowed as I took my glass.

The show began. Another, older merchant explained about the rugs and especially the superior quality of Tunisian rugs. He recited passages about their beauty, history and the different qualities of weavings.

"The government has a system to grade the quality depending on the number of knots per square centimeter. The tighter the weave, the higher the grade. See this label?" He turned over the corners of several rugs already spread on the floor. "We sell

SNAPSHOT: THE MAGIC RUG PALACE

only the top three grades. Please, tell me which ones you like. There is no obligation."

Suddenly, he motioned to an accomplice who rolled out a carpet that magically stopped inches from my feet. Our host pulled up leather ottomans and suggested we sit closer to the floor, all the better to examine the rugs' knots and feel the texture of real silk.

He continued his monologue as one rug after another was snapped out before us in military precision. The stack of possibilities thickened. I had long ago finished my tea.

The merchant went back through the carpets. Even though we were not obligated to buy, he asked which rugs we liked so the others could be cleared away. Many still remained. We worked through the selections, having become serious buyers without knowing it.

By now I assumed we were not just passing time but were intent on buying a couple of rugs. Staefan and I walked up the stairs, at the merchant's urging, and leaned over the banister to better appreciate our chosen carpets from above. We each had picked out one the other hated.

The negotiations began. We continued to wander around the room looking at other possibilities.

As Staefan and the merchant sparred, I realized the game was becoming dangerous.

I had fallen in love with my rug. It was a Berber with a red background, stylized gazelles and geometric patterns in heraldic symmetry. I had to have it. It would be the focal point of my living room, the perfect foil for the black leather couch I had not yet bought, clearly visible through the Noguchi glass table I would one day own, and a major conversation piece if I ever decided to throw those intimate dinner parties I was always reading about in glossy magazines.

Merchants should be grateful to women like me. I was ready to pay any price for this rug that did not even turn my head a few minutes ago. I rationalized: What price could one put on such an experience as this? I could never find such a rug at home. I could go without lunch for, say a month, to pay this off. I needed to go on a diet anyway. And those gazelles; how precious.

I was bursting at the seams, afraid we would not come to an agreed price. I would die if I did not have this rug.

Staefan, fortunately, had remained calm. He walked around the room, humming, feigning indifference and casual interest in other rugs, completely ignoring the salesman. Finally, he told the merchant we wished to buy two carpets and expected a discount. He offered another last and best price.

The merchant left the room in the company of three of his cronies. He returned to announce he had consulted with the manager and they would make a best and final price for two rugs. Staefan shook his head: It was still too high.

My companion continued his act. "That price is for one carpet. We want two. I am making you an offer for two," he said. Such a businessman. It was a reasonable, if not low offer.

The merchant made a great show of distress. He called for the manager who entered the room screaming in Arabic, apparently dishing out verbal abuse to the poor salesman for even considering such low prices. His three cronies scoffed at our ridiculously low price by making gestures and hissing sounds. When the manager left the room, the salesman shrugged his shoulders as if to say: See? What did I tell you. Now, I'm in trouble so you'd better buy one.

The salesman offered another last price and best price.

Not bad, I thought. They had come down a considerable amount. Let's grab it!

Staefan, however, was unimpressed. He decided to brood some more. Obviously, he was enjoying this mind game. I was only becoming more nervous because I could see this macho wheel of fortune coming to a head.

I would lose my Tunisian gazelles, my living room would be declared a disaster area, all future dinner parties would have to be cancelled, and I would slip into a mild depression for the rest of the trip.

Staefan offered his last and final price.

The merchant again left the room to consult with the manager, returning boldly a moment later to announce: "Impos-

SNAPSHOT: THE MAGIC RUG PALACE

sible. The manager already made you his best offer." The chorus of men affected looks of, boy, have you screwed up this sale!

Staefan shrugged and got up, slipping on his jacket. I was crushed. We said goodbye, offered thanks for the tea, and walked slowly toward the doors.

Just as my foot crossed the threshold, the merchant miraculously reappeared.

"Come with me," he declared. He was very insistent.

I wondered what we had done wrong. Did I walk off with something by mistake? Were we going to jail like in "Midnight Express?" We followed him back into the room.

"OK," the salesman announced with a great deal of anguish, "we will accept your price."

I couldn't believe it, the gazelles were coming to America after all.

The three men proceeded to fold the five by nine rugs (fringe included) into tight little bundles that could easily fit into any suitcase. They wrapped each bundle in brown paper and tied them with blue cord the color of Tunisian skies. Staefan sat at the desk as the merchant processed his Visa card. Somehow I had expected an abacus and gold coins.

As we collected our packages, the merchant told us it was traditional to give two dinars to the chorus for the wrapping. "It is good luck for the rugs," he said.

Staefan, keeper of the coins, missed this entirely and we walked from the palace to subtle hisses of disgust. Staefan insisted he never heard it.

Weeks later when I unwrap my rug at home, I will swear this was not the one I drooled over in the magic rug palace. It looked different, somehow. The stripes on each end were of varying widths, the colors weren't as bright, the gazelles weren't as graceful, and the symmetry was gone. Probably an apprentice's project.

The distractions of the rug palace, the hundreds of rugs rich in history, design and color, the exotic tea, and the young boys waiting on me hand and foot had its intended effect. Still, every time I look at my red Berber with the asymmetrical rows of long-necked gazelles, I remember what a magical carpet ride it was.

5

ALGERIA ON THE HORIZON

We left the high walls of Kairouan behind hoping to make Gafsa before dark. Already we were edging the desert where rain is scarce and little grows. Tomorrow we would enter Algeria and encounter the *Grand Erg Occidental,* the massive sea of sand that occupies thousands of square miles of eastern Algeria.

This night would be our first in the MOG. Everything was still packed in the cases we had shipped from Dallas, including our kitchen. We had yet to develop a system or a routine. When finally we pulled off the road under a massive eucalyptus tree on the outskirts of Gafsa, it was pitch black. We had driven too long.

Wearily, the Princess and I opened tins of sardines by flashlight, broke apart a loaf of bread and washed it down with Tunisian wine before burrowing into our sleeping bags. Tomorrow, we agreed, we would have to get organized.

When we awoke two small Tunisian girls, seven or eight years old, in faded Western-style dresses that hung from thin shoulders were leaning against the eucalyptus watching us in silence. I went about fixing my breakfast of instant coffee, a packet of oatmeal and local bread.

The Princess asked them: "Are you on your way to school?"

They shook their heads. Their brother was in school, they said, but they stayed home to help their mother work. As the climate warmed they edged closer.

"Where do you live?"

They pointed over their shoulders toward a small dirt-colored concrete house across a bare and dusty field.

ALGERIA ON THE HORIZON

As we prepared to leave, I handed them each a piece of candy and a pen. The older one tested the pen on the palm of her hand. Satisfied, she looked at me, stuck the pen in her mouth and made the motion of smoking. "Do you have any cigarettes?" she asked in French.

Of course, I thought, how silly to think an eight-year-old would be satisfied with a mere pen. At this rate, we would soon be out of cigarettes and have pens to burn.

At mid-day we stopped in Tozeur for a lunch of chicken, fried potatoes and brochettes at the *Restaurant du Paradis*, one of the many sidewalk cafes recommended in a guide book. I didn't know it at the time but our quickly consumed lunch would be the last satisfying restaurant meal I would enjoy for the next several weeks.

Tozeur was an oasis town with flat-roofed buildings sheltered by groves of palms on the edge of a dried lake bed. It was the last Tunisian town of any consequence before the border and a major point of embarkation into the great dunes, which were barely visible on the Western horizon.

The energy of the town was infectious. The sandy streets were alive with tourists and four-wheel-drive Toyotas equipped with special air cleaners to guard against flying sand. Biblical goat skins of water hung from their sides. Street corner signs offered camel rides.

The faint of heart could charter a vehicle for the day, be whisked twenty-five miles to the nearest dune, spend a few minutes crawling over the sand, and return home with wonderful stories of their adventures in the Sahara.

Only a handful of serious desert travelers were about to do what we had in mind. You could pick them out by the glint in their eyes, the ruggedness of their vehicles and the extra tires, gas cans, sand ladders and spare parts carried on their roof racks.

While I retained a few doubts, the Princess and I were as prepared as we could be. The sky was a matchless deep blue. A warm breeze was blowing from the northeast. My blood began to pump with the realization that in another hour we would be crossing the border into Algeria, launching ourselves on the

On the Algerian border, the Tunisian oasis of Tozeur offers artesian water and date palms for shade.

adventure we had come for.

All was ready except we had yet to christen the MOG. This presented a quandary. What would we use? Champagne was not available. Wine was, but was rather common. Cokes were pedestrian. They would never do. We settled on the one commodity which was both available and of the greatest value — bottled water.

The Princess found a liter of Italian mineral water we had

ALGERIA ON THE HORIZON

brought from Genova, cracked the lid and with the proper incantations, poured a stream over the front bumper. Properly blessed with Italian Holy Water, we felt quite secure. We were immune from misfortune and the MOG from mechanical failure.

Checking out through Tunisian border control was almost uneventful. The customs officer gave the truck a quick scan, opening the doors and poking his head briefly here and there. It might have taken longer but mid-way through his search I offered him a pack of cigarettes, which he accepted with great delight abandoning the inspection. The police, on the other hand, were having some difficulties with my passport.

We had overstayed our welcome. When we had entered Tunis, the port police had placed a notation in my passport that we had forty-eight hours to transit the country. We were several days past our limit.

"Where have you been?" the policeman asked in French, consternation on his face. "You should have left Tunisia four days ago. This is very bad." He pointed to the restriction penned in my passport.

I shrugged ignorance and replied in English: "I only speak English. I don't read French."

He struggled to explain our predicament in his few words of English. I listened with great satisfaction pretending to be confused. A smoke screen of ignorance is bliss.

The Princess and I had decided on a language strategy for the trip: If someone wanted something from us, we spoke only English. If we needed something from them, we would use French. By and large, this strategy worked well, particularly as a defense against harassment by police, the prying demands of border officials or the unwelcome advances of hustlers.

I waved my tourist card and said: "Two weeks. I do not understand. We have two weeks."

The policeman huddled with his colleague. Together, they studied my passport and the conflicting tourist card, which had two weeks written in it. After a few minutes he stamped us out with a shake of his head. The policeman followed us outside. "Do you have any water?" he asked in slow, broken English.

"The water here is terrible."

We handed him our last bottle of Italian mineral water. His eyes lit up.

It had taken us only thirty minutes to clear Tunisia. It would take the rest of the afternoon to enter Algeria.

Most of us, when we become tourists, are accustomed to flying into a country and clearing all entrance formalities in a few minutes at the airport. Even when traveling to Mexico, U.S. Customs is typically on the north side of the border, Mexican officials a few feet away on the south side. Not so in North Africa. Between Tunisia and Algeria, and other countries we were to visit, the border posts were separated by several miles of real estate known as no man's land, an apt description.

A lot of wild thoughts went through my head as we left the Tunisian border post behind.

I had heard rumors of travelers who had checked out of one country and crossed no man's land only to be denied entry into the next. Since they had already used their single entry visa, they couldn't re-enter the country they had just departed and were stuck in no man's land without a legal right to go anywhere. I generally don't put much stock in such rumors, but they can't be discounted, either.

I thought back to the problems we had in obtaining our Algerian visas. Trying to plan ahead, I had mailed our passports to the Algerian Embassy in Washington and waited about two weeks. When the return envelope arrived, it contained only my passport. The Princess' was missing. Only four days remained before our flight to Europe.

I called the Algerian Embassy.

"Oh, yes," the official said in excellent English. "It is here on the desk. We wondered who it belonged to." They returned it by Fed. Ex.

The day before we were to leave I happened to open my passport to the Algerian visa and noted with horror that the Princess' passport number had been entered into my visa, and mine into hers. I was quickly on the phone.

"Oh, damn!" muttered the Algerian Embassy officer in his

ALGERIA ON THE HORIZON

relaxed but educated English.

"What do I do?" I pleaded. We leave tomorrow. There was a pause on the other end.

"Do you have white out?" he asked.

"You mean that little bottle of white liquid used to correct typewriter errors?" I replied, not quite believing what I knew was coming.

"Yes, that's it. Just white out the wrong number and write in the correct one, but use a black pen. Do you have a black pen?"

"Yes, I do. Are you sure that will do it?"

"No problem. Have a good day."

We were crossing a stretch of absolute waste land toward the Algerian border post with altered visas. I didn't say anything to the Princess about my concern. I was fairly certain she had no idea this could be a problem. It was better that way. Her show of genuine surprise and indignation, if it came to that, might come in handy.

The miles of no man's land clicked by. The sides of the road were littered with the carcasses of cars that had been abandoned and stripped for parts by their owners rather than be driven into Algeria and be subject to the obscenely high duty levied against automobiles.

We arrived at the border post two hours before sunset, plenty of time, I reasoned, to fill out a few simple forms, pass out a few cigarettes and be on our way. What we didn't count on was a bus of Japanese tourists that had arrived moments before us.

We filled out our entry forms, stuck them in our passports and handed them to the single immigration officer behind a wood desk in a dirty concrete building. He slipped our passports under those of the twenty-five Japanese tourists.

The Algerian official wrestled with the stack of Japanese passports. He would slowly search through each one trying to decipher the critical information, which was in Japanese and English, and fill out each immigration form in long hand in French. I calculated he was working at a speed of ten passports per hour. It would be dark before he got to us. I trudged back to the MOG and broke open a book.

Dusk was settling in when there was a tap on the door. It

was a customs officer. He wanted to inspect the MOG, he said, and handed me a declaration form.

"Put down everything of value you are bringing into Algeria," he announced, "money, traveler's checks, radios, cameras, spare parts—anything and everything."

I filled out the form and handed it back. He pointed to the back doors.

As he searched the truck, he began to check off those items I had written down against what he found. When he uncovered something extra, he would admonish me and add it to the list. In ten minutes, he added a typewriter, binoculars and two spare tires. I had a compact, palm-sized, shortwave radio hidden behind the seat that I didn't mention and he didn't find. Miniature electronics are highly prized in the Third World, particularly by sticky-fingered border guards.

The form was an attempt to keep us from exchanging our dollars or swapping our cameras, radios or spare tires on the black market in the misguided belief that the voracious appetite of the underground economy could be starved to death by not feeding it.

When we exited the country, we were told, another customs official would again search the MOG and check off everything written on the form. If we were short a camera, for example, it would be assumed we had sold it on the black market and we would be assessed a fine equal to the value of the camera.

"Go to town to the bank and change money and come back here to buy insurance," he instructed. "Your papers will be ready then. Do you have any cigarettes?"

I gave him a pack. *"Ah, Americain. C'est bon. Merci."* He vanished into the night.

We drove three miles nearly bypassing the town, which was off the road, set against a low hill. It was so black I could barely make out the buildings. Only two street lights pierced the darkness. No bank was in sight. At the end of one street was a small concrete building with hand-painted letters over the door: *Banque d' Agricole.*

ALGERIA ON THE HORIZON

There was no life. The bank had already closed for the night. We were about to return to the border when the door opened a crack and a hand waved us in.

Inside, we passed through two outer rooms, barren except for a few wood chairs stacked against a wall. The floors were concrete and covered with dust. Our shoes left tracks. In a small, inner office a young man with a large, multi-colored knit ski cap pulled over his ears sat behind an old desk. A cassette player spouted American rock. We sat opposite in two uncomfortable chairs.

"Passports?" he asked. "Ah, American," he beamed. He pulled off his hat and a thick mane of long braided hair fell to his shoulders. He was the spitting image of Bob Marley, the late Jamaican Reggae star.

"What are you doing in Algeria?" he asked in perfect King's English, reaching to turn down the volume of the cassette player.

We explained our trip. He began to make small talk.

"How do you like my English?" His face was all smiles.

"It's wonderful. Where did you learn it?"

"I studied at the British Consul in Algiers. It's pretty good, isn't it?" We agreed.

"What do you think of my long hair? Never thought you'd see an Algerian with hair like this, did you?" He shook it out and ran his fingers through the braids.

"That's right," we assured him. "It is certainly unusual."

He chuckled with glee.

"It is the rule that all tourists must change at least 1000 Algerian dinars when they enter the country," he explained, tapping his fingers to the rock music.

"How much in dollars?" I asked.

"The official exchange rate is eight-to-one." He pulled out a hand-held calculator. "That would be $125. Each," he announced. "How much do you wish to change?"

"The minimum," I answered. I didn't want to be stuck with a bunch of worthless money when we exited the southern border. In spite of his assurances that excess dinars could be converted into dollars as long as our currency exchange form was in order, I knew better than to believe him. It never worked that way.

Chances were there would be no dollars available at the border, even if we found a bank. If an exchange were possible, we would be required to wait a week while the paperwork was sent to Algiers for approval. Countries like Algeria are so starved for hard currency they invent a million excuses for hanging on to every penny. The paperwork approval game was just one.

As soon as our banker friend mentioned the mandatory exchange rule, several things ran through my mind: a worthless currency, severe inflation and a raging black market. In short, an economy in chaos. All in spite of Algeria being a major petroleum producer.

It seems to be a rule that currency exchange coercion is only practiced by state-run, centralized 'socialist' economies like Algeria's, a subtle government admission that the economy was so badly mismanaged it was necessary to shake down tourists to help balance the books.

The street value of the dinar, as I was to learn, was not 12½¢ as dictated by the government, but closer to 4¢. We should've received 3,000 dinars for our dollars, not the 1,000 we were handed.

Ironically, Algeria, with all its oil wealth, was the only country we were to visit with a black market. Most West African countries (at least those formerly French colonies) have joined a monetary union that uses the CFA franc, a West African version of the French franc. It is underwritten by France at a constant ratio of fifty-to-one.

Someone bringing 1,000 French francs to Nigér or Senegal would automatically receive 50,000 CFA. Excess CFA can be changed back into francs without hassle, either before leaving the country, or later in Paris.

This system not only provides most West African countries with a hard currency but also inextricably ties them to France. Political colonization has been replaced by a form of economic colonization.

The French, for the price of underwriting these near bankrupt economies, has secured a captive market for their goods.

ALGERIA ON THE HORIZON

With the exception of a few Japanese and German consumer goods, most everything is imported from France. Goods from the U.S. are virtually nonexistent. There are plenty of American labels — Coke, IBM, Marlboro, even Apple — but these products are either manufactured under local license or imported from France.

Algeria, after a bloody, prolonged war for independence with France in the mid-'50s, chose to pursue an independent course of socialism and declined to tie itself to France through a monetary union. While this strategy has served Algerian pride, it has resulted in an economic mess with high inflation and a worthless currency.

In spite of government controls, dollars, francs and marks mysteriously find their way into the pockets of those Algerians who want them. In the process, the dinar, like other socialist currencies — the Russian ruble, the Cuban peso or the Tanzanian shilling—becomes a worthless joke.

We had been at the bank nearly half an hour before our Bob Marley look-alike finished the necessary paperwork and handed over our passports with 2,000 dinars. As I tucked the money into a zippered pocket of my bush pants, he pulled the green, yellow and black striped ski hat over his head, and tucked his braids under the fold. It seemed long hair was not welcome in the *Republic of Algeria, Democratic and Popular*, as the country was officially known. We rose to leave.

"Do you have any tools?" he asked, pulling something from a desk drawer. "I have to install this lock in the front door and I don't have tools."

I retrieved my tool kit from the MOG and positioned the truck so that the glare of the headlights illuminated the door. Within minutes I had replaced the deadbolt.

"Thank you. It's been broken for two months. Now I can lock the bank."

When we returned to the border post, it was dark and deserted. A sliver of light came from a small trailer. While the Princess waited in the MOG, I knocked on the tin door. A thin man appeared.

"I've been waiting for you," he said, sleepily. "I have to sell you insurance."

He filled out the forms for liability insurance. It was in Arabic and cost about $10 a day. I had no idea what I was signing. Outside, a different policeman approached with our papers.

"Do you have any cigarettes?" he asked, making it sound like casual banter between friends.

I dug under my sleeping bag and gave him a pack. He squinted to read the label in the faint moonlight. "Ah, American," he mumbled, and then hesitated. "Do you have anything . . . special . . . to drink," he asked haltingly.

I knew what he was after — beer, maybe wine, or something harder, but he couldn't say so. This poor fellow, like so many of his countrymen, caught on the horns of desire yet living in a puritanical society that brands so much of life immoral, was forced to speak in code in the middle of the night.

"Sorry," I told him. "Nothing special." He shrugged slightly and nodded understanding.

There are many crude indices of a country's prosperity. One is the overall appearance of the people, their general bustle, along with the number of beggars encountered in the streets. Another is the number of shops in a town and what's on their shelves. And then there is what the border guards ask for.

When we left Tunisia, a country of relative prosperity, the guard simply wanted a good drink of water; in Algeria, a few miles away, it was cigarettes and a little alcohol. It is a good evaluation of not only what constitutes a luxury, but also relative deprivation.

Snapshot

WONDERFULLY LOST

The dark-skinned Arab reached in the window of the MOG and held out his clenched hand.

"*Pour Madame,*" he said. Smiling, he slowly opened his long, slender fingers to reveal a quartz stone in the shape of a rose. It was smooth and its edges glinted from the bright sun trapped among its sharp petals. Grains of sand still clung to the crevices.

I plucked it carefully from his palm as the MOG began to move and turned it slowly in the light to catch the sparkling reflection.

Sand roses were natural phenomena gathered from the desert. Hard, cold roses of stone were the only sort that would grow here.

How would the desert begin? I wondered, as we drove through the streets of the Tunisian border town of Tozeur. I had come a long way for this experience and I was impatient. Would the Sahara reveal itself slowly, as the peeled back layers of an onion, or would it loom suddenly as a giant sandbox contained within mystical walls?

We had barely escaped the confines of Tozeur, within minutes of the Algerian border, when I reached across to shake Staefan's arm. His eyes were on the road, not the future.

"Look," I shouted above the din of the engine. "Dunes! We're there!"

Giant rolling dunes had sprung up across the horizon as if by magic. We were heading right into them. It was a child's picture book. Sand was piled everywhere, even engulfing date palms up to their necks, leaving only the top fronds to flag their presence.

Sandal-clad figures walked slowly across the sands, their bodies cloaked in white robes that puffed behind them in the wind like mini-parachutes. Some rode mules with palm fronds draped over the animals' backs. They had walked out of the pages of the Bible. These people, Muslim to the core, would not have appreciated the comparison. I felt as if I, like Saint-Exupéry's "The Little Prince," had landed on another planet, far away in time and space.

That was how it began.

The Sahara was not what I had thought. Most think of the desert as a flat, monotonous landscape. "What did you look at day after day?" my friends would ask me. "The desert's just flat, isn't it? You took pictures? Of what?"

Far from being a monotonous landscape, it changed character from day to day, often hour to hour.

We drove for hours across flat, barren salt flats. No matter in what direction I turned, there was a flat view of the world unobstructed by any vertical form except the mirages that danced insistently before our eyes. There were other hours spent skirting giant sand dunes, smoothly undulating like a Brancusi sculpture as they took their shape at the hand of the volatile winds.

In other parts, rock formations and craters looked as if they belonged on the moon. Some vistas were so prehistoric I expected dinosaurs to rumble across our path. Colossal boulders in the shape of ragged elephants, their surfaces oddly wrinkled from centuries of living, stood at silent attention as we drove by.

The massive volcanic Hoggar Mountains rose thousands of feet above the sand while thorn trees grew in the crumbling hills at their base. Their silhouettes in the yellow light of afternoon reminded me of giant bonsai trees, graceful, yet strong, spreading their meager umbrella of shade and dropping thorns onto the sand below.

We threaded our way over pools of powdery sand, around outcroppings of jagged rock, through narrow canyons, in and out of dried river beds and across miles of incredibly flat, denuded, hard packed earth. It was never a case that there was

SNAPSHOT: WONDERFULLY LOST

little to photograph, only the realization that pictures would never tell the story.

How can you photograph the deafening silence of solitude beneath a broad, sheltering sky?

In the cool of early evening, we would camp surrounded by giant sand dunes two and three stories high, their surfaces patterned in wavy ridges like ribbons of silk moire. I would struggle up the sides, my feet sinking into the powdery sand, to sit on the top and become one with the night. The neon-bright stars exploded from the blackness above me. An eerie silence prevailed. Except for the noise coming from Staefan.

Far below, a pool of warm light from a butane lamp spilled onto the desert floor. Staefan had set up his portable typewriter on our camp table and was madly tapping away, oblivious to his surroundings. How small was one man's world. There he was tucked behind a dune like a ferret, at work illuminating a tiny corner of the world.

Outside the pool of light I felt detached, separate, not of his or this world.

In my search for darkness and silence, I would walk farther and farther down the spine of the dune, far from the artificial light. I wanted to embrace the sky and send wishes to the stars that dangled just above me. I wanted to be alone in an incredible stillness, enveloped by a quiet that defied silence. The stars were speaking to me. I could almost hear them. I listened hard to the whisper of the night breeze.

I often ventured out of the truck before dawn, awakened by a bright light falling into the side window. I would put on my shoes and crack open the door. As always, there was no one but the night and a brilliant white moon. A solitary explorer in an empty land, I walked out into the moonlight, savoring the solitude of a beautiful, silent night created just for me. My eyes drank in the silvery waves of sand and the cold heat of the moon. I wanted to burn their images onto my mind so I would never forget. When I couldn't bear the cold any longer, I crept back into my sleeping bag and dreamt.

I had visions of fierce Berbers astride camels waiting to

whisk me away. A lone, mysterious Arab stood on top of the dune waiting for me, his cloak slowly waving like a flag behind him. His body and face were covered, only two dark eyes pierced the night to stare at me. What did he want? He would reappear in my dreams throughout the desert.

There was always a sense of being lost, wonderfully and totally lost in that great void known as the Sahara. It was like an infinite confessional box and I my own confessor. Meditation at its highest, oblivion at its most surreal, a chance to judge my life from a distance. I had re-entered the womb, the cradle of mankind where I was the only judge of my character.

I saw that I was happily lost in the Sahara, but sadly lost in my own life. A born-again bon vivant, I had no 'project' as Sartre referred to it, no life theme of any great importance. Like Dante in the "Divine Comedy," I had reached a dark forest in the middle of my years and was lost. His way out was through hell. Perhaps a two-month journey through Africa would serve me as well. Was the mysterious Arab to be my guide toward knowing myself?

This all seemed appropriate, as I neared midlife, to journey to the greatest expanse of nothingness on earth and have it play with my mind. I had half-a-life to go. How would I choose to fill what was left?

6

PLAYING THE BLACK MARKET

Two hundred miles into Algeria the Princess and I were swept by our first sand storm.

I had read about the *Harmattans*, the sand storms that raged in the Sahara raising massive clouds of dust particles miles into the atmosphere, obscuring the sun with a yellow-brown haze, but didn't believe it would happen to us.

All the way from Tunis the weather had been ideal; the sky was a crisp, pure blue with temperatures in the low 70s. Magically, I believed, life would continue as it was. We would weave our way through the perils of the Sahara and be spared the displeasure of hours of choking sand and dust.

The storm enveloped us from behind, from the northeast. The wind accelerated gradually sending sand across the road in spurts, then in graceful wavy patterns. Date palms rocked violently as the wind gained force. The MOG shuddered with each blast. Sand swept us in sheets, waist-high at first, then rising until everything was obscured in a yellowish curtain of sand and dust.

It is near impossible to escape a sand storm. Either you stop and let it blow over, or drive out of it. Had the wind met us head on, I would have been forced to turn the MOG around and stop so as not to clog the radiator. As it was, with the wind at our hind quarter, my concern was one of visibility.

Slowing to a crawl, I drove cautiously for more than an hour straining to make out the limits of the tarmac road, which by now was a sheet of solid sand that blended with the general landscape. Now and then a car or truck would creep by in the

82 THE LION IN THE MOON

opposite direction, bursting from a wall of sand only a few feet in front to be swallowed instantly behind us.

Visibility dropped to near zero. I slowed further fearing collision with one of the massive drilling rigs that float across Algeria on huge balloon tires loaded with fifty-foot sections of drilling pipe that extended several yards over the rear. If a truck decided to wait out the storm in the middle of the road we could run into the pipe before we ever saw the rear of the truck.

Mysteriously, the sky turned from a yellow haze to a bizarre shade of black. Drops of rain appeared on the windshield mixed with the sand and became a blizzard of mud. The wipers struggled to clear the glass. Quite unexpectedly, the wind stopped and the sand disappeared. Only the rain lingered. After nearly three hours, we had outrun the sandstorm.

It was already mid-afternoon. We were miles short of Ghardaïa, our day's destination. If this storm were an indication of what was to come, I feared we would be thrown days behind schedule. Already we were hearing reports of worsening conditions deeper in the desert—the widespread shortages of gasoline and the rapid deterioration of the road. A few travelers talked of being stranded for days in small oasis towns waiting for gas; others spoke of being bogged down for hours in seas of sand. I had wanted to get slightly ahead of schedule to put some time in the bank, just in case.

Ghardaïa was a surprise. It was nearly invisible until the last moment when we broached the brow of a hill and descended a steep, winding road. There was not one but five separate towns facing each other from opposing hillsides. A stream ran through the valley separating the towns and nurturing small orchards of date palms and olive trees. The houses were typically biblical, squat, flat-roofed and drably mono-chromatic.

The campground was a rectangular plot of ground surrounded by a high wall squeezed between two buildings. There was sufficient room for about a dozen rigs in two rows of six along each wall. Eight or ten palms provided some relief from the blazing sun but did nothing to shelter us from the dripping rain.

Ghardaïa was known for its 3,000 deep artesian wells, the

Algerian fast food: drinks, pastries and ice cream at the Cafe Labaraka. There was little to choose from inside.

availability of fresh vegetables and the best mechanics in Algeria. One guide book suggested facetiously, that if we were planning on breaking down, do it here. While parts were impossible to find and mechanics inept most everywhere else in Algeria, we would enjoy a slightly greater chance of success in Ghardaïa, due to the presence of a small Islamic sect of Mozabites.

The Mozabites have developed independently from the rest of Algeria refusing even to fight against the French during the Algerian war of independence. About 100,000 of these people inhabit the narrow valley sticking pretty much to themselves. Merchants by tradition, orthodox in their beliefs, they are a hard-working, entrepreneurial people who have developed an aptitude for mechanics and a speciality of locating hard-to-find spare parts.

We were not in need of repairs but did need extra engine oil. In Tunisia, both gas and oil had been plentiful at prices comparable to Europe. Assuming petroleum products would be even cheaper and more plentiful in oil-producing Algeria, I had not bothered to stock up. In the morning I would take care of this oversight.

During the night the storm overtook us with a fury. The howling wind and constant drumming of the rain on our metal cab made it difficult to sleep. It was still raining at daylight and continued hard all morning forcing us to stay in our bunks to keep dry. Toward noon, out of frustration, I pulled my coat over my head and headed into the narrow, serpentine streets looking for motor oil.

Electricity at the only gas station in town had been knocked out for hours. A single attendant was frantically pumping gas by hand. Cars were lined up for two blocks, some had already run out of gas and were being pushed forward a few feet at a time. A crowd of people carrying small plastic containers milled about in excited confusion trying to grab the nozzle from the attendant before it was stuck into another car. Everyone was limited to four liters — just over a gallon.

I watched all this from the shelter of a doorway across the street becoming increasingly worried about our own gas situation. I had always taken availability for granted, until now. The next gas, according to reports, was in El-Golea, a small oasis town 150 miles south.

We were still operating on our thirty-five gallon internal tanks. I had not yet filled our jerry cans. I calculated sufficient gas for 175, perhaps even 200 miles, if we were lucky. I couldn't buy gas here. More would be consumed waiting in line than I would be allowed to buy. I decided to concentrate on oil.

Two hours later, I finally stumbled across a man who agreed to sell me oil from a drum, if he had any left, and if I brought my own can. The mechanic tipped the drum upside down and drained what was left into a discarded can charging me forty-eight dinars, the equivalent of three dollars a quart.

On the way back to the campground, I poked my head behind some heavy wood doors into the dimly lit interiors of a few shops to see what was for sale. The unpainted wood shelves were inhospitable and practically bare — packets of crackers, dates, small cans of condensed milk, a few sardines, tins of tea and an Algerian brand of instant coffee in a knock-off Nescafé label. It was pretty dismal. If these shops closed and never

PLAYING THE BLACK MARKET

opened again the people wouldn't be any worse off.

The rain continued in a steady drizzle. The Princess was perched on her throne in the cab writing in her journal as I slogged into the campground. She was adapting much better than I had anticipated. Always in good humor with a ready smile, she brought a bit of sunshine to an uncomfortable, cramped situation. Would it change later on after days of sand and sun? And further south after we crossed into black Africa, when we hit tropical heat and mosquitos, would she still have that sunny smile?

When we had checked into the campground the attendant had assured us of hot showers. After hours of constant cold drizzle, a shower seemed the only way to warm up. I grabbed my towel and dodged rain drops to the low concrete shower building at the end of the compound, stripped off my clothes and turned on the faucet.

A slow trickle of cool water seeped from the pipe. I waited patiently for it to warm up. Nothing happened. The pressure dropped and it got colder. It was then I noticed there was only one faucet. I dressed and walked to the office.

"You said you had hot showers," I complained to the attendant. "The water is cold."

He glanced out the door into the gray drizzle and shrugged. "We have hot showers when the water is hot. The water is cold now because it is raining. It will be better after the storm when the sun is out." He pointed to a large, solar barrel on top of the shower house.

I crawled into the MOG and relayed to the Princess my tale of woe.

"If the showers are anything like the toilets," she commented, "I can wait. Have you seen those toilets?" They were French style, where you squatted over a hole in the ground.

If there is one mechanical invention that should be sainted by the Catholic Church it is the flush toilet. It's an ingenious product that simultaneously washes away waste and seals in odor eliminating the insects commonly attracted by such odors.

It is sanitation that most clearly separates the U.S. from the

Third World in general and Africa in particular. For the most part, Africa is an open sewer with all the consequences—mosquitos, flies, smells and a dozen unpronounceable diseases.

With Africa's high growth rates, people are created faster than are the means of disposing of their waste. The streets are awash with garbage, people (men mostly) urinate at will, usually against the nearest wall. Faded signs spray-painted on walls read: *Forbidden to urinate on wall. Fine, (so much)*.

But there are no options — no public bathrooms. Sanitation is a luxury. After living for weeks with open pit toilets it was easier to understand our society's near pathological obsession with clean bathrooms and the enormous obstacles faced by a people who are born into societies that lack even the basics.

Camped around us were a collection of Europeans. I struck up a conversation with a tall, long haired Swiss man with two earrings in his left lobe and a four-inch braid woven from the beard of his left cheek. He was heading south to Nigér with a small Mercedes truck, which he hoped to sell. He too, was fed up with the weather.

I queried him on what lay ahead.

"This storm does not go very far south," he said. "Those Germans" — he nodded to a couple of men camped across the way — "have just come from El-Goléa. It is possible to drive out of the rain in five or six hours."

I wanted to leave, too, I told him, but I needed dinars for the trip. There were no banks open. Did he have any to sell?

He glanced around the campground with a wary eye, and said softly: "I have brought dinars from Europe. They are very cheap there. I can sell you some, maybe 1000."

"How much?" I asked.

He thought a minute. "Forty dollars."

That was the black market rate — 25-to-1. I was delighted and reached for my wallet.

"No, no," he hissed, laying a hand on my arm. "Not here."

We moved casually to the front seat of his truck.

"You must be very careful. That man over there," he nodded toward a Dutchman sitting in the front seat of a Peugeot

PLAYING THE BLACK MARKET

station wagon. "He was caught at the border with 7,000 dinars in his sock. He brought it from Europe. The border police fined him three times what he had and made him pay at the official rate."

The Swiss was twirling his pig-tailed beard as he talked. "The dinars cost him maybe $200 in Amsterdam. The fine cost him $1000. An expensive trip, I think. He was stupid."

The risk of our being caught with black market dinars was minimal. Traveling with the Princess gave me greater legitimacy than if I were with a group of men who were always suspect. All we needed to show at the border was that we had legally exchanged sufficient funds to traverse Algeria. As we were camping and only needed money for gas, the $200 we had already changed should prove sufficient.

Cautiously, I slipped the Swiss two 20s from my stash of unreported funds. In return, he handed me a roll of dinars. We now had enough local currency to buy gas for the entire trip. Instead of $2.25 a gallon, we would be driving on 75¢ gas. With the MOG drinking fuel at an astounding rate, 10-to-12 miles per gallon, this was more to my liking.

We left the campground around three and slowly wound up the steep, curvy road out of the fertile valley to the desert plain. The sky was still ugly. We were heading straight south now, on the main road into the Sahara. The wind was at our back pushing us a bit faster than our normal forty-five miles per hour and our gas consumption would improve. We might make it to El-Goléa after all.

7

THE SANDMAN BRINGS NIGHTMARES

From Ghardaïa at the northern edge of the Sahara south to the Algerian border town of En Guezzam, a distance of nearly 1100 miles, there are only three oasis towns: El-Goléa, In Salah and Tamanrasset.

These are small settlements of a few hundred people who congregate in narrow valleys formed by the confluence of barren hills. Sweet artesian water flows to the surface supporting groves of date palms and small-scale hydroponic farming yielding plump, large-celled vegetables with a spongy crunch, and a spattering of livestock, mostly chickens, goats and camels.

The surrounding hills are criss-crossed with sand fences of palm fronds stuck in the sand in a desperate attempt to thwart the inevitable march of the great dunes across the landscape. Each morning farmers, shovels in hand, march to their small fields on the edge of the oasis to push back the sand from the base of their crops.

Between these oases there is nothing.

I have driven many times across the great expanse of West Texas thinking there was nothing out there. In terms of people, it's generally true, but there's plenty of plant life. Compared to the hundreds of miles of desolation between these oases, West Texas is the Garden of Eden. The Sahara was a revelation in redefining my concepts of desolation and distance.

Few appreciate the immensity of the Sahara, which very near blankets all of North Africa. If this great desert were placed

THE SANDMAN BRINGS NIGHTMARES

over the United States it would displace the entire heartland of our country, from Dallas to Chicago and Las Vegas to Louisville, Kentucky, more or less. Very little fertile land would be left for crops. Tens of thousands of square miles would be desolate wasteland. Each year thousands would starve due to lack of rain and depleted soil.

Even fewer grasp the mind-numbing enormity of Africa, which is over twice the size of the continental United States, or understand its political and geographical divisions. Misconceptions abound.

For starters, Africa is not a country; it's a continent with fifty-two independent countries boasting a combined population of about 600 million, twelve percent of the earth's population (twice that of the United States). Algeria alone is three times the size of Texas and still not the largest country in Africa.

"I'm going to Africa," is a statement uttered by many who are actually heading to the game parks in Kenya, one of eight countries in eastern Africa. There are seven countries in northern Africa; twenty in western Africa; eight in west-central Africa; and, eight in southern Africa.

Africa is not a homogeneous continent. The geographical regions have little in common, people-wise or culturally, although most of the continent tends to be relatively flat. If there is one commonality, aside from black skin in the sub-Saharan portion, it is the general absence of water.

Two-thirds of Africa loses more water to evaporation than is gained from rain, except in the equatorial rain forests, a thin strip that straddles the equator, which are deluged during two rainy seasons. This strip constitutes the famous jungles of Africa.

Many believe Africa is synonymous with jungle. Not true. Most of the continent is farmland or desert. There is some jungle along the southern coast in West Africa and in East Africa along the Indian Ocean on either side of the equator; none in southern or northern Africa. And the jungle, where it still exists, is rapidly giving way to coffee, cacao, pineapple and banana plantations.

Another misconception is that if you dared step from your vehicle you'd likely be consumed by wild animals. Africa is full of people, not animals. Animals are, in fact, a rarity. The few left are herded together onto a handful of game parks, most of which are in East or Southern Africa, much as the remnants of our native animals, the buffalo and elk, have sought refuge in the national parks of our West.

Those animals romantically linked with Africa — the lion and the elephant — have dwindled rapidly and are considered endangered. With human birth rates in Africa twice the world average and three times that of the United States, and with society's insatiable appetite for farm land, the animals don't have a chance. In West Africa in particular, people are virtually all you'll see.

Finally, there is the misconception that Africa is a land of barbarian tribes intent on massacring whites.

The foundation of African society is the tribal unit. But the days of tribal wars are pretty much over. Africans are mostly cattle herders, farmers, shopkeepers, laborers and beggars — a pretty benign lot on the whole. This is not to say an occasional Idi Amin will not pop up and incite traditional tribal rivalries as a means of gaining political control. This may serve to reinforce the stereotype, but the cliché of spear-chucking natives on the rampage is passé.

The people generally are friendly, gracious, easy-going with great humor and willing to help. The exceptions are limited mostly to those with a little authority — border guards, police, petty bureaucrats of all kinds — who can become obnoxious now and then, just like petty officials anywhere. Threats of bodily harm, however, are rare, particularly in the countryside. In the cities, the risk increases with the level of poverty, as it does in cities everywhere.

The campground at Ghardaïa had afforded more shelter than I realized. As we climbed out of the valley the storm unleashed its full fury turning our afternoon drive into a harrowing experience. Forty mile-an-hour winds blasted the MOG driving sheets of wet sand across the road blurring our vision. When the sand relented we were drowned in cloudbursts of driving rain. Numerous small lakes submerged the road requiring slow navigation.

THE SANDMAN BRINGS NIGHTMARES   91

At one point as we descended into a shallow valley a flash flood of muddy water raged across the road cutting it in half. Cars and light trucks were stalled on either side. A small pickup had been swept over the bank and lay broadside to the current. Several people had thrown the driver a rope and were yelling encouragement as they tried to haul him ashore.

What were the risks in crossing? I judged the river to be a hundred feet wide and two or three feet deep. If it were deeper than I thought our engine might flood shorting out the electrical system even though I had been assured the electrical components were sealed. The middle of a churning river was not an ideal place to learn the truth.

If the current were stronger than it seemed, we might be pushed over the edge to join the small pickup. On the other hand, the MOG weighed three tons with considerable ground clearance and was designed to accommodate this depth of water.

Quick calculations suggested we might be pushed sideways one foot for every fifteen to twenty we advanced. At that ratio, if my computations were valid, and I had no confidence they were, we could cross the hundred foot width and remain on the road. It was a gamble. Either we went for it, sat for hours as the water receded, or returned to Ghardaïa.

I slipped the MOG into four-wheel drive, pointed the nose slightly against the current and edged into the water at a point high on the road. My heart was in my mouth. The current hit broadside rocking the MOG. I could sense the tires slip. The river was stronger than I anticipated, and deeper. Only the tops of the tires were visible.

We began to slide sideways. I wanted to tromp on the accelerator, but increasing our speed, even if it were possible, would throw more water over the engine. Slowly but surely, inevitably, we forged across to higher ground. The men tugging on the rope stopped to watch us pass. The small American flag decal on the lower left fender glistened with water, though I doubt anybody noticed.

An hour later, the rain stopped. The clouds had lost their ominous black threat. It might be possible to drive out of the storm, after all. Blue skies would be wonderful. Still, we were fifty miles shy of El-Goléa and it was getting dark. The drive would be risky.

A prime rule of the road in Africa is never drive at night. It is dangerous enough in the daylight when you can see. At any given point the road could be washed out or you might slam into a rock barrier or a stalled vehicle.

So many African cars are held together by tape and wire that they break down frequently. When it happens, they are often abandoned where they sit. Sometimes the drivers thoughtfully place rocks across the road behind the vehicle as a warning. Unfortunately, when the car is finally moved, often the rocks aren't, creating a minefield.

Many have no head or tail lights. At night, particularly, there is no warning of their presence. Driving in the day is living on the edge. Night driving is one notch short of suicide.

By six-thirty, when it turned dark, we had cut the distance to thirty miles. A few stars lingered above us suggesting the storm was spent. But the wind had picked up, and with it, the sand. Our headlights were useless. The beams hit a wall of flying sand twenty feet in front, then fractured and dissipated into the night. When I switched the lights on high beam, the sand threw the glare back in my face. I slowed to twenty miles per hour, then fifteen.

Without warning the needle on the speedometer cranked sharply to the right, hit the small restraining post, bent in half and stayed stuck. The numbers on the odometer ceased to move. The flying sand had claimed its first victim. What other part would be next? Would the air filter clog choking the flow of oxygen to the carburetor? Would the radiator become a wall of caked sand over-heating the engine? I remembered the Toyotas in Tozeur with their externally mounted air filters. Now I knew the reason.

The road gradually ascended through a pass. El-Goléa lay on the southern flank of this low mountain range. The sand was blowing in blizzard-like intensity. Suddenly our headlights picked up a large truck stopped dead ahead in the road. I swerved left and crept past. Beyond was another truck and then another.

THE SANDMAN BRINGS NIGHTMARES   93

Traffic had come to a standstill. We edged forward past a stalled bus. The lights were on inside. Some of the passengers were reading; others were playing cards.

In front of the bus the road had completely vanished into a sand drift three feet deep. Beyond the drift a large truck and trailer lay broadside to the wind, hopelessly mired. The wind had blown an eight-foot drift against its side and was blowing sand over the top, as if the truck were a dune. By morning, if the storm continued, it would be.

I turned off the engine not knowing what to do. We could stay put, crawl into our bunks and wait out the storm, or try to push through. Off the road, to the right and left, I could barely make out the faint pin point lights of stranded cars. Some had already left the road to try a run through the open desert, only to become mired. Our options were less than promising.

Climbing down from the MOG, I tried to trace on foot what used to be the road. Just how deep and long was this drift? Was it a temporary barrier, or did it extend for a considerable distance? How far would we have to drive to regain the tarmac?

The blowing sand bit into my face and hands. I pulled the collar of my leather jacket around my neck and burrowed my hands deep inside my pockets. After a hundred yards I gave up. The sand was even deeper. I had lost all track of where the road should have been.

When I headed back toward the MOG, I realized I was totally disoriented. Fortunately, I had left the headlights on, but there were a half-dozen other pairs discernable through the flying sand. Which were mine?

I picked out a set and began to walk, leaning into the driving wind as I stumbled over the ground. The sand, now blowing full in my face forced my eyes shut. I shielded my face with my hands. Every few moments I would stop and squint through my cracked fingers for bearings.

I had picked the right set of lights. The Princess and I sat in silence neither of us quite knowing what to do. It was now almost eight. We were on the verge of accepting our fate and bundling down for the night, when to the far left I noticed a pair of creeping lights. Someone had found firm ground. There was hope. It would be a gamble, but I was slowly gaining confidence in the MOG's ability to surmount obstacles.

The key to desert driving is speed and momentum. Once you start, never, never stop. If you lose forward thrust the sand has a way of sucking you down. I locked the differential, placed the gear in crawl, revved the engine to high RPM and released the clutch.

Like a battle tank, we lurched forward at a roaring five miles per hour, up and over the embankment and into the open desert. I kept the peddle to the floor. The engine roared. We bucked and churned our way over invisible rocks, through pools of soft sand, in and out of deep gullies toward the set of lights that were still moving on the horizon.

We passed one, two, three stalled cars. Shadowy figures hunkered against the wind hopelessly digging at their wheels with shovels. I had no idea where we were going. The point was to keep going. I turned this way and that by instinct, without much thought.

The sides of the pass formed a funnel. If we kept pushing ahead, I reasoned, we would eventually discover the road, if it wasn't buried and we simply drove over it. If that happened, we would encounter the other side of the pass and be forced back. Sooner or later as the pass narrowed, we would merge with the road. At least, that was my hope.

We drove across the open desert through pitch darkness for what seemed an eternity, but was actually closer to fifteen minutes. There were no landmarks; no evidence we were making progress. That road had to be somewhere. I was beginning to question my own sanity.

With a terrific lurch, we bounced over an embankment and pitched forward down the other side onto a flat hard surface and stopped. By pure luck we were on the road. It was well marked and clear. A few minutes later we negotiated the pass and began to descend the southern flank. The wind was cut off by the mountains behind us. The clear, black sky was full of stars. On the horizon were the blinking, beckoning lights of El-Goléa.

THE SANDMAN BRINGS NIGHTMARES

Later I learned we had been fighting a freak of nature, a sand storm combined with a major depression over the Mediterranean that had dumped torrential rains over most of the North African coast and deep into the northern Sahara. Massive flooding had been reported in Algiers and Tunis; both countries had asked the United Nations for emergency relief.

It was nine when we found the campground and turned off the engine. My hands were limp from hours of white-knuckling the wheel. The clatter of the engine still rung in my ears. The Princess and I looked at each other in the quiet darkness of the cab, too tired to talk, too tired to move. It had taken us five-and-a-half hours to cover 150 miles, all but a few in a blinding sand storm.

We had come for adventure, and had found it.

Snapshot

GOOD GUYS WEAR BLACK

Being alone in the Sahara can be a frightening experience. It can be even more frightening to see another human being.

Staefan and I had just stopped for the day beneath a magnificent sand dune, its golden walls curving gracefully, sheltering us in a sacred space of desert. I had climbed to the top of the dune and was basking in the solitude and vastness of the desert when I caught sight of them, quite by accident: two black specks on the horizon.

Impossible, I said to myself. We were literally a thousand miles from nowhere. A chill came over me. If they were real, and not a mirage as I first suspected, were they good or evil?

A scene from "Lawrence of Arabia" popped into my head. A thirsty man, wandering in the hot desert, stopped at a well he knew belonged to an enemy tribe. As there was no one around, he took the forbidden water. Within moments, a speck appeared on the horizon and arrived in an instant.

It was Omar Sharif, sinisterly draped in black. As the man cowered, Sharif shot the intruder for drinking from his well.

I squinted my eyes to focus. The two specks were real and growing larger as they progressed slowly towards us. I slid down the dune.

"Arabs approaching," I announced to Staefan, grabbing the binoculars. Through the heat shimmers all I could make out were two men in flowing robes: one was tall, the other short. One was wearing black, the other, gray. Were we on their property? Ridiculous.

SNAPSHOT: GOOD GUYS WEAR BLACK

"What are they doing out here?" I thought out loud.

After days of solitude, company was a nonsequitur; it was out of place. This couple had no transportation. They were on foot. In the desert? It wasn't right. They simply didn't belong here.

They were coming closer. I suggested to Staefan we should at least get into the MOG, probably leave and find some place else to camp.

Staefan began to drive in the direction of the specks. I didn't think this was a good idea. They flagged us down, as if we could miss them. As unnerving as this situation was, it would have been worse to ignore them. The first rule of the desert is to offer help. We slowed.

Their car was stuck in the sand, the tall one in black explained. "Just over the hill." They had heard our engine and came for help. Likely story, I thought to myself. I didn't see any car and "over the hill," wherever that was, was a long way away. No one could have walked that far so quickly.

Reluctantly, we agreed to help. The one in black wanted to ride in the truck. There was no room, I tried to explain, unless he sat on my lap. But he insisted and rode spread-eagled on the roof, gripping the edges to hang on. The other one walked back. They were afraid we would leave them stranded. Every few minutes the one on top would pound on the roof, lean over the side and point a slight change of direction.

"This is a trick," I told Staefan. "They're leading us to an ambush. What if we're robbed and left in the desert to die?"

Staefan didn't say anything. Perhaps I was being overly dramatic.

There was a car, a Toyota 4 X 4, and it was stuck. Two other men were futilely trying to budge it. Staefan hooked it up to the MOG and began to drag it out.

Meanwhile I sat in the sand with the Arab in black, who offered tea from a thermos.

"Weren't you worried no one would find you?" I asked.

He shook his head. "No. It was meant that you would help."

He had the Arab attitude known as *mektoub*, meaning "that which is written," or fate. Being stuck in the sand was meant to happen and so, we should sit and have tea and make the best of it. When the MOG failed to dislodge their Toyota, my new Arab friend became excited.

"Now we can all have dinner and camp together!" he exclaimed.

As if that were all the motivation he needed, Staefan managed to extract the car and the Arabs went on their way. We headed back to our dune, the echo of their motor and shouts of joy still hanging in the air. I felt foolish for having thought the worst of them.

Black clothes don't mean what they used to. *Mektoub.*

8

BLUE SKIES AND MORE

I awoke the next morning and lay still, holding my breath, afraid to peek out the little window of our sleeping compartment. I couldn't handle another day of black skies and flying sand.

It was very quiet outside. The wind had ceased, but what of the sky?

Slowly, I rolled over and squinted through the window. The sun was just cresting the eastern horizon. The day would be clear and blue. After three days of miserable conditions, over 500 miles into the Sahara, we had finally outrun the storm.

I lay back in my bunk, breathed deep sighs of gratitude and listened to the Muezziem, the Islamic holy men, as they called the faithful to prayer from the minarets of the town's mosques. During the bustle of the day, these calls went unnoticed. In the solitude of sunrise, they were pleasantly hypnotic, soft and melodic, like the gentle, distant call of a songbird or the Sunday morning church bells in a New England town. Unconsciously, I would listen for these reassuring chants in every Muslim town we were to visit.

The Princess and I spent the early morning luxuriating in the warm sun, devoting a disproportionate amount of time preparing our simple breakfast of instant coffee, tea, instant oatmeal with dried fruit and bread.

Our other meals were equally unpretentious. Even though we tried to frequent restaurants when they were available to sample local cuisine, we had brought a hundred pounds of dried foods with us just in case. Lunch was usually dried soups, bread with pâté or Italian dried salami, and dried fruit, fresh if we could find it.

The Princess accomplished small miracles for dinner: Pasta camouflaged twenty-five different ways — a la sardines, tomato sauce, tuna, with vegetables, mixed with soups, chicken, beef broth, and for variety, plain, or in olive oil.

I was in the middle of cleaning up the kitchen after breakfast when I remembered the warnings I had received about the shortages of gas. In Tunisia, and in the black African countries we were to visit further south, most of the world's major oil companies were represented — BP, Texaco, Shell, Exxon. Not so in Algeria. Only NEFTA, the state-owned oil company, was allowed and as a rule there were only one or two stations per town.

Immediately, a small wave of panic swept over me. Buttoning up the MOG, I drove off in search of petrol. The closest NEFTA station had only diesel. The operator suggested I try the remaining station on the other side of town. When I arrived there was already a line. After a thirty minute wait, I pumped sixty gallons into the internal tanks and five jerry cans.

Back at the campground, I finished my chores and set off on a quick stroll looking at the odd-ball rigs and people that had accumulated during the night.

Saharan campgrounds are a mini-United Nations with decals and license plates from nearly every major European country. As we were part of this crowd, it was always assumed by inquisitive North Africans that we were also European. They would approach us time and again wishing to strike up a conversation, or hoping for *cadeau*, a small gift, by asking if we were German.

When I shook my head, they would squinch up their face and pause, then point to our German license plate. I would smile and shake my head. In puzzlement, they would throw out a long list of European nationalities. I would continue to shake my head until they ran through every country on their list. A few, with greater knowledge of geography, would even name the eastern European countries until they ran out of those.

One young Algerian in particular, who managed one of the

BLUE SKIES AND MORE

campgrounds we visited, had exhausted at least thirty countries in this guessing game, before he finally stopped, cocked his head in puzzlement, looked at me out of the corner of his eye, and asked with an air of disbelief: "You aren't Algerian, are you?"

I laughed and shook my head. "No, I'm American."

His eyes grew wide, the inevitable reaction to this revelation.

"American?" he exclaimed. "We never see Americans here. Why is that? Why don't Americans come here? It is always the Germans and French."

"Algeria is very far away," I suggested.

"Perhaps that is so," he responded. "But I think it is because we are socialist. Americans don't like socialist countries. Look what they did to Khadafi. I think that is the real reason." He had a look of satisfaction on his face.

"Khadafi may be part of it," I admitted. "But I think Americans don't speak French and Algeria is very far away. Unfortunately," I added apologetically, "most Americans don't know where Algeria is, let alone that it's a socialist country."

That stumped him. "How could they not know of Algeria?" he responded, finally.

Yes, I thought. How could they?

Ironically, our conversations often took place in front of the MOG with the small American flag in open view. Very few seemed to recognize the flag.

I had thought hard about putting an American flag on the fender fearful it might invite inflated prices, an increased clamor for handouts, or even subtle retaliation for our government's continual interference in the Middle East. It made more sense to travel under the anonymity of German license plates, much like in the '60s, when many of my generation traveled Europe during the Vietnam era with a Canadian flag sewn to their backpacks.

Surprisingly, we had little to worry about. The flag evoked a few curious looks, but little more. When it was recognized, we were treated as novelties with a great deal of friendliness. It was a pleasant feeling to be so far from home and able to travel incognito with the knowledge that few Americans had done what we were doing. In our two-month trip we never ran across

At an outdoor market in an Algerian oasis, the men do the buying and selling.

another American, outside of one or two embassy types, who don't count.

At the far side of the campground I spotted the Mercedes truck owned by the Swiss with the braided beard who had sold me dinars in Ghardaïa. He had arrived sometime during the night after we had gone to bed. I was curious how he had gotten through the sand blockade in the pass.

He and another man, wearing sandals and a dirty, but bright shirt, were squatting around a small fire trying to heat water when I approached. They were an odd couple.

In the northern and central sections of the desert most of the travelers were male/female couples. The further south we progressed, the tougher it became and increasingly, all we saw were men — young men like this Swiss with a cavalier attitude toward risk. Time, distance and hardship effectively weeded out the women.

"When did you arrive?" I asked.

"It was very late. About one in the morning." His English

BLUE SKIES AND MORE

was good, but slow and halting. "I was in the sand and had laid down on the seat and gone to sleep. Someone knocked on my window and woke me up. A big sand plow was there. It had cleared the road. The man put a chain on my truck and pulled me free. Here I am."

He nodded toward the MOG across the way. The Princess was rummaging in the back, fixing herself a peanut butter sandwich and more tea. "With your Mercedes, you do not have trouble, I think. They go everywhere."

"What do you have in the truck?" I asked. It was small and enclosed, like a furniture delivery truck. I had been curious from the first, but had not pried out of politeness. Now that I knew him a little better, I had to know.

"Refrigerators." He laughed and pulled on his braid. "I will sell them in Nigér. And then I will sell the truck and go home."

"How did you get a truck full of refrigerators through customs?" I asked incredulously.

"With refrigerators. It cost me one refrigerator for each border, so I bring three extra for the customs people. The customs people don't care as long as I leave with the same number that come in. Three isn't bad. In Nigér I sell them for enough that it doesn't matter." He stoked the fire and repositioned the pan of water.

"I was to take these to Nepal. This type of Mercedes is very popular in Nepal. I could get a good price. But I would have to drive through China and the Chinese would not give me a visa. So I am going to Nigér." He shrugged. "It is all the same."

There were many like this Swiss, young French, German and Dutch men, single, tough looking, bearded, hippie-types wearing sandals, dirty shirts and jeans, who were running contraband across the Sahara destined for Nigér, Burkina Faso, Nigeria or Cameroon.

They would buy used Peugeots and Mercedes, or small trucks, anything that would run, even buses, load them with spare parts, new tires and tools, and lots of gas, pack some food and a sleeping bag and drive like hell.

As they made their way inland from Tunis or Algiers, others

would join to form convoys for the frenzied dash across the heart of the desert. If one got stuck in the sand or broke down, the others were there to rescue him.

There were men on motorcycles, too, small groups dressed head-to-toe in Mad-Max suits of reinforced black leather wearing Darth Vader helmets with built-in air filters, steel-toed boots and heavy leather gloves. They rode exotically equipped cross-country motorcycles, Hondas or Suzukis, with oversized gas tanks and tires.

Packs of five or six would roar by in the distance at break neck speeds, hell bent for somewhere, spewing plumes of desert dust. They were the Saharan version of the Hell's Angels.

Further south, long after the road had disappeared, we even passed a man on a mountain bicycle peddling slowly in the mid-day sun, wearing shorts, a light shirt, baseball hat and goggles. He waved feebly as we passed. He was small and thin and looked Japanese.

About mid-day, after a leisurely early morning stroll through El-Goléa, a nondescript oasis town of a few low buildings built around a desert military post, we made our way out of town passing the station where I had bought gas three hours earlier.

The hoses hung limply over the pumps like tired snakes, a sign they were out of gas. Several vehicles were parked to one side, their occupants leaning against the fenders or sitting on the curb, waiting.

I made a mental note. The first thing we would do, day or night, rain or shine, when we entered an oasis was to buy gas, whether we needed it or not. If I had waited even one more hour it would've been too late. Two or three days would pass — perhaps more — before that station would be pumping gas again. The further south we progressed the greater the scarcity of fuel.

On the outskirts of El-Goléa we passed a bright black and yellow sign: *Have a good trip*, it said in French and Arabic. Underneath was the logo of NEFTA.

It was ironic. The further we drove into the desert and the greater the scarcity of fuel, the more new gas stations we observed under construction and the more NEFTA signs we passed wishing us a wonderful trip

I could only conclude that NEFTA assumed if we could buy enough gas to get this far, we must be having a good trip.

Snapshot

THE OASIS OF MY DISCONTENT

It is a painful experience to have one's illusions lanced.

In my languorous daydreams, the same mysterious Arab in black who now haunts my Saharan nights charges down the steep, glistening dune, sand flying, his angry white steed snorting, tossing its head and chomping at the silver bit that ravages its mouth.

As the exotic stranger sweeps me off my feet, I am tucked in front of him, his arms locked about my waist. We ride through the wind, my face half-buried in the folds of his elaborate cloak, scented with sweet incense and myrrh.

We gallop far across the rolling dunes into an oasis of fragrant gardens. Gently, he sets me down beside a sparkling pool of artesian water that bubbles to the surface amidst floating orange blossoms.

Shedding my Western clothes, I float with sybaritic abandon in iridescent waters. As other women dress me in sheer, flowing garments, a feast is spread in the shade of the date palms.

I dine across from the man in black surrounded by camel traders and merchants who speak in quiet tones of marvelous adventures in the unforgiving desert. Their eyes skim my body.

As I prepare for sleep, the man in black sweeps into my tent and sheds his robe with the poetic twirl of a bullfighter's cape. We share passion on layers of silk rugs and immense pillows while above, the white canopy flutters in the night breeze. I fall asleep to the sounds of a young boy playing a flute.

Such were the oasis dreams of my imagination.

SNAPSHOT: THE OASIS OF MY DISCONTENT

107

Even as I prepared for this trip, immersing myself in articles and books on North Africa and the Sahara, my naive vision of an oasis remained remarkably intact. My imaginary world, however, would soon collide with reality.

I did encounter occasional men in black, but not the one of my dreams. The ones I found were proud Tuaregs and Berbers with leathery hands and blue-black faces swathed against the merciless desert sun. Astride their four-legged desert cruisers, they ambled down the dusty streets with a rolling, loping gait, heads erect, not bothering to recognize the presence of a mere woman.

I watched as one Tuareg, enthroned high on his one-humped, dusty brown camel with faded red spangles dangling from its halter, moved beyond the security of the oasis toward the dunes. At an imaginary point, the camel changed directions quite deliberately and struck a predetermined course into the open desert. I watched with admiration as they disappeared. Both camel and rider moved with a certainty of direction inspired by faith in their internal compasses and a lifetime of wandering.

And I did find water, though I never floated among orange blossoms. Sweet, pure water is, after all, what an oasis is about. It seeps to the surface in shallow ponds attracting wading goats, dogs and other livestock seeking shelter from the intense heat. Irrigation brought life to grass, groves of date palms, small olive orchards and just enough agriculture to sustain a few hundred permanent dwellers.

After the harsh wasteland of the desert and hours of being jolted in the front seat of the MOG, oases were a welcome respite of fresh green in a vast sea of browns. As refreshing as they were, Palm Springs they were not.

Typically, a cement arch would rise from the desert sands welcoming visitors and forming an imaginary line that separated the oasis proper from open desert. The arch was visible from miles away. Before the green hue of palm fronds appeared, before I had any inkling of the existence of humanity, the arch would stretch its welcome across the horizon.

It was almost accidental that the road ran through the arch

In an oasis deep in the Sahara, one always lives under the shadow of the towering shifting dunes.

and not to one side or another, which would have been just as convenient. As we drove beneath it, my first sight was not of fragrant gardens but of a gas station: two pumps stuck in the sand with a small cement building set to one side. Next door was the bus station, another squat, dreary concrete building. A few men draped in gray loitered about the door. I didn't realize bus service existed in the Sahara. Later, when a truckload of men passed, I realized the bus service was really truck service.

We followed a low wall made of concrete block and palm fronds stuck upright in the sand. It paralleled the road, then deviated sharply left to encircle a mosque with a white-washed minaret that rose sufficiently above the canopy of palms to make its point. Attached to the tower were small loudspeakers. Cassette tapes called the faithful to prayer in this modern age.

We turned right and drove down a dusty lane lined with gnarled olive trees and thirsty pines. Small garden plots were visible behind rickety fences. A few goats were tied here and there. A donkey hugged a section of crumbling wall as he

SNAPSHOT: THE OASIS OF MY DISCONTENT

attempted to scrunch every square inch of himself into the only slice of shade available. At the end of the lane a small settlement of crooked, flat-topped, mud-bricked houses were concentrated under a grove of palms. Perhaps this was the oasis of my dreams.

Except for the rustling fronds, it was extremely quiet. A few Arab men, their bodies and faces wrapped in fabric, rested under the trees. There were no sparkling waters in which to float, no crisp, white tents billowing in the wind, nor youths playing flutes to lull me to sleep.

Instead, there was a walled campground with an iron gate at the far end of the oasis, dangerously close to an enormous sand dune that seemed poised to envelop the entire community. The campground provided a few spaces for vehicles to park between palms and a concrete cube shower that the proprietor swore had hot water but didn't.

A tourist registration card asked for nationality, occupation, and the nature of our trip. Occupation was a tough call since I didn't want to arouse suspicion by claiming to be a journalist or a writer of any sort. I decided I would be a caterer, *traiteur*, and marked the blank accordingly. This brought puzzled questions from the proprietor, who had no concept of catering. I made a mental note to be a teacher in the future.

As to the nature of our trip, my notation, 'tourists crossing Sahara,' brought an up-lifted brow, or did I imagine it?

The oasis included a small, mud-walled military outpost in a miniature fortress-like setting reminiscent of "Beau Geste," and a small office of *Air Algerie*. Each oasis we encountered had a small airstrip that was served by regular, low-cost domestic flights on those days the sand was not blowing. Not even the Algerians wanted to endure the harsh realities of desert travel.

The oasis surrounded a town square hemmed in by drab concrete buildings with arched portals. In the early hours of morning it became a farmer's market. Long-gowned men in white and gray, some wearing coats of red and blue, sat cross-legged on straw mats with their produce spread before them in attractive displays. Each hoped to catch the eye of other men who were doing the shopping.

110   THE LION IN THE MOON

A customer would select a few tomatoes, a carrot or two, or a bundle of greens that the merchant would carefully weigh in an old-fashioned balance scale before placing them in the client's bag. Gossip and politics were part of the process. There were no women in sight.

There was only one bakery that sold out of everything by the time the sun had peeked over the horizon. There was one small café as well with bare floors, two or three wood tables and an odd collection of chairs. The inevitable small black-and-white television featuring instructional films on animal husbandry or agriculture droned on mercilessly in Arabic in the corner.

Often, walls were covered with pictures of top American and European models torn from magazines. I recognized them immediately: stunning Paulina from Esteé Lauder ads; Elizabeth Taylor extolling the virtues of Passion; Cindy Crawford, Brooke Shields, Princess Caroline and others, a reminder of a world left far behind.

Contrary to the secret world of the Arab female, these women flaunted their beauty with makeup, elaborate hairstyles, jewelry and revealing clothes. They smiled down on their pedestrian Arab male viewers, looking them directly in the eye as if to say, buy my perfume, buy me. On these barren Muslim walls Paulina, Liz and Cindy seemed as provocatively daring and exotic as a Playboy centerfold. The magazines must have been bought abroad, for I never saw any magazines or newspapers for sale.

The trickle of tourists and shortages of a variety of foods dictated a redundant menu in this and other oases cafés: chicken or skewered lamb, french fries, and couscous. A soup might be served before the meal and coffee afterwards, if you had the patience. Inevitably, the waiter had to start a fire to heat the water.

The small, dimly lit shops were sparsely stocked with only the barest of necessities. Couscous grain was sold from large sacks. A few small tins of Algerian sardines, powdered milk, instant coffee, small cardboard boxes of sugar cubes, and several rolls of local toilet paper were arranged neatly on a dusty shelf behind the counter. Under the counter glass were school supplies: a handful of pencils and sheaves of paper, all made in

SNAPSHOT: THE OASIS OF MY DISCONTENT 111

China. Next to the pencils was a pile of cheap plastic toys, also from China.

There were none of the family size, price-saver goods so common at home, nor the range of brands and colors. A shopper typically bought two or three small items at a time. There was no need for shopping carts. There was neither room to push them nor enough food in the entire shop to fill one.

In twenty minutes, maybe thirty, it was possible to walk the perimeter of an oasis and obtain a vague sense of what living under these confines must be like — the sun, the sand, the emptiness and isolation.

Having done that and digested the realization that all life, mine included, hung by a thread, or rather, a trickle of water, I came to see an oasis for what it was: A place of water that in turn attracted a collection of mud buildings, a few acres of palms, some goats, camels and a few humans.

Had I been flying over, it would be less than a speck on the windshield.

9

AN EVENING ON THE TOWN

We had barely departed the outskirts of El-Goléa when a dilapidated, grey Peugeot pickup appeared in my rear view mirror. The driver was flashing his lights and waving frantically.

Fearing a serious mechanical problem, I quickly pulled to the side of the road. The pickup swerved off ahead of us. The driver hopped out and was standing beside my door in his long, Arab gown before I had time to turn off the engine.

"Yes? What's wrong?" I inquired.

His face lit up. "Oh, English!"

"Yes, we speak English. What is wrong?"

"Do you have anything to sell? T-shirts. Jeans. Cigarettes? Anything. Parts for the truck? Tires. Tools?" He rattled off an endless list. I kept shaking my head, not believing we had been stopped for this.

Finally, he smiled and shrugged, returned to his car and took off like a shot.

This incident was one of many small reminders that Africa is a dry sponge capable of absorbing the least particle of wealth. The deeper we burrowed into the heart of the continent, the more desperate the people became. From faded T-shirts to used bars of soap, ballpoint pens, even mildly tainted food, all would disappear at the turn of a back.

Not that we would be pulled over again — in the future I would ignore such a ruse — but whenever we stopped, for gas, at a restaurant, for a rest, wherever there were people, we would be asked to share our wealth, not in pleading voices but assertive

AN EVENING ON THE TOWN 113

tones, as if ours was destined to be theirs. They need only ask. No matter how meager we thought our possessions, we were, after all, driving a Mercedes through Africa. They drew their own conclusions.

The oasis of In Salah was 250 miles ahead. By all indications it would be a tough trip. Travelers had warned us the road deteriorated rapidly and we would find driving in the open desert more advisable. The next few miles belied this grim prediction. The highway was beautiful, wide and smooth. We rode in comfort.

Abruptly, just as I was getting a little smug, the pavement crumbled into a series of potholes; not little dents in the surface, but major excavations several feet across and half-a-foot or more deep. Caught off-guard, we pounded headlong into the first hole. Both of us were thrown out of our seats with a neck-breaking crunch as the front axle collided with the frame.

I slowed quickly trying to control the MOG while navigating between the gaping holes. Within a hundred yards the blacktop vanished completely except for chunks that stuck out of the hard packed sand at odd angles creating a mine field of deadly debris.

A barricade of sand blocked the center of what remained of the road thwarting our advance. Beyond lay a vast expanse of open desert.

Much of the desert has a hard crust an inch or so thick that covers pools of soft sand. In addition to speed, one survives the desert by steering clear of the ruts of earlier vehicles, which have already broken through this crust.

Many times, this proved impossible. The rocky terrain would funnel us into a narrow pass of powdery white sand. Before I could react the sand would stop the MOG dead in its tracks.

When this happened to other desert travelers, even those with four-wheel drive, it meant grabbing a shovel, unpacking the sand ladders (long planks of corrugated aluminum) and digging for hours.

There were times when I thought our situation hopeless; when it didn't seem possible that a small six-cylinder engine

By sunset the gates were closed tight at "Camping de Palmeraie" in the oasis of In Salah.

would have the power to ram 6,000 pounds of steel through a sea of sand as fine as powdered sugar.

The MOG, fortunately, was a different animal. With its ultra-low crawl gears, high torque engine and lock differential, we could power our way through even the most treacherous pool of sand. At a mighty three mph, engine revved, cab shaking violently, tires barely moving, we would inch our way forward while the sand sucked and pulled and constrained us in every way imaginable.

The Princess would brace one foot on the dash pushing herself against the back of the seat, holding onto anything solid for dear life. I dared not let go of the steering wheel praying the machine would not explode.

Even as my confidence in the MOG's performance increased, my apprehension of the unknown desert ahead never diminished. I always wondered if we had seen the worst or if it were yet to come. We had barely made it through the last crisis. Would the next be our last?

AN EVENING ON THE TOWN

Unexpectedly, the black hard surface would reappear and we would roll in comfort for a few miles more before being cast again into the open desert.

Word was the Algerian and Nigériene governments had made plans to finish the trans-Saharan highway sometime before the end of the century. No mention was made of 'which century.'

Saharan sand storms and heat are as inhospitable to highways as they are to humans and the Algerian method of road construction virtually guarantees a short life. Being in a hurry and not having a great deal of money to spend, roads are constructed by building up a bed of sand and rock, rolling it flat and paving it with a layer of sand and oil.

Within months the new surface begins to crumble from heat, erosion, and the incessant pounding from over-loaded trucks. After a year, the highway is so full of potholes that it's safer and smoother to drive in the desert.

Occasionally we would encounter stretches of virgin highway, sometimes forty or fifty miles, from which vehicles were totally barred. We would plod for hours through miles of rutted and rocky desert within a stone's throw of a beautiful silky black snake of a highway, totally deserted. There was no explanation.

It was speculated the highway had to season for a few months before it could take the weight of traffic; others claimed these stretches were reserved for emergencies. A Frenchman told me they were for military use and we would be fined if caught driving on them. No one really knew.

I had drawn my own conclusion: The government had finally learned, after years of frustration, that new roads lasted considerably longer if no one was allowed to use them.

Eight hours after we had left El-Goléa the minarets of In Salah appeared on the horizon.

In Salah was as close to being at the dead center of the Algerian Sahara as any place could be. If there was any spot on earth that evoked fantasies of Arab traders dozing beneath the shade of date palms while their camels drank from a pool of sparkling water surrounded by giant dunes of golden sand, In Salah was it.

116 THE LION IN THE MOON

Historically, In Salah, meaning 'salty source,' was a great trading center where caravans from the south laden with ivory, gold and slaves met those coming from the north carrying European cloth, iron tools and spices for barter. The architecture is Sudanese-style. The buildings are of reddish-brown mud with few windows and small wood doors designed to keep out the heat. The wide, sandy streets are lined with ancient, almost prehistoric olive trees.

The oasis is now the home of a few hundred inhabitants — mostly men from what I could tell — a small military outpost, a hotel, two or three restaurants, a gas station, campground and the important office of *Air Algérie*. Due to vast distances and terrible road conditions, air travel between Algiers and the interior is frequent and inexpensive. A round trip between most any point in the country was less than thirty dollars.

In Salah is noted for creeping sand dunes that have migrated to the very edge of town. The dunes are said to advance at a rate of a foot a year, quickly enough, that with the help of a little imagination one might actually see them moving. While there is little fear of waking in the morning half-buried in sand, the movement is constant and determined.

In a generation, I was told, it was possible to witness a dune absorb a small house. The occupants, rather than fight the sand, move to the far side of the oasis and rebuild with the sure knowledge that what the dune covers it invariably will uncover. Sometime in the future, in seventy-five or a hundred years, the house will be revealed as the dune moves on its way. Ownership is re-established and that family's living relatives have the right to move back in.

In Salah is also the home of a small number of blacks, the first I had noticed in North Africa.

Tall and statuesque, these people are descendants of the Berber and Tuareg nomads that roam the Sahara and sub-Saharan regions of Africa. With deep, blue-black skin and fine features that reflect generations of cross-breeding with Arabs and Moors, they are both a buffer and a bridge between the olive-skinned Arabs of the north and the Negroid tribes of the

AN EVENING ON THE TOWN

tropical south.

At In Salah, we were crossing that invisible line in the desert that marked the beginning of the end of white Africa and the encroaching influence of black Africa.

The campground was a large sandy compound, typically high-walled with a scattering of palm, olive and eucalyptus trees for shade. As it was too late to sightsee, we unpacked our folding camp table, strung a rope for wash and settled in for the rest of the day.

Even in late January with temperatures in the cool eighties old habits die hard. The desert ritual of resting behind closed doors during the heat of the day meant the town closed down after noon not to open again until early evening, if at all. Touring was limited to early morning hours.

This schedule did not mesh well with our travel habits of sleeping past sunrise and relaxing during the cool morning hours. When finally we began to explore about ten or eleven, doors and windows would mysteriously close and the town would empty of all living souls.

In Salah's single bakery sold its limited production of bread by seven each morning. This proved a particular hardship on the Princess who had acquired a taste for peanut butter sandwiches for breakfast and required a baguette a day to sustain her habit.

It was due to her insatiable quest for bread that we met Moulay.

The Princess had returned from a small shopping excursion with two baguettes under her arm in the company of a tall Algerian in his fifties dressed in a white flowing gown over long pants and a white head cloth. His face was deeply creased by the desert winds. The campground was his and he had generously offered her two of his baguettes for our evening meal.

Moulay had obvious eyes for the Princess. They talked at great length while I occupied myself with small chores around the truck.

"Moulay is taking me to town to find a wedding blanket," she announced. The two departed abruptly.

When the Princess returned she had a large blanket under

THE LION IN THE MOON

her arm. It was a handsome piece, hand woven of white cotton with red and orange geometric designs.

I returned to my chores while she spread the blanket over her sleeping bag. The nights were getting colder the further we went into the desert. The extra layer would be welcome. I resisted asking if the blanket were for a special occasion of which I had yet to be informed.

Later on, the Princess commented that Moulay had invited us to his house for couscous, if we should decide to spend an additional night. The invitation was too good to pass up. The next evening we accompanied Moulay to his home for dinner.

Our Algerian host collected us in his dilapidated black Peugeot pickup. He had to unwire the passenger door so we could slide in. The moon had not yet risen and the truck was without headlights. We crept through the narrow, inky black streets past shadows of people and trees. One tire was out-of-round causing the truck to sway back and forth. Everytime Moulay turned left, my door would fly open and he would chuckle.

We parked in front of a high, mud wall and entered through a small wood door into an inner courtyard. I stopped to stare into the brilliant, star encrusted night sky. Moulay disappeared into a long hallway. I stumbled along after him unsure of my footing. The Princess was somewhere behind me.

We passed through a series of inner courtyards into a large, dimly lit concrete room with pastel walls. A fine layer of Saharan dust covered a blue and pink tile floor. At the far end were three large, very old overlapping rugs and several pillows.

We removed our shoes and made ourselves comfortable on the rugs propping the pillows under our elbows. It was an awkward arrangement. Being over six feet with long legs, I don't fold easily. I shifted continuously, but it was impossible to get comfortable. While the Princes and our host conversed, I surveyed the room.

It was spacious, 25 X 40, or more. The ceilings were high, at least twenty feet, designed to absorb the heat. Cobwebs ornamented each corner. Two naked fluorescent tubes on opposite walls cast just enough light to see. Next to the rugs was a

AN EVENING ON THE TOWN

brass tray on a stand. On one side were two simple wood chairs; opposite the chairs was the front seat from an old car. A suitcase lay open behind the seat suggesting that a trip was imminent. Quite possibly we had interrupted someone's packing. These were the only objects in the room.

"Will you be traveling soon?" I asked, deciding to participate in the conversation. Moulay glanced at the open suitcase.

"Every year I spend a month in Europe — in Paris, or Bern or Rome. I visit friends. I will leave again, soon."

"We have interrupted your packing."

He waved his hand. "No. I will not go until summer."

Summer was five months away, although from the looks of it, he was ready to go tonight.

His annual trip to Europe obviously was an event of considerable importance. The suitcase lay open like a beckoning shrine. I could imagine Moulay looking at it every night as he ate alone in this big room dreaming of escaping the harsh austerity of oasis life.

We talked for an hour while the food was being prepared. Never once did he mention his wife or family. He always spoke in the first person, never the collective.

"Does your wife travel with you?" I inquired. I already had a notion of the answer.

Moulay gave me a strange look. "No, she must care for the children."

"How many children do you have?"

He thought for a moment. "Ten, maybe more," he answered with hesitation. "My wife knows."

"How old are they?"

Again, he hesitated. "The oldest is twenty. He is in Algiers. The youngest is," his voice dropped away. "Perhaps four. My wife knows. The others are between."

When Moulay had invited us for dinner, I assumed it was to be a family affair. This was not the case. It was dinner with Moulay, served by his children while his wife stayed in another room in a different part of the house babysitting. As the man, Moulay represented the family. Dinner with him *was* dinner

120 THE LION IN THE MOON

with the family.

After rinsing our hands in a pail of water provided by a son, one of his daughters entered with a large ceramic bowl of steaming couscous and three tablespoons. She set the bowl on the rug between us. I mentally divided the bowl into thirds and carefully ate from my portion. We ate in silence.

The daughter reappeared with another dish, a small bowl of chicken parts, which our host tore apart with his wet fingers and passed to us. The last course was a bowl of lettuce leaves and sliced tomatoes in oil and vinegar.

"We always have salad at the end," he explained. "It helps settle the stomach — good for digestion."

The son returned with the pail of warm water and we rinsed and dried our hands. Then his daughter entered with a small tea tray. Moulay poured the tea, handed each of us a full glass, picked up his own and drank with loud slurps. I mimicked his behavior. It was hard to do and not feel conspicuous. The tea was mint flavored and sweet, very sweet.

He placed his glass on the tray, satisfied. "Tea helps you sleep," he counseled. We finished ours.

Two times more he filled our glasses, but only added a touch to his own. The pot was small. Like a good host anywhere he sacrificed his own portion to make sure we received ours.

When we had finished our third glass, he handed the Princess a present, a small basket woven of reeds and plastic. We had brought gifts, too. When the exchange ended, our host rose. The evening was over.

He dropped us off at the campground about ten. It had been a leisurely three-hour evening of talk, simple food and tea. Had he been with true friends, it might have lasted longer. The length, it seemed to me, was modest considering there was little else to do.

I leaned against the MOG and stared up into the crystal clear night at the white wash of stars and thought how far we were from home. To Moulay, In Salah, a small oasis of palms and mud buildings buried deep in the Sahara, was home. It was, after all, only an hour-and-a-half by air to Algiers; three-and-a-half to

AN EVENING ON THE TOWN

Marseilles, four hours, at the most, to Paris — no greater than flying from Los Angeles to Chicago.

Standing under that broad sea of stars, I felt hopelessly lost, perched precariously on the edge of the earth, about to plunge into the abyss. Who had ever heard of In Salah? What if we were to disappear in a sea of sand? Would it matter? We weren't important people. A search, if launched at all, would be half-hearted.

I had this overwhelming urge to get back in touch with my world. I crawled into the cab of the MOG and tuned in BBC on my short wave radio.

"The World Health Organization," the voice said, "has just announced that for the first time in history more than fifty percent of premature deaths in the Third World are life style deaths, and not due to traditional killers such as malaria, yellow fever, cholera and TB. Life style deaths are those deaths caused by cancer and heart disease: diseases due to fat, sugar and stress."

I turned off the radio and reflected on Moulay's family perched in front of their black-and-white TV. I wondered how long his wife would be content to babysit while her husband played in Paris.

I thought of all the TVs I had seen in huts around the world spouting their revolutionary messages of greed, consumption and change. Television was now the driving force behind politics, diplomacy, market economies and life-style changes. The world was coming together into a global culture faster than we could possibly comprehend. Third World political instability was both proof and byproduct.

While the pen remains mightier than the sword, television is worth a thousand pens.

Snapshot

MY DINNER WITH MOULAY

Moulay wore a white dress and his eyes were rimmed in heavy black kohl. His skin was the color of peanut butter and his head was perpetually swathed in a maze of thin, white muslin that he would constantly rearrange to cover his mouth.

When he talked to me, I was forced to look into his dark eyes. Over his white robe, he wore a tweed blazer, a Western touch that was very chic and original.

A heavy silver ring adorned each hand; he was quite proud of his large wristwatch. Besides being an ornament, it gave him the distinction of being a businessman, of having some place to go, something to do at an appointed time. Moulay was a man of affairs.

His full name was Moulay Abderrahman and he owned the Camping de Palmeraie at the oasis, In Salah, where we had decided to camp.

I liked Moulay because I understood his French, and he mine. So many others had heavy accents, or mixed French with local dialects. They were hard to understand unless they spoke very slowly. Moulay spoke perfect French, to my minor ear, and so we talked. I could expect a visit from Moulay several times during the day.

One morning I informed him I wanted to find a Tuareg wedding blanket. I had read about them and wanted to acquire one, but wasn't even sure what they looked like. Did he know where to find one in In Salah? I inquired.

"Of course," Moulay replied. "They are difficult to obtain.

SNAPSHOT: MY DINNER WITH MOULAY

But I have a friend who has a small shop. I will take you there."

He led me out of camp down a dirt road lined with softly boughed pines to a plaza bordered with ancient olive trees.

On a corner was a musty shop painted blue inside. Behind the counter, a statuesque black man swathed in multi-striped cloth presided over floor-to-ceiling shelves sparsely filled with clothing and household goods.

Moulay and the merchant exchanged words in a language I did not understand. In short order a blanket was produced from a stack in the corner. The merchant handed it to Moulay, who presented it to me.

The blanket was much longer than wide, of white cotton striated with an unusual color combination of green, orange and maroon. "What of the other brightly colored blankets?" I inquired. They were not Tuareg, Moulay answered. His attitude suggested he did not deem them worthy of my consideration. The one I held in my hands was made in Timmimoun in the depths of the Algerian Sahara, he told me.

Since Moulay was part Tuareg and married, I could only assume he knew his wedding blankets. On the other hand, he was a merchant and I was his pigeon. I wasn't sure I really liked the one I had been given, or that indeed it was truly a Tuareg piece. I decided to show it to Staefan. In the meantime it might grow on me.

Moulay and I chatted as we walked slowly back to the camp. He moved gracefully with the blanket neatly folded in the hook of his arm. Each time he wanted to emphasize a point he would stop walking and turn on me full face with his dark eyes.

"Life must be experienced through the soul; you must taste it, drink it up," he would say in his soft voice, but with an undertone of urgency. "You have the means to do it, but not with him," he nodded towards the campground. "He will tie you down."

"I will introduce you to my friends," he told me again as he stopped walking to make the point. "I will put kohl under your eyes, take you into our culture, teach you what the Sahara is."

Thankfully, the campground was not far. Staefan was work-

Our host Moulay discusses the value of the Tuareg wedding blanket with the Princess.

ing on the truck. He thought the blanket beautiful. It would keep me warm at night and it certainly dressed up the drab interior of the MOG.

"Would the merchant accept dollars?" I asked Moulay, knowing the answer in advance. Algeria had a very active black market.

Moulay nodded his head deeply: "Any amount you offer in

SNAPSHOT: MY DINNER WITH MOULAY

dollars would be gratefully accepted."

I didn't know how to respond. Any amount? I was tempted to shoot back: $10! I'll give you $10. What a steal!

The merchant's price for the blanket, in official currency, was about $200. I didn't want to insult my new Algerian friend, yet the price was clearly inflated. Apologetically, I offered $40, fully expecting him to laugh. Moulay accepted my offer with a deep bow of his head. I unfolded two crisp twenties from my secret stash. They looked very strange after dealing with the large and colorful money of Algeria.

With a polite thank you and a thin smile he tucked the bills into the folds of his gown. He traveled each year to Paris, he explained, and needed money for his airplane ticket, which could only be purchased in hard currency.

I had my Tuareg wedding blanket, which I folded and laid over my sleeping bag. From that night on I was never cold. Come nightfall, I would lay in my bunk and dream of the nomadic Tuaregs sleeping under their blankets just like mine. It was a slim thread of communion with a people I would never know.

Moulay returned later after the mid-day heat to invite us to his home for dinner the following night. We had already made plans to leave the next morning on our journey south. This was truly a shame, Moulay lamented. His voice was tinged with sadness. He asked me to think about it over night.

A bright new moon cast its light through the small vents of the MOG. I lay awake listening to the soft pine boughs dust the metal roof.

"You must experience life in the Sahara." Moulay's words haunted me. I decided, yes, we should spend another night.

Moulay was very glad. When he saw our truck in the morning, he informed me, he assumed we were staying and told his wife to start the couscous.

A little past sunset Moulay called for us in his pickup. It was very dark; there were no street lights. He drove cautiously out of the campground and down the dirt road without headlights. I was stuffed between the two men: The Algerian pressed on my left; Staefan's large body squeezed me on the right. Only the

126   THE LION IN THE MOON

silent stars were visible as we pulled alongside a high dark wall.

Moulay opened a small, faintly blue door. We followed, still in the dark, through a black curtain into a room with a sand floor. A large pan filled with glowing coals was set in the middle. A black woman, whose head was wrapped in gray cloth, sat on the floor beside the coals holding a lifeless baby in her arms. More children of varying ages were sprawled on several thin mattresses covered with fabric. A portable black-and-white television played quietly in the corner.

We were introduced to Moulay's wife and children. Staefan, convinced the baby was dying, inquired if it were sick. It was only sleeping, Moulay reassured him. How embarrassing, I thought, as Staefan continued to look at the child with great concern. What a bleak picture this was, this huge family living in a one-room house with no furniture but a TV. I was looking for a place to sit when Moulay commanded us to follow.

We trailed behind down a dark hall past many dark rooms. *"L'electricité ne marche pas,"* he explained.

We passed the kitchen on the right, a small room lit by a single, bare light bulb. One of his daughters, who looked to be sixteen, was squatting on the floor squeezing couscous between her hands and piling it into a *couscousiére*.

I was fascinated at the thought of an Algerian kitchen and asked Moulay if we could go in. He agreed reluctantly. It was a sparse kitchen with high bare walls, a sink, a few shelves with round trays, a tea pot and a few other utensils. The small stove and oven reminded me of a Suzy Homemaker kitchen set. There was no refrigerator.

I wanted to talk with the girl, to learn about couscous and the mechanics of Algerian cooking but had the uneasy feeling our host did not relish us in the kitchen. He stood impatiently in the door, half turned and ready to lead us on our way. Obviously, he saw this as women's work, a task and place below himself and his guests.

We continued our trek through the house. I wondered where we were going and when this house would end. We passed through yet another room where the ceiling was filled with stars. What a magical place, I thought, pausing to stare. It

SNAPSHOT: MY DINNER WITH MOULAY

was not a room but an inner courtyard with a clothesline strung across it. I was looking into the heavens.

A few more stairs and we arrived in the main salon, a large room painted the palest of Mediterranean blues with a white ceiling. Cobwebs hung high in the corners and the inevitable dust of the desert powdered the floor. A cobwebbed chandelier hung from the center of the ceiling, its two working bulbs emitting a soft glow. Built-in banquette seats marked each corner. There was no furniture in this large room, nor was there anything on the walls.

This was a huge, empty house, yet the family huddled together in one small room around warm coals, as nomads would in a tent on the desert. They did not know what to do with such a large house.

Moulay led us to the far corner of the room where two rugs of different design and coloration were rolled out next to each other. He slipped off his shoes and sat comfortably cross-legged on the rugs. I wrestled with my shoes. Reeboks were more difficult than sandals. Clumsily, I untied each shoe, standing on one leg, then the other, leaving the shoes in the corner. Fortunately, my socks were clean and without holes. How foolish it had been not to wear sandals.

Our host invited us to become comfortable. I tried to affect an easy, reclining pose, leaning against the hard banquette, legs casually pretzeled. Dinner had not yet begun and already I could feel my left leg going to sleep.

Again, I was seated in the middle. Staefan shared the rug on my left; Moulay was perched on a pillow to my right. As the conversation began I realized I would have to work at this party. Staefan asked long questions in English which I struggled to translate into French. Then I had to listen very carefully to what Moulay said before translating the answers back to Staefan. The only consolation to the arduous evening was that we'd need only a third of the conversation normally required for such social occasions.

Moulay told us he had opened the campground because it was good business and because he could meet all the interesting people coming through the Sahara. He had made many good friends. His favorite city, he confided, was Paris where he spent a month each year with friends on the Left Bank. From Paris he would continue on to Germany and Switzerland, again visiting and staying with friends. He always traveled alone. His wife and children remained at home.

Moulay did not know exactly how many children he had; ten or twelve he guessed. As for their ages, he could remember the month and year of each child's birth and would try to calculate their ages from that.

"Will you arrange marriages for your children?" I asked.

"Things have changed now," he said. "Girls marry whomever they want. There are no more arranged marriages."

"Where do boys and girls meet?" I pressed, since there seemed so little social life that included women.

"They know the places," he smiled, rolling his eyes. "At school, in passing, they know."

"*Coup de foudre*?" I suggested.

He nodded. "Love at first sight is still the best way."

A teenage son entered the room carrying a pitcher of water, a bowl and a towel over his arm. He knelt next to Staefan and placed the bowl with a colander-like cover on the floor. I was grateful not to be the first in this charade and watched carefully.

Staefan placed his palms up over the bowl. The boy slowly poured warm water over them as Staefan rubbed his hands together as if he were washing them. As there was no soap I wondered, was this for cleanliness or social ritual? The son handed Staefan a towel to dry his hands. The procedure was repeated with each of us, the towel being passed from one to the other before the boy left the room.

Minutes later, the daughter entered bearing a tray she set on the floor in front of us. It held a large ceramic bowl of steamed couscous with a sauce of carrots and turnips and three spoons. I waited for Moulay to begin and then proceeded carefully eating only my share from the communal bowl. It was better couscous than any restaurant had served us.

We ate slowly. No one appeared to be greedy or too hungry.

SNAPSHOT: MY DINNER WITH MOULAY

Perhaps like the proud characters in "Don Quixote," we pretended not to be famished. Rather, we talked and took the food as an accessory to the conversation. What a pleasant way to eat.

Staefan passed a jar of yellow-green pickled peppers. I selected one and popped it into my mouth. Moulay looked stunned. He held his breath and watched my face. I smiled and asked for another.

"Mais, tu as l'habitude!" he announced with pleasure breaking into a rare, broad smile that showed stained teeth. He passed me the jar so that I might take another.

I noticed that Moulay cut his pepper with the edge of his spoon and ate small pieces with a spoonful of couscous. I asked for yet another pepper so that I might try this as well.

"Three, then, stop," he warned, saying stop emphatically in English. "You may have one more, three is good. But I am worried about your stomach."

There was also a small dish of chicken parts on the tray. I was tempted to spoon up a piece with my couscous, but wisely decided to wait.

In due time Moulay passed out small cloth napkins which were on the tray and instructed Staefan to help himself to chicken. Staefan obliged by picking up a piece with his fingers. Moulay took over, picked up a juicy piece and tore off a portion which he handed to me. We ate the chicken with our hands.

Staefan broke the silence with a question: "Is it true about eating with only the right hand? I have read that the left was reserved for personal toilette."

"Now? You want me to ask him that now?" I shot back in a bare whisper, hoping Moulay truly didn't understand English.

"Yes, ask him." Staefan prodded. "I want to know. It's one of the great mysteries, along with the pyramids."

I tried to phrase the question as politely as possible, as Moulay was eating away with both hands.

"No truth to the rumor," he responded between bites.

Staefan had me ask him again, thinking Moulay did not understand. I rephrased the question as delicately as possible, to which Moulay replied, "If you are left-handed, you eat with the left hand. If you are right-handed, you eat with the right hand."

"C'est bon," I replied, feeling extremely provincial for asking.

As if on cue, the daughter returned with the cleansing water ritual that her brother had performed earlier. The tray was removed and another one put in its place. This one had a glass bowl filled with dark green lettuce leaves and sliced tomatoes lightly dressed in a vinaigrette that glistened beneath the chandelier's soft light. We selected leaves with our fingers. The tomatoes were sweet and rich, unlike those I had ever tasted at home.

"The best tomatoes in Algeria come from In Salah," said Moulay proudly.

We repeated the water ritual a third time to cleanse our hands from the salad. Yet another tray was set before us. This one held a small enamel teapot and three delicate glasses. Each glass was of a different shape and design. Moulay began the tea ceremony by pouring the mint tea into one glass, then pouring the tea back into the pot. He did this twice with much precision.

"It's to mix the sugar," he explained. "You can do it two or three times."

He then poured a tiny bit into a glass and tasted it to check strength and sweetness before serving his guests. When it met with his approval he filled the three glasses lifting the pot high into the air so the stream of tea arched directly into each glass without spilling a drop.

Our host said something in Arabic and sipped his glass with loud slurping noises as was customary. I tried my best to imitate him without feeling self-conscious.

Twice more Moulay filled our glasses for the traditional three rounds of tea, which according to Arab hospitality meant we were honored guests. If he had offered only two rounds we would have been guests but not honored; four rounds were reserved for his best friends.

Abruptly, Moulay rose and left the room. I looked at Staefan wondering if we had offended him in some way. Perhaps we had not slurped loudly enough. He soon returned with a present for me, a colorful woven basket.

We, too, had come bearing gifts: Lucky Strike cigarettes for

SNAPSHOT: MY DINNER WITH MOULAY

Moulay; ballpoint pens, peppermints and balloons for the children; and Paloma Picasso perfume for his wife.

I had brought several small bottles of beautifully boxed perfumes, gifts from hefty cosmetic purchases at Neiman Marcus. It seemed odd to give a gift of designer perfume to desert dwellers. I wondered if his wife would think it gaudy. Moulay excused himself to deliver the gifts to his family.

"Allez-y," he said upon his return.

We struggled awkwardly from the rugs and pillows, which by now had become quite comfortable, and retraced our original steps through the dark maze of rooms, through the starry courtyard and up and down stairs stopping to visit at the family room.

Madame had not moved from her place on the floor, the sleeping baby still in her arms. She held out her rough, calloused hand to me. I bent down to shake it and looked into her tired eyes thinking how oppressed she looked. At that moment she broke into a beautiful, wide smile showing all her white teeth and thanked me for the perfume which sat in her lap. I liked her immediately and wished I could have spent a few days beside her in her daily routine.

The evening was over and Moulay, once again, was quickly whisking us away from his family and into the dark.

On the ride back to the campground Moulay asked me to stay another day. We would decide in the morning, I told him.

As I was fixing my breakfast tea, I caught sight of Moulay heading toward me with four *baguettes* tucked beneath his arm, more than we could possibly eat in one day. In the dry Sahara bread turns to stone within hours.

He handed me the bread and asked if he could do my eyes with kohl in the traditional Arab fashion. There was so much he wanted to show me, he said.

Staefan interrupted with a no, we just had to go. It would be a long drive.

Moulay was very sad. We said our farewells, climbed into the MOG and drove out the campground gate. I watched Moulay disappear in the rear-view mirror — a man in a white dress with kohl around his eyes.

10

A LITTLE DETOUR IN THE DESERT

The howling wind was beginning to take its toll. The MOG was acting up, its carburetor slowly choking on sand. I had to pump the gas pedal continuously to gain power. Still it ran, for which I was immensely grateful.

I had no idea how many days it would take us to reach Tamanrasset, the crossroads of the Sahara, over 400 miles to the south. The reputation of this oasis was considerable. At a higher elevation on the edge of the Hoggar Mountains, it was a favorite watering hole of modern trans-Saharan trekkers, as it had been for camel caravans of earlier centuries.

The red line on the map indicated an improved, all-weather road the entire route. That meant little, as I had painfully learned. In fine print were thin red arrows pointing towards sections of the highway with the words, *revétement détérioré*. In French it meant the road was in poor condition. To me it meant: This road exists in someone's imagination.

The road out of In Salah had been in modest shape. Typically, within a few miles, the pot holes reappeared and shortly beyond the pavement ended abruptly. Car tracks split off left and right into the desert following the path of least resistance.

I edged across an embankment into the open desert slipping in and out of four-wheel-drive as we alternated between pools of sand and hard alkaline plains.

There was absolutely no vegetation to be seen, not a twig, leaf, or blade of grass, dead or alive. There was flat sand and rolling sand, and miles of hard encrusted sand giving way to

A LITTLE DETOUR IN THE DESERT

Hungry? Pick a dune, stop and open the kitchen.

alkaline dust and then more sand sometimes interrupted by jagged, saw-tooth outcroppings of volcanic rock.

We stopped for lunch in the middle of a vast plain. The horizon was perfectly flat, so flat I could observe the curvature of the earth on all sides. The largest objects in sight were small, round black rocks the size of baseballs. They spread before me like a sea of marbles.

In the afternoon, the terrain changed again. Sand dunes reappeared, the classic kind in the shape of a perfect crescent, their backs arched against the wind.

The Sahara contains several independent seas of sand. They are labeled on the map just as the Pacific and Atlantic oceans are labeled. In Western Algeria lies the *Grand Erg Occidental*; in the Eastern part along the Tunisian and Libyan borders, is the *Grand Erg Oriental*. The trans-Saharan road splits them.

Other great seas of sand exist in the extreme Western Sahara, in Mali and Mauritania. These seas move and change their shape, expanding outward, consuming more and more of the North African landmass while reaching down into sub-Saharan Africa, although at a rate imperceptible to the eye.

The classic dunes, the ones made famous by Lawrence of Arabia and popular literature, are often isolated phenomena. Some of the smaller ones we encountered were two or three hundred yards long and forty or fifty feet high. They travel across harder surfaces, alkaline or volcanic plains, pushed by the wind, taking on the shape of a roving croissant. The constant pressure of the wind, which whips the sand from the back over the tops and around the edges, gives them an almost perfect symmetry forcing the wings outward in a graceful curve, as if it were a giant crab claw in search of dinner.

As often as possible, we would park the MOG in the sheltering arms of one of these marvelous monuments, if for only a moment, to walk the length and marvel at the purity of its design and majesty of its simplicity.

After a tough nine hours of travel in which we had covered barely 150 miles at an average speed of 17 mph, we camped near Arak. According to the map it was a small oasis settlement, but we could find no trace of its existence. What we did find in the middle of a long, naked canyon was a thorn tree. Its protective canopy seemed the perfect place to spend the night.

There is something odd about the human urge to find shelter. We were turtles carrying our shell and could have stopped anywhere but for some reason we always sought the backside of a cliff, the hooking arm of a dune, a half-dead tree or a pile of rocks. This night it would be a tree, not just any tree, but the only tree we had seen for several days. As we approached, a small herd of wild camels ambled off.

The setting sun cast the barren east wall of the canyon in shades of pink. The silence was deafening. Air molecules vibrated against my ear drums.

After dinner I sat at our small dining table and typed notes. Giant moths dive bombed the butane lamp at my elbow. This was our fourteenth day of travel. We were 1,000 miles south of Algiers, yet still only half way through the Sahara.

I snuggled in my leather jacket as I pecked away at the keyboard. Instead of getting warmer, the nights were getting

A LITTLE DETOUR IN THE DESERT   135

colder. Our sleeping bags were too thin, so we slept in our clothes.

The Princess and I tried to get an early start the next morning. If we could push through to Tam we would spend two or three days resting. But it would be a hard drive. I had not given serious thought to a mechanical breakdown since we entered Algeria, but as I crawled behind the wheel and reached for the ignition, I realized I was becoming a religious man.

What if the engine failed to start? What would we do? The rule of any travel, mountain or desert, is to stay with your vehicle. We had sufficient food and water for at least two weeks. Chances were someone would stumble across us.

We might be rescued, but what would happen to the MOG? Only a larger truck could tow us; parts were impossible.

Looking back, I suppose I would have left it to the camels. As soon as it was discovered, the MOG would have been stripped clean of every useable part down to each nut and bolt, its frame left to oxidize slowly, very slowly, in the desert heat. At the time, the whole issue was too ugly to contemplate.

The next morning, as we emerged from the long canyon, I stopped to take our bearings. Numerous tracks wove around us so we were far from lost, yet there was no certainty we were where I thought we were, or should have been. In these moments you need to rely more on your compass than on instinct. But ironically when instinct is in doubt, so is faith in your compass. It is also at those moments when you realize just how terribly alone you really are.

At the every edge of the horizon I thought I detected a moving object progressing at great speed. You can never be sure of these sightings because the desert plays tricks on your vision. I steered southeast across a flat crusty surface in the general direction of the object, which in the meantime had long disappeared.

After about fifteen minutes I was on the verge of turning back thinking I had been suckered by a mirage when we lurched over a high mound of sand and onto a newly paved road. It was absolutely the last thing I had expected.

There are never road signs, markers or other indications that a road exists. Except for that chance flicker of movement I had presumed was another vehicle, we could easily have paralleled this highway for many long hours and never known of its existence.

My joy was short-lived. In a few minutes a barricade appeared. A crudely painted arrow detoured us to the left off the road, which proceeded straight ahead to the horizon. In Algeria a detour sign is not an invitation to take an alternate well-marked route. It is an abrupt warning that the road is closed and you're on your own.

I debated driving around the barricade and continuing on. The road beckoned. It was straight and beautiful as far as I could see. What harm could it do? Chances were we would encounter no one of authority. Even if we did, we were dumb, lost tourists who couldn't read French.

Behind us a large tanker truck appeared and swerved off the road into the open desert heading for a series of low hills. Algerian truckers knew this desert route like their backyards. If he had left the road it was for a good reason.

I turned about and followed in his tracks believing if I stuck close he would blaze the trail. That was a mistake. With his huge sand tires and savvy knowledge of desert driving, we were quickly outdistanced.

Once again we found ourselves wandering in the open desert. Occasionally, an abandoned oil drum with a painted arrow and the word Tam scrawled in white paint would appear in the distance providing temporary guidance. More often, there was nothing. I had the sense we were driving in a large easterly loop around some mountains. They seemed to go on forever and I couldn't figure out how to get back to where I intuitively felt the road had to be.

The Princess continually searched the horizon with field glasses trying to pick out a landmark — anything, but it all looked the same. The heat shimmers rising from the sand distort everything beyond a few hundred yards.

There was very little conversation between us. There was

A LITTLE DETOUR IN THE DESERT

nothing to say. Either we knew where we were or we didn't. As long as I stayed within range of the criss-cross of tracks and were able once in awhile to see some sign, like an old tire rim or a piece of car, I retained some sense of assurance we were headed in the right direction. It was when the tracks completely disappeared and we hadn't seen an old tire for a couple of hours that I began to develop a funny feeling inside.

It was after an extended bout of insecurity that I stopped on the brow of a ridge to study the landscape in earnest. I stared through the binoculars into the vacuum of space for many minutes, searching for a sign. Suddenly, a flash of light. The sun was reflecting off something, a windshield, maybe. I slapped my knee with a great sense of relief, slipped the MOG into gear and headed for the pinpoint of light.

In twenty minutes we were on the road. It had been a four-hour, hundred mile detour. How many miles had been in circles and how many toward our destination I had no idea.

Two Germans told me later the road beyond the barricade was in excellent condition but was reserved for the Algerian Army, who used it only occasionally. The road wound through a stretch of mountainous terrain the army probably considered strategic so they decided to keep it for themselves forcing us, and numerous others, to grope about in the desert like blind mice.

The Germans had done what I had wanted to do — bypass the barricade and stay on the road. They had been stopped within a couple of miles by two army guards who threatened to arrest them for trespassing, and would have, except the Germans graciously bestowed many fine gifts upon their reluctant hosts.

In gratitude, the Algerians had let the Germans pass. They rode all the way into Tamanrasset in style.

Snapshot

DESERT TREKKERS

You meet all types in the desert rendezvous of Tamanrasset.

Two young women, one blonde, the other brunette, shuffled into the campground at Tam, deep in the Algerian Sahara. They walked tilted slightly forward from the weight of the towering backpack each carried. In their mid-twenties, they were fulfilling a dream: backpacking across Africa.

As they threw down their packs and collapsed into the chairs next to mine, the brunette gave me a tired look and groaned, "I'll never do this again."

A journalist from New Zealand, she was the more assertive of the two with short, curly hair, flushed cheeks and a determined manner. Her companion seemed younger and a bit ingenue. Maybe it was her long blonde hair. Whatever, they were good friends and a perfect match as traveling companions.

They had mapped out an ambitious plan that was to lead them across the Sahara, through West Africa, then southeast across the continent to Kenya and the game parks. They had been dogging our tracks down the length of Algeria, stumbling into a campground a day or two after us, just in time to wave goodbye as we drove out.

Six months was their allotted time to see Africa and they were determined to do it all. They were several weeks into their journey, only halfway through the Sahara and already discouraged. Hitching rides was consuming more of their valuable time than they had anticipated. It had not been as easy to catch rides as they had thought.

SNAPSHOT: DESERT TREKKERS

They would solicit rides from other trekkers offering to chip in on gas, but most had no room to carry two extra bodies. When that failed they would pay Algerian truckers to let them ride along, even in the back with the cargo. But that rarely worked. The truckers made their own way through the desert. It was impossible to flag them down.

As a last resort they would hop a bus, or try to. "We've waited hours, even days, for these buses," the brunette sighed, "they'd never show up. When finally we'd corner one, it would drive right by because it was so overcrowded. I figured, if all else failed we could use public transport. It was the worst."

Paperbacks sustained them. At each campground they would move down the row of campers trying to swap their just-finished tome for another English-language paperback. Considering most trekkers were Europeans, English wasn't the language in demand.

The brunette pulled a paperback from her backpack. "Have anything to trade for this?"

"Sorry, wish I did."

"The Thornbirds" was up for grabs, a book I'd wanted to read for years. Unfortunately, attempting to travel light as a feather, I had discarded the thick book I now pined for. It was impossible to buy a book in the desert, let alone one in English. The first place I saw a few paperbacks was near the end of our trip, in Togo. Old and pre-owned, they were kept inside a locked cabinet and sold for $10 each.

She sighed and stowed it inside her pack. I lusted after that book. I wanted to grab it from her and run.

"You know what I miss most?" the blond asked. "Water."

"God, there's so much desert," the brunette added. "It's so hot! I'd give anything for a swim and an ocean view."

"Where are you heading after Algeria?" I asked.

"We're heading straight for the beach. Probably Togo. It's supposed to have pretty good beaches."

Surprisingly, they did arrive. Several days after we had set up camp on a beach in Togo the two Kiwis trudged through the gate. I saw them every day on the beach, floating in the sap-

140   THE LION IN THE MOON

phire waters and reading books.

A week later when Staefan and I departed Togo for Paris, they were reclining against a palm tree, reading. I wonder if they ever made it to Kenya . . .

* * * * * * *

"He won't bite ya," said Laura in her heavy British accent as she scooped up her small dog. Her long blond hair and pudgy, sunburnt face nuzzled into his. "He's our baby, aren't ya luv?"

Laura and her husband, Dennis, had long ago given up the idea of returning to their home in Jersey, England. They had adopted a dog, a mongrel actually, and now were doomed to wander the globe. Jersey forbade them to enter with an animal acquired abroad. Rather than jettison 'Jeff,' who by now was part of the family, they would stay out of Jersey forever, if necessary, and only travel to those countries that allowed parents to bring their adopted children with them.

The three of them travelled in a white VW bus outfitted like a miniature home. Curtains, carpet, and a kitchenette provided, if not all the comforts, then the very basic ones, at least.

True nomads, they travelled wherever they wished finding work along the way. North Africa was actually a vacation. They had already lined up summer jobs on the French Riviera where Dennis, a mechanic, would work in a garage and Laura would work as a maid at a deluxe campground. Jeff would be resident mascot. Until late spring, they were free as birds.

It worked well for them, as they had been traveling in this fashion for several years. Laura did not mind doing menial jobs. And a mechanic was handy anywhere.

The Brit's VW bus, equipped with city tires, often got stuck in the sand. We had pulled them out once, for which they were eternally grateful and thanked us with an invitation to pop by for dessert when next we met, which I knew would be soon.

A week later the five of us (including Jeff) sat scrunched in their van with Dennis in the driver's seat, swiveled around to face us. Laura poured tea and passed biscuits without getting up

SNAPSHOT: DESERT TREKKERS

and Jeff sat quietly in the passenger seat waiting for something to fall to the floor.

"We're not proud," she said to me. "We do what we have to do. Dennis and me, we're buying a life style, so to speak."

"Being a mechanic, I'm in high demand," Dennis added. "I can find a job about anywhere. I carry my tools everywhere I go. Everyone needs a mechanic. Look at these blokes." He waved a hand at the campers outside. "There are half-a-dozen lorries broke out there. Soon as I walk outside someone will be asking me advice. Trouble is, I've got me own problems." He looked at Staefan. "You don't have extra tubes (shock absorbers), do you? Mine are busted. I've searched the whole bloody town for them."

Staefan shook his head. "Sorry. Even if I did, they wouldn't fit a VW."

"I'd make 'em work," Dennis smiled. "There's always a way."

I first spotted Dennis under a truck. Wearing a white jumpsuit, he was laying flat on his back tinkering with something under a neighbor's camper. Dennis was the polite British sort who could never say no, so he spent much of his free time fixing other people's problems.

He seemed to love being in demand and he loved the quick camaraderie that formed among the men. Perhaps because they were all strangers in a strange land, the men felt their strength in numbers. Dennis would take a look at their engines, the men would discuss the fine points of tuning or whatever, and they would all have a beer, which someone had managed to ferry across 1,500 miles of desert.

Dennis and Laura had simple tastes and simple clothes and could live a long time on what they made in the summer. In the last few months, they had driven through Italy, Greece and Turkey. I marvelled at how much they had seen, but also at how little they could possess. Memories were the only things that could fit in their tiny VW. But oh, what memories they had tucked away . . .

* * * * * *

142 THE LION IN THE MOON

Malcolm and Jean were a different breed of British.

They passed us on the desert one day after we had crossed from Algeria into Nigér, going faster than the wind. Their white Land Rover Safari was in line for border inspection behind ours. It was quite a rig: turbo-diesel, solar panels for heating and electricity, infrared water filtration system, air conditioning , . . all that was necessary to travel in style.

Jean was tall, slender and elegant with a sheer scarf that she held about her face to keep the sun off. Malcolm had graying hair, a quick gait and an air of breeding. They were gentle, educated people who seemed very much at home in the desert.

Staefan and I had crossed the border first, but they soon passed leaving us in a stream of dust. We caught up with them a few hours later on the brink of sunset setting up camp beneath a majestic sand dune. Inviting us to share their dune, we set up camp in a spot that would not invade their privacy and joined them for tea.

Jean had arranged a card table with lawn chairs directed towards the western horizon. As the four of us sat beneath the igniting sky sipping hot tea and munching crackers, we gazed out into infinity and talked about home and travels.

Jean and Malcolm had been missionaries for twenty-eight years in Ethiopia and Kenya. Malcolm's interest lay in agricultural engineering. He was torn between heading back to school to earn a doctorate or continuing on in West Africa to experiment in arid agriculture.

Their two children had grown up in Africa and it remained their home. On their first visit to the States, they had complained, "But Mommy, where are all the flies?"

They were now attending college in California, but were not completely happy. They missed the closeness of family and the strong sense of values they had grown up with in Africa.

Malcolm and Jean would eventually head to California to visit their children but could not resist the pull of Africa, their spiritual homeland. After a short stay they would be back.

"I do like America," Malcolm said quietly. The sky was a

SNAPSHOT: DESERT TREKKERS

flaming orange. "It is a grand place with giving people. We have many fine friends there. But it's not a place to stay. Really, there's nothing like Africa."

* * * * * *

A row of painted black camels walked in single file across the side of Hans' Hanomog, a Mercedes vehicle similar to our UNIMOG. It was an imposing vehicle, as imposing as Hans himself. Tall and muscular, he was a virile German with a handlebar mustache and a thick shag of dark hair. He spoke very little English, but his companion, Marta, spoke it perfectly.

Marta, who was much shorter and smaller than Hans, cared nothing about her appearance. Her face was wrinkled and swollen from too much sun, her short hair fell into whatever shape the wind blew it, and her clothes were baggy and "sensible," she said.

Marta had only one purpose in life: to get to Benin where she would build a house and farm. She thought Benin was the end of the rainbow, a magical place where all her dreams would come true. Listening to her, I could only think how hopelessly misled she was.

I could not figure out the relationship between the two. Hans was obviously more than a friend. He was driving her to her destiny, to homestead alone in a poor West African country, but would not be staying. He would return home to Germany leaving Marta alone in a strange country to pursue one of the most difficult and uncertain livelihoods on earth: farming. How could anyone allow her to do it?

Together, two vehicles forming a short caravan, we drove outside of Tam to the Hoggar Mountains, a mystical place that has wooed many a monk to keep a lifetime vigil on its precipices.

That night, Hans cooked dinner, a German specialty of whipped potatoes with corned beef and hard boiled eggs. Marta passed jars of red cherry peppers and we sipped lukewarm African beer.

In the cool silence of the desert, we gathered around the

warm flame of a lantern and talked of ourselves. We each told our life story, shortened to the most interesting details, and how we each came to be sitting in the middle of the Sahara at this exact moment.

It was our only night together and we knew we would probably never see each other again. We revealed our innermost thoughts, perhaps moved by the awesome environment that surrounded us, or perhaps we knew our secrets would be safe with strangers passing in the night.

The next morning we continued on across the desert in tandem for a short while. They drove very slowly, absorbing everything, stopping every half hour. It was as if Marta wanted to savor all of life before she reached her final destination. We parted finally at midday, driving on steadily, leaving them behind, a diminishing speck in our rearview mirrors.

I often wonder if she made it to Benin. Was she now walking to market with a basket full of fresh carrots pulled from her garden? Or perhaps she was farming on a much larger scale, employing farmhands to pick cotton that she would sell by the bale to factories that weave the beautiful African cloth?

Or did she give it all up and return to Germany with Hans? Wherever she is, I hope she found her dream and knew how to hold on to it. And I hope she has kept my secrets, as I have kept hers.

11

SAHARAN CROSSROADS

If there is a tourist mecca anywhere in Algeria, it's Tamanrasset.

As deeply buried in the Sahara as any one place could be, it is a pleasant oasis town with considerable appeal. Inhabited mostly by the nomadic blue-robed Tuaregs driven here by the continual state of drought in the Sahel, Tam has a population approaching 30,000, not counting the thin stream of European tourists who drift in and out.

Set in the foothills of the Hoggar Mountains at an elevation of 4,300 ft, temperatures rarely exceed 95 degrees even in the summer, making it more livable than Tucson or Phoenix and giving the town a resort-like atmosphere.

The streets are broad, lined with olive and eucalyptus trees. Under their considerable canopy, Algerians and a few tourists sip tea at numerous sidewalk cafes barely turning their heads as strings of camels lumber by.

As in other Algerian towns, restaurant menus are lengthy but what is available is not — chicken, couscous, *pommes frites* and maybe a vegetable. It's always fun to ask for the other items on the menu if for no other reason than to watch the waiter shake his head and repeat, "Yes, we have green beans, but not today."

The only decent hotel in Tam, the state-run Hotel Tahit, is second class by most standards, but an oasis in itself. A sign in the bar lets you know that alcoholic drinks are served to hotel guests only and not to those who might stumble in driven by thirst.

From the hotel, tourists who are not motorized can arrange

an excursion fifty miles northeast to the Assekrem plateau high in the Hoggar Mountains to visit the Hermitage of Charles de Foucauld, a French Christian Missionary who came to the Hoggars at the turn of the century. The sunrises from the Hermitage are enough to make anyone religious.

The Hoggars are an interesting phenomenon in themselves as they deny the logic of the Sahara, which to most minds is a flat, endlessly boring continent of shifting, drifting sand. Few realize that deep in the bowels of this desolation lies a spectacular range of moon-like mountains with 9,000 ft peaks that often wear a coat of snow in the winter.

If I were a tourist not intent on crossing the Sahara, yet wished to taste the experience, I would fly from Algiers directly to Tam and spend a week exploring the desert, the Hoggars and the 8,000-year-old rock paintings in the Tassili caves, which are also within a day's drive.

Virtually every trans-Saharan trekker stops at Tam for at least one night, usually three or four, to shower, wash clothes and talk to people. The walled campground is several acres in size and large enough to accommodate a hundred vehicles and several hundred people. It is not only a staging area for outbound expeditions, but a travel advisory center, repair yard and swap shop for spare parts. The small campground restaurant served Coca-Cola flown in from Algiers, the only Coke we had seen since Tunis.

We camped near the wall next to a tree where we could fashion a clothesline. Around us was a collection of every sort of expedition vehicle from pedestrian VW campers and low-slung, six-wheeled military looking trucks loaded with jerry cans, sand ladders, shovels and extra tires, to souped-up motorcycles.

Against the opposite wall I spotted two other MOGS. A small crowd had gathered around one. I wandered over.

Three men covered in grease were squatting around a tarp. Spread before them were a series of gears and a clutch assembly.

"What's going on?" I inquired. One of the men looked up at me with a hint of interest.

"You're Canadian, are you?" he asked in a difficult British accent.

Though 4 X 4 Toyotas are the modern camels, the image of a nomad and his dromedary captures the romance of yesterday.

"American."

"Not many of you around these parts. Camping out here, are you?"

I nodded toward our MOG across the way.

"Any spare parts?"

"Spark plugs, set of points, filters, not much more," I answered.

"Not much help here."

"This your MOG?" I asked. It had German plates, so probably wasn't.

The Brit looked across the tarp at another fellow who was absently arranging and rearranging the gears, as if he were deep in thought. Standing behind him was a woman with a great deal of sadness in her face.

"Can I help?" I asked the German.

"Not unless you have an extra gear box," he responded quietly, in fair English.

The German couple had been 200 miles north of Tam when their transmission bearings burned out, gear by gear. They had driven the last 150 miles in fourth gear and now the whole box was spread out on the tarp in the vain hope that the problem wasn't as serious as they had feared; that somehow, something could be jerry-rigged and they could manage the 1,400 mile trip back to Algiers.

"Any hope?" I asked in general.

"Afraid not," the Brit replied. He was a mechanic from the island of Jersey traveling around Algeria with his wife on holiday. "At any rate," he added, rising. "I've got my own problems. Lost all my tubes on the way down. You wouldn't have any tubes, would you?" He didn't wait for an answer.

"I've got three Algerians combing Tam for tubes. I could probably make anything work. Bloody hate to drive north without them."

"What will you do about the gear box?" I asked the German.

He scratched his head slowly before answering. "I am trying to get a box from Munich. We are making phone calls now."

"How can you do that?"

"The German Automobile Club offers this marvelous service," the Brit interjected. "You can buy a policy that covers repairs anywhere in the world. They will fly parts anywhere. They have an agent in Algiers who will clear the box through customs and put it on a plane for Tam. The problem is getting through on the phone and then finding a used box."

"What will happen if you can't find one?" I asked.

No one said a word.

The German looked over at our MOG.

SAHARAN CROSSROADS

"Had any problems with your gear box?" he asked.

"No," I replied, uneasily. "Not yet."

"It's a diesel, is it?"

"No. Gasoline."

He whistled low and shook his head. "Gasoline. How many kilometers per liter?"

My reply, about five, brought another low whistle with the clear connotation that I must be wealthy.

Five kilometers per liter translates into roughly eleven miles per gallon, which is what we averaged. Europeans measure consumption by the liter, while we use gallons. His question to me was the same as if I had asked an American: "How many miles do you get per quart?"

We laugh at quarts. Not the Germans. With gasoline at $3 per gallon, gas consumption in Europe is measured in tea cups, which is one reason their societies are more efficient than ours.

Our gas-guzzling Congo Crusher was adding to the reputation of Americans as the energy hogs of the world. Our greatest single expense, in fact, was gas. In two months we spent over $1,000 just to feed the MOG's insatiable appetite, twice what it cost to feed ourselves.

I left the disheartened Germans and walked the perimeter of the campground. Other groups of men were huddled here and there working on engines, changing oil, rotating tires, repairing, splicing, taping and mending. Always, after my nationality was established the conversation turned to spare parts. What did I have to sell? What could I spare? For what would I trade?

Four days later when we left camp heading south, the German was still tinkering idly with his disassembled gear box and the Brit was still scouring Tam for shocks.

We used our time in Tam to rest, wash and wander the town in search of small adventures. There was little to buy and what was available — rugs, blankets, some nomadic jewelry —was priced in inflated dinars, which were geared to black market rates.

It was common for a shopkeeper to quote the official price in dinars, wait a moment, glance about nervously, and then suggest in a low voice that marks or dollars would get special consideration.

150   THE LION IN THE MOON

The price quoted in hard currency was cut in half.

One of our needs was to obtain visas for Nigér and countries beyond. Most guide books and travel agents suggest obtaining all visas in the U.S. before leaving home. If we were on a prearranged schedule or visiting only one or two countries, this would have been our strategy. But we weren't sure of our itinerary, the dates we would be entering countries or our direction of travel.

If we headed west to Senegal, we would need visas for Burkina Faso, Mali and Senegal. If we opted for a southerly route to the Gulf of Benin, we could do without Mali and Senegal. In our situation it was best to obtain visas en route.

As both Mali and Nigér had consulates in Tam, this was an opportunity to obtain both.

Early one morning we approached the Malian Consulate for a visa and were told to fill out a long form in duplicate, enclose two pictures and $25 U.S., each. They refused to take Algerian money. I could smell a racket.

Many Third World consulates (and embassies) are partially supported through visa fees. My hunch was that the consular officer, after collecting our dollars, would sell them on the black market for dinars tripling his take.

We cancelled the Malian visa. Chances were we could obtain it somewhere ahead and probably for less money, if we needed it at all.

We walked two blocks down the street to the Nigériene Consulate. We could come back at eleven the next morning and pick up our visas, the Second Secretary informed us in a friendly manner. It would be 80 dinars and we could pay in Algerian money. At the official rate our visas would be $10 each; at the black market rate, about $3.50. I liked Nigér already.

The next morning a few minutes before eleven we were cooling our heels under a palm frond awning in the outer courtyard of the consulate. A high wall separated the consulate from the street. From somewhere down the road came the muffled roar of chanting.

I cautiously poked through the gate and watched a small

SAHARAN CROSSROADS

group of demonstrators, less than a hundred, advance towards me. They were mostly women. Those in front carried placards in Arabic. Police milled about. A handful of tourists hugged the walls as the demonstrators approached.

I retreated back into the courtyard thankful for the high wall that separated us from the events outside. It was a political demonstration of some kind, not meant for tourist participation. Third World demonstrations are not the media events we have in the U.S. They are serious affairs that could get you killed. This one could turn nasty at any moment.

The chanting passed. I edged out to the sidewalk and stood next to a tall, blond Dutchman. He was visibly agitated.

"What was that about?" I asked. Not that he would know.

"They took my camera," he gasped. "I was standing right there," he pointed to a spot against the wall. "When the people came by I tried to focus my camera. I wasn't going to take a picture. I was just focusing. A policeman took it. He ripped it off me and took it."

"Go to the police station later. Maybe you can get it back."

He stared down the road without replying.

Incidents like this helped remind me I was not at home, but in the *Democratic and Popular Republic of Algeria*. The role of the police in this, as well as in so many similar countries, is to squash dissent and make sure the country stayed 'democratic and popular.'

The incident was also a reminder of the general difficulty of photographing anything, not only in Muslim countries, where photographing the human image is strictly forbidden and most difficult, but in Africa in general.

Most all these countries operate in a pitched state of paranoia over security matters. Almost anything a tourist might want to photograph — buildings, streets, bridges, airports, dams, water ways — is on somebody's list of strategic importance and thus, off limits. Tourists often don't know what is considered strategic until their cameras have been confiscated.

On those occasions when the Princess and I did walk the streets with our cameras, they were discretely hidden beneath jackets and brought out only at the last moment. I shot a lot of useless pictures of houses, trees, donkeys and camels.

A few days earlier when we had shot pictures of the central market in In Salah, I hid my camera under my coat with only the lens sticking through at waist level. As I walked the market feigning indifference, I was pressing the shutter release at random. Even that was risky. It's amazing how far the click of a shutter will carry. Some of the pictures proved acceptable; most cut off heads, arms and legs. Better theirs than mine. We had brought 60 rolls of film but due to these constrictions, shot only half.

Having secured our visas to Nigér, we could resume our trek south. This would be the toughest part across the exact heart of the Sahara into Nigér and black Africa. We would be on our own. No roads. No signs. No gas. Nothing.

12

CROSSING THE LINE

We left Tamanrasset after a four-day rest for our final leap, a five hundred mile death march across the heart of the great desert. I had no plans on expiring in the Sahara, but considering the unknowns, the dramatic element of survival was paramount in my mind.

"It isn't that bad," several different people had told me. "Just use common sense. Follow your compass and try to stay in sight of the tracks left by others. There will be markers — some concrete posts — here and there. You should be all right."

On the outskirts of town was a large sign in French, Arabic and bad English. It warned:

- Drive robust vehicles in perfect state well equipped with special tires for these particular roads and a filter against sand (oil bath).
- Drive in daylight and in groups of at least two vehicles.
- Have an extra food of at least two days in addition to your need, a reserve of fuel, a medical first aid case, and a sufficient reserve of drinkable water.
- Never leave the main road and in case of breakdown never get far from the vehicles.
- Before setting out your journey it's wise to consult the authorities of the security services for information about the conditions of the roads.
- It is vividly advised to tourists to avoid crossing the great south in the estival season, that's from June 1st

to September 15th, and that's because of the high temperature and the wind storms.

It was a sobering reminder.

The paved part of the road out of Tam quickly ended and we made our way along a sand track that was still well defined. Within a mile or two the sand road melted into the desert to disappear forever.

I stopped the MOG and looked over the hood into the endless expanse of desert that stretched before us from horizon to horizon. I wanted some guidance, just a small sign of where to go. Should I turn right? Left? Continue straight ahead? How would I know? I simply couldn't comprehend the fact that *there was no road* .

Roads offer security. They channel travel and lead to a defined destination. Roads eliminate guess work and risk. But this road had ended. I had to make my own choices and it was frightening.

I searched the horizon in indecision hoping by some small miracle someone might come along and I could follow, but we were alone.

I took a deep breath and gave the engine some gas driving conservatively, endeavoring to stay close to the tracks of others out of fear that if I lost sight of them we might spin off into the desert never to be found.

Gradually, I began to cut my own course relying on intuition as to how far to go in one direction before turning in another while continuing to peg the compass on a southerly course.

The Princess would sweep the horizon with her binoculars trying to pierce the heat shimmers and flying sand for the concrete pylons we hoped would mark our route. Some appeared frequently, every five or ten miles; other times we drove two or three hours and saw nothing.

When it seemed hopeless tire tracks would appear from one side, zigzag under the MOG for a few hundred yards then disappear off to the other side. A few miles on others would reappear, cross and criss-cross and disappear again. They were

When the road ends in the heart of the Sahara, there remains only desolation and trepidation.

small, reassuring signs.

In the late morning the rolling terrain flattened into a hard alkaline plateau that stretched for miles. I eased the MOG to top speed, about 50 mph and held it for almost an hour. We were hurtling through a vacuum stunning in its simplicity: There was no motion, no sound, no life.

Quite unexpectedly, fifty yards to the left, a long, black Mercedes with darkened windows passed with a fury leaving us engulfed in a vortex of alkaline dust. It was easily pushing ninety miles per hour. Piled on the roof were several stacks of tires. In a few seconds it had disappeared. I had seen that car before, but wasn't sure. Perhaps on the ferry from Genova.

It was that evening, when we were safely curled in the arms of a quiet sand dune that I made the discovery about the sun rising and setting without making a sound. It was to be the single most lasting impression of the entire trip.

The border town of In-Guezzem was a hard three-day push from Tam, long hours of pitching and swaying, aching muscles and ringing ears as we ground out the miles. We would roll for awhile, bog down in a sea of powder sand, fight free and drive on for a short distance before being sucked once again into the sand.

It was almost noon when we finally rolled out of the sand into In-Guezzem. I had no idea what to expect of this border outpost and so expected nothing. Unfortunately, my expectations were more than realized.

In-Guezzem was a shriveled nothing of mud huts and a few tents pitched on the sand. Dozens of nearly naked children intermixed with goats and camels. There were no discernable streets and no sense of permanence.

Along the main street were a few tumbled mud buildings, a gas station and a small hut that said customs. A dozen cars were parked, or abandoned, in every direction. It was hard to tell the difference.

As we stopped across from the gas station, several Europeans approached.

"Benzine or diesel?" one asked.

"Gasoline," I answered.

"Do you have some to sell?"

"No, I'm afraid not. We barely have enough. Is the station empty?"

"There has been no gas for five days," he answered. "We have been waiting for five days."

"I wish I could help. Sorry."

He waved and turned back to his friends. I understood why the cars looked abandoned. They were out of gas.

"Which way is the border?" I asked after him.

He pointed in a general direction out of town.

I followed some tracks that disappeared over the top of a sand dune. To the left a Toyota Land Cruiser came racing around a dune and headed into town. Assuming it had come from the border, I headed in the opposite direction.

The sand gave way to a flat plain. After fifteen minutes, I could make out two or three low buildings snuggled into the rolling sand. They turned out to be portable metal buildings on

CROSSING THE LINE 157

pylons. In front were two upright oil drums about twenty feet apart with a rope stretched between them. This was the border.

We entered the building marked police. After checking our papers, the official stamped our passports and directed us to the other building, which was customs. As I tried the locked door, several officials piled into a car behind us and drove off toward town. It was noon. The border was closed.

It would be three hours before customs would reopen for business. I crawled into the cab of the MOG and opened a book. A small caravan of nomadic Bedouins loped by on their camels, circumvented the rope barrier, by-passed the police and customs buildings and angled off into the open desert as if they knew precisely what they were about.

I watched until they had diminished to specks on the horizon. Like their forefathers, they were a self-contained people, not constrained by artificial boundaries, political or otherwise. I wished we could do the same.

At precisely three, two official vehicles roared up in a cloud of dust. The border was open for business. We waited in line for customs. When it was our turn the officer scrutinized our papers carefully checking our currency declaration forms calculating in his head if we had exchanged enough currency relative to the time we had spent in Algeria.

Satisfied, he stamped our passports and told me to bring my car around to the side for inspection. Another customs official looked half-heartedly through the cab and into the sleeping quarters.

"How much gasoline do you have?" he asked, noticing five jerry cans lined up in one of the storage compartments.

"About sixty gallons."

He thought for a moment then waved us on.

The smuggling of cheap Algerian gas into Nigér for resale was big business. If customs determined we had too much for the trip, they might assume we were smuggling and could levy a fine equal to twice the value of the gas.

I was just beginning to steer around the building for the open desert when the official waved me down and pointed to the rope barrier. To make our exit from Algeria official, we had to pass through the barrier.

I drove around and waited in front of the rope. It was too ludicrous to be funny. We were in a vast sea of sand with nothing in sight for thousands of square miles and I had to drive precisely between the two upright oil drums. Obviously, the official had his instructions. There are certain procedures that give a job its dignity.

The rope was lowered and we passed through the drums into no-man's land. Legally, we were no longer on Algerian soil, yet, it was still fifteen miles to the Nigériene border post, if we could find it. There were absolutely no markers of any kind, not even tire tracks to follow, as if, now that we had left Algeria we were no longer anyone's concern. I set the compass on south and drove on. If we didn't hit something within thirty minutes we were in trouble.

The Nigériene border post of Assamakka appeared ahead, a mere bubble on the horizon. Except for a couple of trees, it was no different than the town we had just left. Again, we were confronted by two oil drums and a stretched piece of rope.

A kid appeared and instructed me to stop directly in front of the rope. He demanded our passports, made sure the pictures matched our faces, and departed clutching them between his thin fingers leaving me with unsettling feelings. As a rule, whenever I travel in the Third World, I never let my passport out of my sight and I never, ever give it to a kid.

There is no more vulnerable position than to be deep in the bowels of Africa without identification. As the unimposing figure of the scrawny kid disappeared into a small police hut, our fate — our very survival — was clutched in his hands. I fantasized he might disappear into his burrow forever, adding our passports to hundreds he had already collected.

An official informed us that while we were waiting for our passports we could be obtaining the necessary permits and insurance. He pointed across an open field to a row of mud buildings. Each, as it turned out, was a fleecing station assigned to relieve us of our money.

CROSSING THE LINE

At the first building, I was assessed $75 for one month's auto insurance; at the second, $8.50 each for a tourist tax. In building number three, I was charged $15 for a *Carnet de Transit*, sort of a bond that guaranteed I wouldn't sell my car in Nigér. In the fourth building, we coughed up $16 each in custom's fees. The last building was the police station where our passports waited.

In short order, the Princess and I had been clipped for $140, nearly all the cash I had. I needed money. Someone directed me back to the insurance agent. Yes, he said with a hospitable smile, he would be delighted to cash my traveler's checks. But, he added, apologetically, I wouldn't be happy with the rate.

He then launched into a long explanation of how this was all a favor for me; that we were hundreds of miles from a bank and it might take him weeks to get his money back; that no one else would accept my checks because of the risk; that he might run out of money himself, and so on.

The jist of his windy speech was that he had me by what counted and could damn well give me whatever rate he pleased. He had a point. There was no bank and no black market alternative, at least for traveler's checks. The official exchange rate was 280 CFA to one dollar. He gave me 240, with apologies, of course.

I found the Princess sitting under a tree by the police station. A dozen other tourists were sitting on the ground around her. I joined her for the wait.

Across an open dirt tract a group of brightly dressed women with large tin platters balanced on their heads were peddling fresh baked loaves of bread. There was something unusual about this scene, but I didn't put it together for several minutes. Suddenly it hit me.

I was watching a group of women engaged in commerce. Not men, but women, dressed like peacocks in bright cotton cloth with exposed faces and arms. Gone was the men only society; gone were the dreary head-to-foot gray and black robes; gone were the Arabs. Not only had the people changed, but the very flavor and tempo of life had dramatically altered.

160 THE LION IN THE MOON

A policeman emerged from his dark hole and handed us our passports. We had to clear customs, he informed me. I turned back toward where the MOG was parked. The Princess wanted to stay in the shade, but I wanted her with me. I anticipated trouble. The presence of a woman might give me an advantage.

There were two rows of cars stretching back from the rope barrier. We were at the head of one line. Three scruffy German men in a heavily loaded black Mercedes were next to us. It was not the same Mercedes that had passed us a few days earlier. A group of customs officers, wearing sloppy army uniforms, ambled towards us. They wore stern expressions.

The one who approached us had a small American flag in his lapel. Either it meant he spoke English or it was costume jewelry. He wanted to look in the truck, he said in French. I replied in English. A smile came over his face.

"English?" he asked.

"American," I replied.

He began to giggle as he motioned for me to open the back doors. Still smiling, he commenced to poke into every nook and corner of the truck, opening bags, unzipping suitcases, unraveling this, sniffing at that like a curious cat in an increasingly mindless and pointless search. He had no idea what he was looking for. He was just looking. He unfolded a small, metal bag.

"What is this?" he asked, with unrestrained curiosity.

"Film."

He nodded his head in understanding and then looked at me point blank. "I have a camera. I don't have film." He waited, his face an image of innocence.

I thrust two rolls into his hands. "*Cadeau*. A gift for you."

He beamed thanks. "Now I can take photos of my family."

I stuck a pack of cigarettes in his other hand. Now that both hands were full he had to leave us alone. He waved us on and turned his attention to the black Mercedes. Two other customs men were already zeroing in for the kill. They were sifting through the trunk with a fine tooth comb, laying things aside they wanted.

The Germans were delivering the car to a wealthy busi-

CROSSING THE LINE

nessman in Cameroon who had bought it in Germany and had arranged to have it delivered overland to save duty. Cars brought in through the Cameroonian port of Duoala, the normal way of importing cars, were subject to one hundred percent duty. Delivering the car overland through the back door meant a customs official at some out-of-the-way border crossing could be bribed to impose a lesser duty, perhaps as low as ten or twenty percent. The savings was worth the beating the car would take crossing the Sahara.

As we drove away, one of the Germans was arguing heatedly with a customs man. The official had found a tool box he coveted. The question under debate was how much the German would 'charge him' for the tools? My guess was very little.

After the Mercedes, the officials would move down the line systematically vacuuming the remaining eight or ten vehicles for anything that struck their fancy. From their perspective, there was more wealth in that short line of cars than they could ever hope to collectively accumulate in their lifetimes. Anyone rich enough to be driving a car through Africa wouldn't miss a few tools, sun glasses or a radio.

We had been lucky, in part due to the novelty of being Americans in a world over-run by French and Germans, and to the presence of the Princess, who made us a family. Africans have great respect for families.

Snapshot

INTO THE BLACK

The Nigériene border post of Assamakka appeared like a lump on the flat horizon. As we drove closer, I had a premonition there was something vastly different about what lay ahead. We had come only a few short miles from the Algerian border, yet I had this feeling as we progressed further south we were slipping back in time. The scattering of pathetic buildings that were now very much in view would be my first unforgettable introduction to black Africa.

A halfhearted barbed wire fence was strung across the desert in an attempt to delineate a small section of sand as something of significance. Enclosed within the fenced area were several crumbling cinderblock cubicles with patched tin roofs. A lone, twisted olive tree shaded the front of one building; the rest baked in the hot sun.

Staefan parked in front of the gate, a shredded rope stretched between two oil barrels, and waited. There were no signs instructing travelers what to do so we sat in the MOG, hoping someone would notice us. I searched the compound for life.

A few goats wandered aimlessly between two of the buildings, their heads to the ground sniffing at the dust for something to eat. Across the way, a flatbed truck loaded with African men and women was parked on the shady side of another building. They had either just arrived or were about to leave; I couldn't tell which. I watched for some time for signs of movement. The truck didn't move; neither did the people.

Finally, a small black boy ran out of the building by the

SNAPSHOT: INTO THE BLACK

tree to collect our passports.

"You must park over there," he instructed, jumping around and waving his hands, "beside the fence, in a straight line."

He ran over to the spot, showing us exactly where. It seemed nonsensical. We were the only ones waiting. The desert was enormous. We could have parked anywhere.

When the kid was satisfied with our performance, he ran back across the barren earth to the shaded building without further explanation. I was left with time to check out Assamakka.

Crossing the rope barrier, we were suddenly noticed by everyone. From within each dark building an African man emerged, shouted at us, and waved papers in the air.

"Here, here, you must come here first," they would yell like barkers at a carnival. What business could we possibly have with these people? I wondered.

But, then where should we go? There was no official reception area. I had no idea what had happened to our passports. How were we to proceed? Who were all these men? We gravitated towards the closest building.

A black man stuck his head and shoulders out of a small window like the ticket windows at a theater. He flagged us down as we approached. His very muscular torso was covered with a body-conscious, camouflaged uniform. A black beret was jauntily tipped to one side of his head. Behind him pasted on a desk was a page from a body building magazine showing a picture of an equally muscular white male in a blue string bikini.

"You must pay the tourist tax, 2,000 CFA," he informed us.

"Will you take American dollars?" Staefan asked.

The soldier snorted. "No dollars. No dinars. Only CFA."

This was Nigér and like most of West Africa, CFA was the official currency.

"We don't have CFA," I explained. "Is there some place we could exchange money? A bank?" I already knew the answer to that one.

"No bank," he responded. "Try over there." He pushed his massive shoulder through the little window to point across the dirt compound to another building.

164 THE LION IN THE MOON

This seemed the beginning of a lengthy goose chase. While Staefan headed out into the afternoon sun in pursuit of CFA, I turned to the shade of the olive tree. The contorted trunk lay horizontal before branching to the sky. I found a niche and settled in for a lengthy wait.

The tiny frontier hut in front of me was packed with black men milling about. Two officials sat behind makeshift desks, a stack of passports in front of them. They perused each one in the light of the doorway, turning them around as if to better examine the stamps. They took so much time with each one that I wondered if they could read. Perhaps they were putting on a show for their audience, a small group of impatient Europeans who hung around the doorway.

Sometimes the two officials would confer amid the clamoring of their audience. What was going on? Was this an auction of some sort? Was my passport being held up to the black crowd, as if asking for a referendum on whether I should be allowed into their country? It was too hot to think about such things.

A tall, old black man in rags was walking toward me slowly across the sand, dragging each foot as if he were walking through water. Balanced on his head was a square board covered with loaves of bread stacked in a pyramid. I asked for three.

Slowly, he took the board from his head and set it on the ground, choosing my three loaves for me. After I paid him, about 20¢ each, he carefully balanced the board on his head and walked off in the direction he had come. I watched him disappear into the heat. He walked like I felt: slow, listless, without energy. I realized how tired and thirsty I was.

Staefan returned, unsuccessful, and we waded through ankle-deep bleached sand towards yet another building. Michael Jackson's "Thriller" drifted out into the desert heat from the insurance building. The agent, a boy in his teens, sat at a table piled with papers in the middle of a barren concrete room. A boom box was balanced on a chair in one corner and the agent was grooving to the music.

Without missing a beat, he motioned for us to sit in two folding chairs in front of his desk. He spoke some English and,

SNAPSHOT: INTO THE BLACK   165

fortunately, was willing to change our money. I wondered what would have happened if we had not found this boy. Without CFA would we have been sent back to rot in no man's land?

As the agent discussed the necessary car insurance with Staefan, my eyes wandered over the crowded desk. How could there be so much paperwork in such an isolated place as this?

I pointed to some stamps on an envelope that was wedged between papers on the desk. They were of brightly colored tropical birds showing off their feathers in flights of ecstasy. I had searched in vain for the prettiest stamps to put on my letters home. In Algeria, the post offices had displayed a poster of stunning stamps but they were never for sale. "For exhibition only," I was told as they handed me the plainest green and white stamps imaginable.

"Quelles belles timbres," I announced out loud, clearing my throat in the uncomfortable silence that followed.

The boy stopped talking to Staefan to look at me and then at the envelope to which I had pointed. For a moment he seemed alarmed, as if I had been snooping among his papers. I held my breath. In a serious manner, he announced he would give them to me as a gift. He tore off the corner of the envelope, handed it to me, and continued on with the insurance forms.

We left with a roll of CFA only to return half an hour later for more. The entry fees were piling up as we were directed to visit each of the black men who had originally greeted us with their waving arms. On our second visit to the insurance office, the young agent offered us hot tea. I had been dying for a cold drink, but even hot liquid sounded good at this point. Water fountains and Coke machines were distant memories.

The agent and several others had been sharing one large glass. He quickly rinsed it in a bucket of water, filled it halfway with dark tea and politely handed it to me. I accepted the fingerprinted vessel with trepidation. How many mouths had savored the rim? How many strains of disease lurked in the depths of the tea leaves?

The boy was watching, pleased I was about to share his hospitality. I pressed the glass to my lips and drank. The hot and sweet liquid refreshed me as much as an ice cold Coke. I was sure I would be dead by midnight, but at least I would have been polite in the process.

I set the glass down and stared over the boy's head at the dingy wall beyond. Life was changing here at Assamakka. Islam and the silent purity of the desert were gone. A boldness and gaiety had taken their place, yet these traits were polluted with a sense of chaos. I was being sucked into a dark funnel, slowly falling into a world of mass confusion and poverty. I was heading straight for the dark heart of Africa, one of the most primitive areas in the world.

I had not been prepared for this. North Africa, yes. But this?

Algerians were familiar from my college days in Paris and I felt at home with them. And as an introvert, I had felt more at home on the desert than I could have possibly imagined. But I had no point of reference for what Assamakka represented nor for what lay ahead.

I was a single white woman about to enter a world of blacks; an American, assumed wealthy by virtue of my citizenship, about to walk among the poorest people on earth; a gentle soul with a taste for luxury thrust into a harsh environment saddled with the most primitive of living conditions.

I had never been so much an outsider nor felt so out of sync with the reality that surrounded me. For the first time, I was a minority. It was not as if I were scared of these Africans, yet there was a fear of trespassing into their territory where the rules were different. There were no formalities as I knew them: no sanitation, no simple luxuries, no privacy, no small touchstones of sanity. Everything was raw, on the surface and crude. I was not sure I could handle it.

Assamakka was to be only the beginning. As we drove deeper into the black, everything intensified: the heat, the mosquitoes, the oppressive crowds of black cripples and beggars, the extreme poverty, and above all, my own naive reaction.

Culture shock is a legitimate disease and I was being cut down.

13

THE BOWLS OF POVERTY

Still an hour shy of Arlit, the first major town in Nigér, we overtook the black Mercedes that had passed us in the desert a few days earlier. It was stopped dead. Two legs protruded from under the rear end. A young woman climbed out of the front seat. Obviously, they were in need of assistance.

Since entering the deepest part of the desert, we had encountered a number of stranded cars in need of parts, oil, or assistance of some kind, usually a yank out of the sand. As a rule we always tried to help. It's an unwritten law of the desert, I suppose. Being stranded in the Sahara could be life threatening.

The Good Samaritan in me was beginning to wear thin. These stops not only consumed a great deal of time, sometimes an hour or more, but precious gasoline as well. Once freed, the beneficiaries of our largess would pile into their car, yell their thanks and roar off into the desert leaving us to eat their dust. A few miles or hours later we might see them in the distance, stuck again frantically waving for our assistance. We didn't always stop the second time.

Mostly these were young European men running old cars across the desert to sell in Nigér. They were ill-equipped for the crossing, relying on the generosity of others if they encountered trouble. Brave souls on one hand; parasites on the other.

This Mercedes was having mechanical difficulties.

"What's the problem?" I asked, knowing there was probably little I could do.

"We have a hole in our gas tank, from a rock, I think," the

Crossing into black Africa, straw huts and barren soil were reminders of the depths of poverty.

woman said. "He is trying to fix it," she added, pointing to the pair of legs.

A man slithered out. "I think I have it fixed. But we've lost all our petrol. Do you have some we could buy?"

"I could probably sell you twenty liters," I volunteered. We had made better mileage than I had anticipated and still had two full jerry cans with only thirty plus miles to Arlit.

As the German slowly poured the gas into his tank, I checked out the Mercedes. There was something missing.

"Didn't you have tires on top?" I asked.

The man laughed. "Yes. We had eight. Brand new Michelins. We sold them in Algeria."

I was intrigued. "How did Customs let you out of Algeria without the tires?"

"When we sold one the buyer had to give us an old tire in exchange. When we left Algeria we had eight tires, but they were old. Did you see outside of Assamakka a pile of old tires? Those were ours. We threw them in the sand. We sold the

THE BOWLS OF POVERTY

169

Michelins for enough to pay for our trip."

I was impressed with their ingenuity. Algerian Customs had noted their tires on the customs form, but not whether they were old or new. When this couple had left the country, as far as Customs was concerned, they still had eight tires.

When the German finished pouring the gas, he pulled out a 500 mark note. Twenty liters was worth only 100 marks and I had no change. They promised to pay us in Arlit. Reluctantly, we agreed and drove on.

A few minutes later, the Mercedes roared by in a swirl of dust, with a honk and a wave. Within an hour, we passed them, again, dead in the sand. They had run out of gas. The leak had not been fixed after all. It was our turn to honk and wave. We never saw them again and never collected our money.

Nigér requires all tourists to check in with the police at every major town to have their passports stamped in an effort to track the movements of everyone who enters the country. Since Arlit would be the first town since Assamakka, it was important that we check in.

I had heard horror stories of tourists who had been refused permission to leave the country because they had skipped a police check at some small town. They were forced to retrace their route hundreds of miles to get that single missing stamp. It may have been an exaggeration, but it was better to play the game.

The police station, however, was second on our list. First, we wanted lunch and a cold beer. It would be our first cold brew since Tunis. As we stepped from the MOG we were instantly engulfed by beggars — children in rags, old women, cripples, the blind and lame — a small but potent reminder that we were now in the poorest part of the world.

In the days ahead the population crush and poverty would combine to deprive us of the one thing we cherished so much in the desert and had begun to take for granted: our privacy. From this day forward we would no longer be alone. We could not stop for more than a few minutes even in what seemed the remotest section of the country without the vegetation turning instantly into people. Africa truly is a magical place.

The Princess and I ducked into a restaurant and were seated at a large picnic table in an inner courtyard far from the milling throng outside. We ordered beefsteak, fries and quart-sized bottles of cold African beer. We had found a temporary piece of heaven.

One by one, without any apparent design, Africans would wander up and sit at our table. Some would try to talk to us; others would sit silently and watch. Soon, we had accumulated half-a-dozen passengers.

The Princess, becoming increasingly nervous at the encroachment, finally turned to the nearest woman and said: "I hope you don't mind, but we're eating lunch now."

The African woman gave her a languid look: "Oh, I don't mind," she responded, lazily.

No one moved. They sat there the entire meal, mostly ignoring us, but always interested in what we were doing. It was unnerving with strangers at every elbow watching our every move — an invasion of our privacy and personal space.

Americans have a cultural rule about owning the table where they sit no matter the size, and controlling the space around. There might be four empty chairs but still we consider the table ours. Not so here. We were entitled only to the chairs we were in and the table space displaced by our plates. No more, and often less.

I joined the Princess outside the restaurant. She had just traded her wristwatch to a kid for a piece of Tuareg jewelry, and was beaming at her accomplishment. The jewelry was nice, but we would miss that watch. It was the only one we had.

After checking in with the police, we walked the town —dirt streets, mud huts with tin roofs and hordes of milling, brightly dressed people. Arlit was a border trading town — the first place south of Tam that offered anything for sale and the last chance if you were heading north to stock up for the Saharan crossing. It was also one of the largest used car lots in Africa.

Arlit is where all the old Peugeots and Mercedes we encountered in the Sahara ended up. Buyers from Chad, Cameroon, Nigeria, Burkina Faso and Mali congregated to negotiate a deal.

THE BOWLS OF POVERTY

In spite of the poverty, there was a vibrancy of life here entirely missing in Algeria. A kid with a wheelbarrow of oranges followed us for two blocks — plenty of fruit in this town, just no money. Suddenly, I felt quite alive, too.

From Arlit the road was paved all the way to Niamey, the capital of Nigér, 750 miles southwest, close to the border with Burkina Faso. From Niamey a traveler could continue on into West Africa or turn south into Nigeria and Central Africa, all on paved roads.

Nigér is a massive landlocked country three times the size of California with less than a third its population. Only three percent of the land is arable and twenty years of drought have forced the majority of its population of seven million into the slums around the capital city of Niamey and along the fertile banks of the Nigér River, which cuts through the extreme southwestern tip of the country.

Literacy is thirteen percent and the per capita income of $200 a year is derived mostly from cotton and peanuts. There are only two hospitals in Niamey, and a few clinics in the countryside. A lot of babies are born and a lot die. Life expectancy is barely forty-four years. If true poverty exists anywhere in the world, it is in Nigér.

Historically, Nigér was part of an ancient and medieval African empire that stretched from the Sahel to Central Spain. European explorers reached the area in the 18th century and the French colonized Nigér in 1900 after the defeat of the Tuaregs who had invaded the region a century before. Nigér became independent in 1960 but retains close cultural and economic ties to France.

The Uranium Highway, as the road out of Arlit was called, was the only paved road through the country. It was engineered by the French who mined uranium outside of Arlit for their nuclear projects. The money received by the Nigériene Government had built this highway; thus, its name.

It was a gorgeous road, fully paved, straight and wide, but virtually untraveled, undoubtedly the reason it was in such wonderful condition. On the way south to Agadez, we passed an average of one car per hour, which was not surprising considering there are only about 35,000 vehicles in the entire country.

While we encountered few cars, we did encounter more frequent signs of life — small clusters of animal skin tents, herds of goats, a few donkeys, and increasingly, clumps of brown grass and isolated trees.

There was no line where the Sahara ended and the sub-Saharan Sahel began; no place I could look back and pinpoint as the place that marked the confrontation between two climatological zones. The evolution was so gradual, so subtle I scarcely recognized it had happened at all.

At first there were only a few widely scattered clumps of thin grass, not very large or healthy, and mostly brown, but grass never-the-less. Some distance on a tree would appear standing alone, then two trees, followed by several trees and a little more grass.

It evolves this way for hundreds of miles. Life gradually multiplies and builds. Small herds of goats appear, followed by a solitary person, then by a family, a few donkeys, and a cow or two. When finally I awoke to the change, I was surrounded by life but I couldn't remember when it happened.

My first images of Nigér were chilling. Small children would race to the road as we passed with small colored plastic bowls clutched in their thin fingers begging for food or water. Some waved frantically; some made drinking signs with their hands or pinched their fingers together moving them from bowl to mouth imitating eating. Others just stood dumbly with their hands out.

I felt guilty passing the first child, somewhat less guilty by the tenth, and not much at all except curiosity by the hundredth.

The idea of children begging by the side of the highway doesn't compute in the mind of an average American. These things aren't supposed to happen; therefore, they don't.

Nobody is that desperate, I would tell myself, and if they are, it is clearly an exceptional phenomenon. But it was happening. I knew it to be true. Desperate poverty is the norm for the world's masses. Life in America — a life without want — is the exception. Even the poor in the United States are wealthy by

THE BOWLS OF POVERTY

world standards.

We spent two nights in Agadez in our first campground south of the Sahara near a walled Mosque with a tall, square minaret of red-colored mud.

Camping in the open, as we were able to do in Algeria, was impossible now. Not only was it restricted by the police, but by the hordes of people, as well. Campgrounds were welcome as they provided privacy and safety from petty theft.

They would also separate us further from the experience that was Africa.

Snapshot

TEA IN THE SAHARA

He was the most beautifully exotic man I had ever seen.

Dressed in a long, pale blue tunic and pants, Doulah wore a pointed hat of straw adorned with black ostrich feathers and bright strips of leather. A curved sword was slung across his chest and an ornately beaded money pocket hung around his neck.

Doulah was a Fulani, one of a historically nomadic tribe that wanders through the vast stretches of the Sahel, the grasslands that edge the Sahara. They are a beautiful people, almost gazelle-like in their gentle and graceful bearing. Tall with elegant features and dark hair, their origin is unknown. Some believe they migrated centuries ago from Egypt and may even be of Jewish origin.

Doulah's father had been nomadic, herding cattle along the grasslands of northern Nigér like his father before him. Doulah was just a boy, he told me, when the great drought of the early '70s struck the Sahel killing most of the region's livestock. His father's herd was decimated.

Not wanting to end up like his father, Doulah turned his back on farming and the nomadic life. He moved his family to Agadez, Nigér, a frontier town at the southern edge of the Sahara, and opened a shop where he sold Fulani jewelry to tourists.

On this already hot morning he was looking for customers as he walked through the maze of tin sheds that constituted the town's main market. I could not help but be struck by his presence across the sea of people. He was the tallest one in the crowd and his soft brown eyes fixed on mine as he approached.

SNAPSHOT: TEA IN THE SAHARA

"You will come see my shop?" he asked in French as I stood drinking a Coke. I was mesmerized by him, but also by the cold Coke.

"*Oú est vôtre magasin?*" I asked him.

He pointed into the jumble of sheds and I nodded, sure that I would recognize him when I reached his shop. He walked away, turned, and watched me from a distance. I could delay meeting this stranger no longer and headed in his direction.

There were many sheds, or shops, to investigate on the way to Doulah's. Each was fascinating, yet every time I stopped to browse, Doulah would re-appear at my side to remind me I had promised to see his shop.

"It is not much further down the path," he would say in his soft voice. He was afraid I would spend all my money in other places.

When I arrived, he introduced himself and led me toward the makeshift tin doors that guarded his shed. Above the doors was a crudely painted sign: "*Souvenir de Peul Fulani Shop.*"

I crossed the threshold into a black hole. At first I could see nothing. Slowly, shapes appeared from the darkness. Rickety wood tables held boards hung with tribal necklaces, earrings, bracelets and unusual trinkets that glittered in the thin shafts of sunlight through the gaps of the tin siding.

Doulah began to ornament my body with tribal jewelry of the Fulani and Peul tribes. He fastened bracelets of camel leather wrapped with copper wire on my arms and strung brightly colored trade beads, cowrie shells and brass medallions tethered on soft leather whips around my neck. They were crude yet strangely appealing.

I felt like a desert princess but I also knew I was wearing more than I could afford. I chose to keep only two pieces: a necklace of bright trade beads and amber, and a Tuareg Cross of Agadez of pounded silver.

Traditionally, when a son leaves the tribe to seek his fortune, he is given this silver pendant whose shape symbolizes the four corners of the earth. Suspended from a beaded necklace, The Cross of Agadez is believed to be his guide through the

Doulah and his friend Perodje pose in front of his jewelry shop in Agadez, Nigér.

journey of life.

    Returning to the MOG to stash my newly acquired jewels of the Sahara, I discovered Doulah was following me.

SNAPSHOT: TEA IN THE SAHARA

"You will have tea with me at home?" he inquired.

I gladly accepted.

We ambled through the searing heat of midday. A fine yellow dust hung in the air, acting as a filter through which I viewed the turquoise sky above the brown mud walls that delineated dirt streets.

To the left, at the end of a broad treeless avenue, a square minaret of mud adobe rose into the sky breaking the horizontal plane of low, flat-roofed houses.

After several turns, Doulah stepped through a small opening in one of the mud walls into a dirt courtyard ringed by mud houses. Motorbikes shared equal space with scavenging chickens, guinea hens, goats and nearly naked children.

Doulah led us across the courtyard to his mud home. He opened the crude door of tin to reveal an eight by ten room with a dirt floor. Next to the door was a small window shuttered with a weathered wood board.

His wife, who looked no more than eighteen, was seated on a blanket on the floor breast-feeding her baby boy who was obviously sick. She was petite with milk-chocolate skin that almost concealed the ceremonial tattoos on her pretty face.

Her thick black hair was braided into a fanciful hairdo. She wore a Western long-sleeve, black and purple striped T-shirt with a yellow and black Fulani cloth wrapped around her hips. A silver bracelet adorned each ankle, several silver bracelets encircled her arms, and enormous silver hoops pierced her ears.

As we entered, she bundled her baby and made ready to leave. There was room for her, but not according to their customs. We were her husband's guests. Her duty now was to wait on us: to be seen, barely, and not heard.

She looked at me briefly as she quietly headed for the door. I detected a hint of curiosity in her eyes about the ways of Western women, but the thought did not seem to linger long. She exuded the self-confidence of a woman who knew her duties and performed them well.

Fulani women are unique in Africa. Traditionally, they own their own property apart from their husband's. A Fulani woman keeps what is hers. If she should marry into a class beneath her, she retains her class, not that of her husband's.

We removed our shoes and sat on a layered nest of straw mats, striped blankets, and a sleeping bag topped with an assortment of pillows.

Doulah turned his back to us and began to undress. In a single room, privace is psychological, not physical.

He removed his elaborate hat, unwrapped the twisted fabric that covered his braided hair, and lifted the sword and pouch over his head before stripping off his outer tunic. Out of his formal attire, he pulled on a loose shirt over his pale blue pants and left the room.

In a few minutes he reappeared, sat on a pillow next to us, and began to unpack a large leather pouch. He extracted a small, red enameled teapot, a round brass tray, a small glass and a bag of loose tea. From an old newspaper, he unwrapped a coarse block of off-white sugar. With a piece of shiny iron, Doulah knocked off chips that he dropped into the teapot.

From a clay urn he drew water in a plastic cup and offered it to us to drink. I took a sip and passed the cup to Staefan,. Doulah poured the remaining water into the teapot and added a special blend of tea leaves. It was Tuareg tea, he told us. The blend smelled pungent and rich.

Doulah's wife brought a small brazier of coals on which to heat water for tea. She handed it through the door without a sound. When she brought the small tray with three glasses, she leaned through the door and handed it to her husband without a word. Not once, during the three hours we were in the room, did she set foot inside the threshold; not once did she utter a sound. After we left, I realized I didn't even know her name. Doulah had referred to her only as "*ma femme.*"

Our host made a minimum of effort to accommodate her. He would turn about slightly and raise an arm part way and wait while his wife strained and leaned as far as possible into the room to meet his hand. If they were still apart, she would strain further to the point where I thought she would topple into the room.

If it became impossible, our host would consent to lean a bit

SNAPSHOT: TEA IN THE SAHARA

Doulah's wife and young son appeared for parting photos outside their mud house.

further himself to make final contact. It was a man's world, although he did make sure she had a glass of tea, even though it was after we had finished ours and she had to drink it outside.

After fanning the coals to a red glow, Doulah nestled the teapot into the hot embers.

More guests arrived to join our tea party.

Perodje, who worked at Doulah's shop, was a handsome Fulani with fine features and a very bright turquoise cloth elaborately wrapped about his head. Alhadi, dressed in Western clothes, was a student and could read and write.

Perodje produced a small red radio and tuned it to a station from Niamey, the capital of Nigér. Tracy Chapman filled the mud room.

In addition to the radio, Perodje had brought a small brown package that he unwrapped to reveal a neat pile of sliced barbecued sheep's intestines. He laughed with his wide, white smile and popped a juicy piece in his mouth.

Perodje lifted the paper toward me. "You must try this," he implored. "It is very good." I tried a small piece, swallowed quickly, and passed the barbecue around the room.

Doulah had been quietly attending to tea. He removed the heated pot from the coals, poured two glasses and handed them to us. The tea was strong and sweet with a layer of foam. I drank it slowly. We would have four glasses each, bestowing upon us the title of 'very honored guests,' indeed.

After tea, Alhadi the scholar translated a letter he had received from a friend in Switzerland. Doulah and Perodje listened with rapt attention. After the reading, Alhadi wrote a reply dictated by his two friends.

Another American song floated from the small red radio. Doulah asked me if I understood the words. It was in English but I couldn't make out the lyrics. Finally, I caught the refrain: "Roses are red, violets are blue . . ."

The favorite refrain of this song, though, was "I love you baby," which all three men shouted in unison every time it appeared in the song. When the song died, Doulah shouted it one last time out the door to his wife, "I love you baby!"

I doubt he had any idea what the words meant.

"Michael and Janet Jackson are two of my favorite singers," he confided.

Doulah passed around a small photo album. There were pictures of him and his wife as well as European and American friends. He told us brief stories about each one. Being illiterate, this album was his diary. His whole life was recorded in pictures taken by passing tourists. It was one of his few material possessions, besides his clothes.

It was time for us to present our gifts. I gave Doulah's wife a bar of American soap. In Africa, soap is a brown or black ball

SNAPSHOT: TEA IN THE SAHARA

made from animal fat. She was very grateful for the smooth, white scented bar. Clasping it with both hands, she touched it to her forehead and heart in a silent thank you.

We took parting photos of the group against the outer mud wall of the house for our scrapbook. A little girl with braided hair ran by wearing a brightly colored fabric knotted around her waist. As she passed she shouted, *"Bonjour Madame, Bonjour Madame!"* She must have felt herself very brave.

Doulah left us at our truck beside the sea of tin sheds. We promised to write.

One day soon Doulah will be having tea with new foreign guests and Alhadi will read aloud my letter. The photo album will be passed around and Doulah will point out the photo of Staefan and me, his American friends who had come from so far away to have tea with him in the Sahara.

14

FACE TO FACE WITH RAMBO

While the Princess and Doulah and two of his drop-in friends were deeply involved in an animated discussion in French my mind was elsewhere. I couldn't get over the fact I was about to have tea in a mud hut in the most desolate part of West Africa with Rambo.

When Doulah had invited the Princess to his house for mid-day tea I had no idea the treat that lay in store behind those mud walls. I was leaning on one elbow, my back supported by the mud bricks behind. Rambo was directly across the room, a bandana wrapped about his sweaty forehead, his eyes, deep and black. Ammunition belts criss-crossed the rippling muscles of his naked chest. In the crook of his arm was a nasty assault rifle.

We locked each other in a battle of gazes. I, the underdog from my position on the floor; Rambo commanding the high position, plastered as he was across the far wall in a huge poster.

That Rambo was not alive bothered me little except I was deprived of the one question I truly wished to ask: How did your poster come to find its way into this hut, in this village, in this spot, on the edge of the Sahara? It was what the poster repre-sented — the inescapable, almost insidious reach of American pop culture — that both fascinated and terrified.

There is virtually no place left on earth for people to congregate that is not exposed in some small way to American culture. From Michael Jackson to Billy Graham; J. R. Ewing to L. A. Law; from Coca Cola to Levis, the world swims in a sea of American cultural mythology. It's everywhere. Even where it

FACE TO FACE WITH RAMBO

shouldn't be.

On either side of Rambo's slick image were two other posters: One featured mug shots of all the generals in the Nigerian Army (at least fifty); the other, a kneeling Samantha Fox. Samantha didn't quite fit into the military motif but she was blonde and under dressed. No doubt about it. This was a man's house in a man's world.

Concluding that the conversation among Doulah, his friends and the Princess had excluded me for too long, I nodded toward the poster and said, the magic word "Rambo."

Doulah's eyes lit up. "Yes. Rambo is a tough man," he said, or words to that effect. "Is Rambo American?"

Yes, I nodded. There was a moment of silent awe as Doulah's eyes lovingly caressed the sweaty mass of Stallone's body. "Rambo is very good."

Throughout our travels in West Africa a universal respect, if not worship, was bestowed on the military or anything that passed as such. Invariably, the military is the only organized group of any consequence, and as a result, it is responsible for holding these hapless countries together.

The presidents of these countries are often publicly depicted in military uniforms, usually come from the ranks of the military and most likely achieved power via a military coup.

One consequence is that African leaders bestow great favors on the military. Officers drive the best cars and have the money, prestige and status enjoyed by no other social unit. Another consequence, however, is that these same leaders, knowing the military is the only group capable of overthrowing their rule, rapidly turn paranoid fearing every rumble in the ranks is a revolt. To control the military, it is often turned inward against itself.

Countries are divided into security zones with frequent searches of those passing from one zone to another. The main occupation of the police is not crime control — reporting a crime elicits stares and yawns — but the control of internal dissent. No one is to be trusted. Africans, if not from a local village, are suspect. White men, in groups or singly, are potential mercenaries.

184 THE LION IN THE MOON

Equipment that vaguely resembles military issue will arouse suspicion. Knives, canteens, compasses, clothing, knapsacks, even old duffel bags will start a barrage of questions. If the MOG, a civilian version of a German Army truck, had been olive green, black or any dark color instead of red, we might not have made it out of Algeria.

After the sun had begun to descend, we rose to accompany Doulah back to his shop. Outside his home, against the bare mud walls, we took some pictures. I suggested he might want a Polaroid of his wife and baby. He shrugged indifference, as if to say, 'why waste the film?'

Instead, he asked if we might mail a letter for him in Niamey. It was his response to one he had received from Switzerland. I tucked the letter into my shirt.

"How long before you reach Niamey?" he asked.

"Two days."

"Only two days? It is so far." There was surprise and disbelief in his face. Such a trip by camel would take at least fifteen days. I wondered if he had ever been in a car.

At Doulah's shop we talked to a young Peace Corps volunteer from Boston. She was teaching math in the local high school in French and had only two months left out of her two-year assignment. She was terribly homesick and surprised to meet other Americans. After a short but interesting conversation, prolific thanks to Doulah and promises of pictures, we wound our way through the narrow alleys back to the MOG.

We made it as far as Tahoua, halfway to Niamey, and parked for the night behind a restaurant that blared African and rock music until early morning. We were tired and hot—the days were warming rapidly as we approached the equator—and as the restaurant was convenient, we decided to 'eat out.'

Similar to our experiences in Algeria, the menu revolved around chicken and fries. There were a hundred ways to fix chicken, I discovered. Even when we ordered the same thing we never knew what would end up on our plates. It might be chicken roasted, chicken boiled, broiled or fried; chicken in hot sauce or chopped chicken in rice. The head might be attached, the feet or

FACE TO FACE WITH RAMBO

both. No matter how it was prepared it was always tough and scrawny—bicycle chicken, it was called by the Ex-Pats (foreigners living abroad) because the drumsticks were lean and sinewy.

To amuse ourselves and relieve the monotony we often tried to garnish the chicken with side dishes we knew the restaurant couldn't provide. Pearl onions in white sauce was my favorite. Sometimes the waiter would say outright he didn't have it, or he would apologize that they were 'fresh out.' It was fun listening to the excuses.

Sometimes the waiter would record our complete fantasy order as if he had every intention to deliver. When the food came, of course, it would always be the standard *poulet avec frites,* sans pearl onions in white sauce, or the side order of artichoke hearts I had lusted after.

This time when our chicken dinners came, we were surprised again. Usually, a portion consisted of only a piece of chicken—a tough breast or thigh. The waiter had brought us each an entire chicken. It straddled the plate and fell over the sides onto the table. It was great fun and a good laugh. We succeeded in eating only one and bagged the other for later.

When we stopped the next day on the side of the road for lunch, we debated whether to eat a chicken that had spent the night unrefrigerated or throw it away. It didn't take more than a few minutes to decide. We had pulled off the road along a deserted stretch where we hoped for some privacy. True to past experience, within moments, five or six Africans materialized out of the bush to stand a few feet away curiously watching our every move.

I handed the bagged chicken and half a baguette to the closest and told him they must all share. When they opened the bag and saw the feast that awaited them, they began to talk excitedly. One man nearly dropped to his knees at my feet he was so overwhelmed with gratitude. They retreated to a nearby tree and consumed the entire bird within two or three minutes. I think they even ate the bones.

The wind had been blowing stoutly from the south east across the treeless Sahel ever since we had left Agadez. It was warm and unrelenting, drying the land and blowing what little top soil that remained into the sky turning it yellow. This was a land where the wind had blown for years and the people had lost their memory of rain.

As long as we weren't headed directly into the wind, we could make reasonable time at a speed of about forty-five mph with only a small drop in gas consumption. South of Tahoua, however, we plunged directly into a solid wall of wind slowing our progress to a crawl and consuming a great deal of gas.

When we finally stopped at Birnin-Kónni, a trading town on the Nigerian border, it was noon. It had taken us three hours to cover only seventy-five miles. When a fellow on a motor scooter pulled along side and offered us gasoline at a very low price, I was elated.

I followed as he turned off the main road into a maze of back streets finally disappearing into a walled compound enclosing several houses. I parked the MOG next to a small mud building with a tin roof.

"Do you want gas or diesel," he asked in English. Being in Nigeria's backyard, these people also spoke English. Gas, I told him.

"How much do you want?"

This was obviously not a gas station and I wasn't sure about their supply. "How much do you have?"

The man waved at some kids who disappeared into the small hut. They returned lugging five, large black plastic jugs.

"Each one is fifty liters, (about thirteen gallons). It is from Nigeria."

Black market gas. No wonder it was cheap. We were within a few hundred feet of the border. During the night a bunch of kids could easily carry forty or fifty of these jugs across the border through back yards and empty fields and never be spotted.

"I'll take it all," I said, lining up seven empty jerry cans next to the main tank, which was close to empty.

It took two kids to hoist each jug and another to guide the pouring.

"Is this gas legal?" I asked the man. I knew the answer, but why not talk about it.

FACE TO FACE WITH RAMBO

"No problem," he responded with a smile

I watched carefully as each can was filled, checking the level before the lid was screwed on. It would be easy to short each can by a liter but charge me for a full can.

"Do the police know you are selling this gas?" I asked, casually.

"Of course," he replied. "No problem."

It was certainly no problem for me.

At the end of the process, I had bought about sixty gallons, although the man claimed more. He was intent on charging me for the number of fifty liter jugs he emptied while I was insisting on paying for the number of twenty liter cans filled. They didn't match. Either his jugs weren't full or he overfilled my cans.

After a bit of negotiating, we split the difference. I paid him 33,600 CFA, or about $120. At the gas station out on the highway we would have paid at least thirty percent more. We had saved much needed cash and had a bit of fun, to boot.

Snapshot

STILL LOOKING IN TAHOUA

"I'm looking for a new love baby, a new love baby."

Jody Watley sang her heart out again and again from the big speakers at the end of the bar beneath the grove of eucalyptus trees. It was two in the morning and Jody was still looking. A few drunk Nigériens lay slumped in the doorway and sprawled across benches, no doubt hoping it would be one of them.

The boom, boom, boom of the bass reverberated inside the MOG. There would be no sleep for us this night. We had no control over the choice of music or the volume. Watley's fans were the caretakers of the campground.

In a foul state from lack of sleep, I crept out of the MOG in search of silence. Immediately the mosquitoes began biting in the hot moonlight. They were as relentless as I was irritable.

Tahoua, Nigér, for some reason that alluded me, had only recently been opened to tourists. The town was obviously unacquainted with the necessities of the industry. Throughout Nigér, camping was prohibited except in areas designated by the police. I supposed this was for crowd control, but also for the purpose of funnelling tourist dollars through the right hands. In Burkina Faso, with an invitation, we would be able to pull into a family's backyard and spend a quiet night. Not so in Nigér.

Entering a town in Nigér meant heading immediately for the police station to have our passports stamped and obtain directions to the campground. In Tahoua, we had been guided to a campground that looked more like the community recreation center on the outskirts of town.

SNAPSHOT: STILL LOOKING IN TAHOUA

A high wall enclosed a soccer field with amphitheater-style seats. Next to a small gravel parking lot was the Jody Watley Memorial bar and café where we had been instructed to park.

In the five weeks we had been traveling in Africa, I had adopted a liberal definition of what constituted a campground. I had become prepared for nearly everything, but not this.

There was no water for bathing, no facilities for washing clothes, no zeriba huts for rent, and no toilets except for a small closet-sized building on the other side of the soccer field. That, however, did not count for much as it contained a year's supply of mosquitoes that billowed out of the hole in the floor. There were also, as we soon learned, no other campers.

We parked the MOG and still in good spirits, slipped out the front gate in search of a bank. We were down to our last few hundred CFA and getting worried. In Algeria, money was easy to change and gas hard to find. Here, it was the opposite. Gas was plentiful while changing dollar traveler's checks was a challenge. Either there were no banks, they were never open, or they only accepted French francs.

The only bank in Tahoua was behind barred windows in a drab concrete building with a gas pump out front. The front door stood ajar. We were elated as we charged into the room. Finally, a bank that was open.

It was a classic frontier bank, à la Gunsmoke, with a wood counter and small windows with vertical wood bars. In back of the counter were three wood desks piled high with old fashioned ledgers. The clerk, who had been laughing with an elderly man at the far end of the room, interrupted his conference to ask our business. Staefan presented a $100 traveler's check and asked for CFA. The clerk turned serious as he inspected the paper with a suspicious eye.

"I will need your passports," he announced after awhile. The clerk wanted both of ours, not just Staefan's.

"I will need the receipt of purchase that shows the number of this check and which bank you purchased it from and when," he said.

Asking for passports was common, but a receipt? Staefan

Black-robed Fulani women barter in the open market for necessities.

shot me a 'raised brow' look of concern. "I think I threw the receipt away," he whispered.

"The check is good," Staefan reassured the clerk. "You really only need our passports. No one else asks for receipts."

The clerk wouldn't budge. He wanted proof of purchase.

"The receipt is in our car," Staefan explained, "at the campground. I will have to go back for it."

The clerk shrugged. "The bank closes in ten minutes."

Staefan jogged back to the campground, about a mile away. I decided to wait inside the bank just in case the clerk had any ideas about closing early. The next day was Saturday, the Muslim Sabbath. If we didn't change money now, we would be stranded until Monday with no CFA for gas or food.

Closing time came and went. The clerk wasn't sure what to do with me, so he did nothing. Ten minutes after closing, Staefan drove up in the MOG. He had found the receipt.

The clerk carefully compared the numbers, nodded his satisfaction, and counted out our CFA. We felt so fortunate we

SNAPSHOT: STILL LOOKING IN TAHOUA 191

forgot to complain about the high commission he charged.

The sun had yet to set so we continued our stroll around town. It was typically African with its Third World architecture: dirt streets, drab concrete buildings, wood doors and tin roofs, a scattering of concrete power poles supporting two or three naked wires, and hordes of children at every turn.

As was customary in West African towns, a guide had attached himself to us and was now showing us the main sites. The outdoor market was a pitiful assemblage of stalls fashioned from twisted branches covered with fronds and rags. Items for sale included live chickens, baskets of dried grasshoppers and sides of raw meat. There were plenty of vegetables, but with the sun descending, the women scurried to pack up before dark.

Our guide led us into the few shops that lined the town's main dirt road. One sold liquor, the others a smattering of over-priced canned goods imported from France. Across the street, a man was handing out loaves of fresh bread from a small, high window.

I joined the crowd, stepping on a large rock to reach the window when it was my turn. For about 20¢, the baker sold me two blonde loaves of warm bread. I slipped them into an orange plastic bag that had been tucked into a corner of the window and turned to leave.

"*Madame, madame!* " the baker called after me. "You did not pay for the sack. The sack is 2¢."

Startled, I neatly refolded the plastic sack and pushed it through the window to the open enjoyment of the other Africans waiting in line. I had never been charged for a sack before. The bread was wonderful, the highlight, as it would turn out, of our stay in Tahoua.

Darkness descended rapidly. We drove back to the soccer field cum-campground and opted for dinner at the café, a handful of tables and chairs set among the trees. The unimaginative menu was nailed to the side of the wooden cook shack. We ordered the usual — *poulet pommes frites avec legumes pour deux.*

Overhead the stars began to appear and with them came the entertainment, Jody Watley. Boom, boom, boom, our serenity was shattered. Thirty minutes later our young waiter burst from the kitchen with two large platters. I couldn't believe my eyes. On each was a whole chicken splayed across the plate, its wings hanging over the sides. Another large platter was piled high with vegetables and french fries. It was enough to feed four, maybe six people.

We chased dinner with another cold beer and watched the crowd grow by twos and threes. It was nearly ten o'clock, my bedtime, but the party was just beginning. Boom, boom, boom went the stereo. Unconsciously, I began to memorize the lyrics, "I'm looking for a new love baby, a new love baby."

The Africans hadn't come for dinner, but for beer. Now they were singing along with Jody, laughing and arguing loudly. I had a dreadful feeling about what was to come. How long would this go on? I was exhausted and wanted to scream, "This is a campground, damn it. I'm tired. I want to go to bed. Go home!" But, it wasn't a campground and I knew it.

At two in the morning, when I stumbled out of the MOG in a stupor, the Africans were drunk and asleep. No one moved. Jody still sang, her voice melancholy and distantly alone. By moonlight I walked the perimeter of the wall in the shadows of the night. The front gate was closed and locked. Africans and all, we were interned until morning.

Silence. I stopped. Something was wrong. Jody had quit singing. Somehow, mysteriously, she knew no one was listening. "Why bother," I thought I heard her say, and the music stopped.

15

WHERE RELIGIONS COLLIDE

We had been on the road only a short time when we passed a strange sight.

Set among a grove of trees was a large earthen building with a shiny tin roof. On the roof, a white wooden cross topped a small steeple. It was the first Christian church I could remember since Italy. At some distance from the church, on the other side of a village, was a mosque with its own steeple called a minaret, topped by a crescent moon.

The cross and the crescent moon — two small symbols representing the collision of powerful ideas. It would be difficult to tell there was a war in progress in this small village. It was not one of violence, although violence sometimes happened, but a war of ideas, wills, faith and emotions.

The gradual melding of religions and the displacement of one with another was as subtle to the eye as the Sahara giving way to the Sahel. I couldn't recollect any single time or place where the transition had begun. There was no line in the dirt; no sign on the road or any other demarcation announcing we were at the outer perimeter of Islam about to enter Christianity.

The evolution was gentle as we moved south and west, with subtle shifts every fifty or hundred miles. There were only mosques in the northern part of Niger, where Islam was firmly rooted. Two hundred miles further south, while mosques still dominated, an occasional small church would appear, standing alone or off the road partially hidden behind trees. They would not have caught my eye but for the glint of sunlight off their white crosses.

More hours and a hundred miles further on churches gradually began to multiply while the number of mosques diminished until the ratio had been reduced to parity—one mosque and one church per village. Further still, churches came to dominate, physically and numerically.

The next time I consciously studied the landscape, I was struck that I hadn't seen a mosque in several hours. Those hours became days, the days evolved into weeks and without fanfare, Islam was behind us.

We were looking forward to a few days rest in Niamey. It would be our first major city since Tunis, now a distant memory buried beneath layers of Saharan dust. Hopefully, we would find a pleasant restaurant to break the monotony of packaged food, or at the least, a French supermarket where we could restock our depleted stores.

Niamey would also be our first mail stop. As there were no American Express offices in the countries we were visiting, we had distributed a list of the addresses of American Cultural Centers in the belief we could use them as mail pickups. With a little luck we would hear from home.

We parked the MOG in a campground on the outskirts of the city where it would be safe from theft and took taxis about town. After some searching we found the Cultural Center, which had never heard of us and had no mail. I was mildly surprised. We were now more than a month on the road and my family were avid correspondents. We should try the embassy, someone at the center suggested. Sometimes mail gets hung up there.

A taxi dropped us in front of the American Embassy on the outskirts of Niamey. It was a massive white building set some distance off the road behind a high steel stake security fence. Inside was a football field of a lawn. The sprinklers were on. The click, click of rainbirds and gentle spray of water reminded me of home. Sheltered behind a screen of trees were tennis courts and a swimming pool.

We made it through the steel fence and bulletproof front doors to a Marine guard who asked our business.

"We're passing through town," I explained. "Since there's

WHERE RELIGIONS COLLIDE

no American Express office in Niamey, we gave the Cultural Center as a mail drop. They had nothing, but suggested we might check at the embassy."

"Sir," the Marine guard snapped. "No one is authorized to use the American Embassy as an address unless previously authorized. Letters received will be returned to sender."

We stood outside the steel fence on the broad avenue wondering what to do. There were no taxis to take us downtown, so we began to walk. I cast a glance back at the embassy. Even from a distance it was an imposing, ostentatious structure, one that would make Ali Saibou, the President of Nigér, turn white with envy.

The French Embassy, which we had passed on the way out of town, was more modest. Considering the French were the true political and economic powers in the region, the irony was unavoidable.

What could possibly go on behind that white facade, I mused as we walked away, that could justify such a monument to American wealth in this tired little country of filth and squalor? What mischief was being concocted at this very moment?

I was reminded of a saying that the reason there are never *coups de êtats* in the United States is because we don't have an American Embassy.

The Princess and I finally hitched a ride into Niamey with a Stanford Fulbrighter working on her doctorate in anthropology. I related our embassy experience.

"I deal with the embassy as little as possible," she explained ruefully. "The ambassador's not a very open man. That philosophy trickles down." I had the feeling she wanted to say more, but didn't.

It was noon and we were hungry. Believing we could beat the high cost of restaurants, we decided to buy ingredients at the big French supermarket, SCORE, where the foreign community shopped and make our own sandwiches. The front steps of the market were also, unfortunately, a mecca for every cripple and beggar in the city.

We entered through glass doors into air conditioned splendor and roamed the aisles in curiosity. There were mostly French brands of pâté, cheeses, fresh trout, imported fresh fruit, yoghurt, and a selection of French wine that was truly astounding. A French brand of ketchup was labeled 'American Ketchup' and pictured a baseball player.

Only a handful of American brands were available — Uncle Ben's rice and Hunt's Ketchup were two I spotted. Rolling Rock and Milwaukee's Best beer were available at three dollars a bottle; Kellogg's Corn Flakes at seven dollars a box. Old eating habits could be expensive.

From the deli we bought four slices of cheese and ham, two hard rolls, two small Moroccan oranges and a liter bottle of Vichy water. When the check girl at the counter totaled our small purchase, it came to $10. The oranges were one dollar each. When I handed her a large CFA note, she waived it off and insisted on the exact amount claiming she had no change. We had to step out of line to dig through our pockets for the approximate amount. She kept the difference.

On the steps we searched for a place to sit and eat while surveying the milling crowd of hustlers and beggars at our feet. A few minutes passed before it dawned on me there was no place to go. There were no parks, no benches, no picnic tables, not even curbs. There was nowhere we could retreat to prepare our simple lunch. How could we fix ham and cheese sandwiches surrounded by a wall of beggars, all tugging at our sleeves, cajoling and pleading for handouts?

We were trapped in the poverty of West Africa every bit as much as these people, perhaps for different reasons, but trapped never-the-less. The poverty before us was a vast sea that ebbed and flowed but eventually washed everything in its waves.

We couldn't go back inside, so we spread butcher paper across a row of shopping carts, guiltily turned our backs to the ocean of wretched souls behind us and prepared our sandwiches. Our West African picnic was a disaster. In the future we would be forced to confine meals to the campground or retreat inside a restaurant.

Our first project after lunch was to check in with the

WHERE RELIGIONS COLLIDE

Security Police to have our passports stamped. I was a bit apprehensive as I had deliberately bypassed a few of the smaller towns where stopping was inconvenient. If the police decided we had not played the game we could be denied permission to leave the country until we had obtained the missing stamps. I was weighing how much of a bribe to offer as we entered the police compound.

Fortunately, it was siesta time. The officer on duty was sleepy and didn't want to be bothered. His eyes were half-open as he languidly flipped through our documents searching for the necessary stamps. We had the major ones — Arlit, Agadez, Tahoua. He painstakingly entered the information by long hand into a giant ledger and finally, after dallying for half-an-hour, stamped our passports. We were free to leave the country.

For fun, the Princess and I took a short detour through the lobbies of the two major international hotels. Both were high rises with swimming pools of brackish green water as if it had been sucked directly from the Nigér River. We decided against swimming. Their restaurant menus were uninspiring and horribly expensive.

Back at the campground we conducted a thorough housecleaning. The Sahara was behind us. What remained of that big sandbox was in the MOG. We completely unloaded the truck, cleaned systematically and repacked.

While the Princess tucked herself away with her journal, I took a walk.

At the entrance to the campground was a patio restaurant with a few tables under shade. Several travelers were lounging about fighting off the midday heat with cold African beer as they watched the flow of strangers that moved in and out of the gate. I retreated there myself, ordered a large bottle of Nigériene beer and pulled out my notepad. It was a good place to reflect on the trip and on the concept of America.

Most of us, as we travel abroad, refer to ourselves as 'Americans.' In conversations with foreigners they also label us Americans. Canadians are sensitive about being excluded and make a point of referring to themselves as 'North Americans,' particularly when talking with their southern neighbors. Citizens of Mexico, Costa Rica, Argentina and other Latin countries are equally sensitive and make it known they are 'Americans,' as well, although they may be Central or South Americans.

Still, from the world's perspective, 'American' is generally reserved for those from the United States. When our country was named The United States *of America* it was most likely a defensive move designed to geographically place the country on the map. Two hundred fifty years ago we weren't exactly part of the known world. Few, in fact, had any idea where this new country was, or cared.

Of America, then, is a positioning qualifier. Our proper name is The United States. Why is it we are never addressed by our real name? Others are Canadians, Guatemalans, Brazilians. Why aren't we called *United Statesians*?

It seems to me The United States is an awkward — perhaps even ridiculous — name for a country. It's not as euphonious as Australia, Switzerland, or even New York. Functional and pragmatic, yes, but totally lacking in imagination or beauty.

The people who named our country were probably the same ones who named the electric utilities and municipal water works. Pragmatic to the core. Think of it! Our president lives in a 'white house;' our congress meets in, of all places, a 'capitol building.' Our most common street is 'Main Street' and our city council meets in a 'municipal building.'

This approach does fit the American character and what America is about. This country was founded and settled, by and large, with poorly educated European rejects — people with nothing to lose and everything to gain — as a loosely knit confederation of proudly independent colonies, then states.

In keeping with the decentralized sentiment of post-colonial politics, the states were given top billing while the country as a whole was relegated to a minority position. The founding fathers, I suspect, deliberately chose a national name that wouldn't overshadow the lyrical grandeur of the states — Maryland, New Hampshire, Pennsylvania, Massachusetts, Virginia, or the Carolinas.

Who saddled us with such an odd name? It had to be a conscious decision on somebody's part. After a large bottle of Flag beer, I could almost fantasize that crucial conversation between Benjamin Franklin and George Washington:

"What do you think we ought to call this country, Ben?"

"Nothing too pompous, General. It'll give all those Federalists big ideas."

"What about Columbia, or Olympia, or maybe even New Atlantic?"

"Pretty dangerous, if you ask me, General. With a fancy name like that people might get confused. After all, it's not the country that's important. People back in Philly will have a fit if it reads better than Pennsylvania. We need something functional, pragmatic, unpretentious. Something that says it like it is, but doesn't say too much."

"Yes, I see your point, Ben. How about, The Thirteen States of America?"

"I don't know. What if we add another?"

"Well, then, how about, The Amalgamation of Sovereign States?"

"Certainly unpretentious enough, General. But it's too long. Keep it short."

"The United States?"

"That says it, General. Not too long; not too short; not too pompous. Nobody will confuse it with a state."

"I suppose you're right, Ben. But it's a pretty dismal name, if you ask me."

"That's the idea, General."

While this conversation probably never took place, something similar might have. The name of our country suggests an afterthought. But then, what's in a name, anyway?

Snapshot

THE AFRICAN LAUNDROMAT

"Do you have any laundry for me to do?" the African man asked.

"Oh no, I can do it myself," I replied.

"You know how to do laundry?" he asked incredulously. He shook his head as if it were the wildest thing he had ever heard and walked away laughing.

I didn't need to hire anyone. Staefan took care of the laundry. Being an early riser, he would have our clothes washed and hung on the clothesline before I awoke. It was a perfect arrangement. I wasn't about to rock the boat by getting up early or by paying someone else to do what I was getting free.

We had been in the campground outside Niamey for several days when I noticed the laundry was beginning to pile up. I'd open one of the MOG's side lockers only to have soiled socks and underwear tumble out. Someone was falling down on his job. I was out of clean clothes.

When Staefan announced he was taking the MOG to a local service station for a much needed oil change, all I could think of was dirty laundry.

"I'm out of clothes," I announced. That oil change could wait.

He looked at me a long moment as if not understanding the urgency in my cry for help. Then a light went on behind his blue eyes and I knew I was saved.

"Gee, so am I," he said. "Guess it's laundry time."

He opened the side compartment and unloaded a week's

SNAPSHOT: THE AFRICAN LAUNDROMAT

worth of dirty clothes into a woven basket, threw a box of granulated African soap on top, and with a twinkle in those same blue eyes, drove off leaving me standing very much alone between the single hammock I had just strung between two small trees for my morning siesta and the basket of clothes.

Was this a hint? I wondered.

I lugged the bundle across the campground to the laundromat—three deep concrete sinks built around a single cold water faucet. A short, black hose directed water from one sink to another. As fate would have it, the man who had asked to do my laundry was using the sink to my left. He grinned in great anticipation.

I dropped my load into the dust and stretched my sore back. Doing laundry in an African laundromat was not at all like doing laundry back home. Where were the sleek stainless steel machines that whirled automatically day and night? The chairs and magazines? The bundle service? There wasn't even an espresso bar next door where I could wait out the cycle.

Here, there were no machines, nor idle time. I had a hint this might be true since the African detergent box listed only instructions for hand washing. I looked into the deep sink. The stained sides were coarsely pitted. There were no plugs. How did the water stay in? It dawned on me I had no earthly idea how to wash clothes.

I was not about to ask the man.

What I lacked in domestic skills I more than compensated for in pride. I decided to pretend I knew exactly what I was about.

I found a piece of plastic on the ground, laid it over the drain and piled clothes on top to weight it down. Then I turned on the faucet and watched the ice cold water slowly fill the sink. Growing impatient, I dumped the rest of the clothing in, not bothering to segregate whites from colors, and liberally sprinkled them with blue detergent. There weren't many suds so I added more detergent; still no suds. I emptied the box.

I could see from the corner of my eye that the man was watching with an amused expression on his face. Maybe I had put in too much soap. One whole box did seem excessive. With a determined look, I leaned into the concrete pit and did my best imitation of a washing machine: chopping the water in a whirlpool motion, swirling the clothes in a slow circle. I wasn't very forceful as the sink was clogged with clothes. No matter! I was in the delicate cycle.

In less than a minute my lower arm was red and swollen from the icy water and concentrated detergent. I switched hands and continued the whirlpool action while glancing to the sink on my right. A white girl — wearing a tie-dye T-shirt and African fabric wrapped around her hips, her golden hair tressed in the African style — climbed into the sink. Hoisting up her skirt, she began to stomp about in the sudsy water with great exuberance, creating small waves that lapped over the sides. I tried not to stare. I had never seen anyone walk on their laundry before. I felt totally foolish next to this savvy woman.

In the meantime, the man had begun to lay pieces of clothing on the rippled concrete shelf next to his sink. He rubbed each piece with a large bar of chocolate brown soap. I had wondered why the shelf had those ridges. It was a washboard.

Suddenly, I noticed the water was running out. Only inches were left. I hadn't finished! This was awful. Both my hands were numb. My back ached. I had used all the detergent and didn't have a bar of soap. The only thing to do was to skip the agitation cycle and proceed immediately to the rinse cycle.

I turned on the faucet and tried to hose down the lump of wet clothes that lay in the bottom of the sink. Giving up, I held each piece under the faucet and shot a thin stream of cold water through it until all the soap ran off. Laboriously, I wrung each piece out and piled them one by one on the unused washboard beside me. My back was killing me.

I had been the last to arrive at the laundromat and was the first to leave. With head held high, I lugged and dragged the heavy load of wet clothes back to our campsite and draped them over a rope I had strung for the purpose. With the last sock hung, I collapsed into the hammock and waited for my lobster red hands to regain sensitivity.

SNAPSHOT: THE AFRICAN LAUNDROMAT

I was feeling rather smug. I had after all, conquered the system. Suddenly, the wind came up. One by one, all my clean clothes were blown into the dirt. I had not thought about clothes pins.

Staefan drove up in a swirl of dust and jumped out of the MOG.

"What have you been up to?" he asked.

"I did the laundry," I answered, pointing to the half-empty line.

He walked over and fingered the wash. "What's this?"

"Dirt," I replied defiantly. "The wind blew them off."

"Well," he said slowly. "I guess they're clean. They smell like detergent."

That was the last time I did laundry in Africa.

16

THE GREAT OIL SPILL

I had been planning on changing the oil and filter in the MOG at the first major city we encountered after the desert. Niamey was it. Early one morning, I drove the Crusher to a British Petroleum station within sight of the campground and had the scare of my life.

Having experienced the serendipitous way African mechanics attacked their work, I decided it wise to observe the procedure carefully. The MOG, after all, was our life line. But then not much could happen changing oil, I thought.

I drove over the open-air changing pit, selected six liters of 15W50 oil and handed the chief oil changer my own filter, which resembled a roll of toilet paper that slipped inside an aluminum housing. I backed off, leaned against the wall and watched carefully.

Four or five young African boys in their early teens, barefoot and wearing short pants and torn, oil stained shirts, swarmed over the MOG like monkeys in a yarn shop. They were everywhere, checking, probing, pushing and poking. I couldn't keep my eyes on all of them at one time.

One unscrewed the plug on the oil pan. The oil gushed everywhere. A second worked on the filter housing, a bell-shaped piece of aluminum attached to the engine block by a single bolt through the center. A third was checking stuff under the hood — I wasn't sure what. A fourth began wiping windows. A fifth was washing the tires. It was a circus.

The kid removing the filter housing popped out from un-

THE GREAT OIL SPILL

der the MOG clutching it in his two hands. He was covered with oil, as if he'd gone for a swim. He dumped the old filter onto the ground, slid in the new cartridge and disappeared under the truck into the pit.

I crouched down to watch as he began to tighten the bolt that held the housing. He cranked and cranked on the bolt, and cranked again. It didn't usually take that much tightening. I was becoming alarmed. He gave it another crank.

"I think that's enough," I cautioned.

"No problem," he shot back, giving it one last crank. The job looked complete. The kid under the hood poured six liters of oil into the engine and I started it up to test for leaks.

"STOP!" everyone shouted in unison. I quickly shut down the engine and hopped out.

The pressurized oil was spraying in all directions, like a lawn sprinkler. The housing was not sealed.

The kid dove back under the chassis, backed off the bolt, and attempted to reseat the housing. Once again he began to tighten the bolt. He cranked and cranked, and cranked some more. Something was very wrong. Normally, it took only a few turns. Aluminum is fragile material and has to be tackled delicately. Obviously, this kid had no feel for the job.

He cranked one more time. A small flange on the side of the housing started to split. I began to panic. We'll be stranded in Nigér. I could see the headlines: 'American Tourists Die in Deepest Africa Searching for Spare Parts.'

"Stop!" I shouted. "No more!"

The kid stopped and looked at me like I was nuts. He started to give it another turn when I screamed, *"NO! LEAVE IT ALONE! GET OUT OF THERE!"*

Trembling, I crawled underneath to inspect the damage. Carefully, I unscrewed the bolt and removed the housing. A thin flange used to protect the rubber gasket had split off. It was not critical to the oil flow. If I were lucky, it wouldn't be fatal.

Several of the kids gathered around to see why I was so upset. "No problem," they kept saying in unison.

"Let me have it," one of them said. "I can get it welded."

"You can't weld aluminum," I told him. "Aluminum takes a special process." The idea was beyond him.

"No problem," his buddies kept repeating.

One of the kids pointed across the road to an outdoor auto parts yard.

"We'll find another one," he said, confidently.

We walked across the road to a pile of scrap and showed the housing to the old African gentleman who ran the yard. He took one look and shook his head. He didn't even recognize it. The only way I would get one of these was to cannibalize another MOG. The chances of that were zero.

I crawled under the engine and carefully reattached the housing myself. Crossing my fingers, I started the engine and quickly checked for leaks. Dry as a bone. The housing was sealed.

The station manager appeared (where was he when I needed him?) with the bill. It was thirty dollars. Eight liters of oil at $3 each and a car wash for $6.

"What car wash?" I asked.

"The boy washed your tires," the manager replied.

"The engine only uses six liters. You've charged me for eight."

"You used eight," the manager said.

"But two went on the ground. The kid didn't know what he was doing. It was his fault."

The manager shrugged. "The boy has no money. Someone has to pay."

I looked at the kid. It was obvious he didn't have any money. He barely had clothes.

"You used eight liters," the manager repeated. "You pay for eight liters." The matter was closed.

I paid and was grateful. It was just money. If I had not been there at all when the oil was changed, if I had just dropped the MOG off like I do at home, it would have cost more than money. It would've cost our trip.

When I returned to the campground the Princess was waiting, alarmed.

"You've been gone nearly two hours," she exclaimed. "I

THE GREAT OIL SPILL

207

was getting terribly worried. I thought something had happened to you, that you'd been in an accident or broken your leg. How would I even begin to find you? I wouldn't even know how to start."

She was right. If I had been in an accident and was rotting unconscious in some public hospital, it might take her days to find me. The police would never know, and if they did, wouldn't care. She would have to report me missing to the embassy. By the time someone found me I'd probably be dead. If the accident hadn't killed me, the hospital would've.

Accidents were something we had planned for only marginally and tried not to think about. We had a substantial first aid kit prepared by her father, a retired physician, and an Army survival handbook. These would handle minor ailments, not crushed bones or internal injuries.

To be admitted to an African hospital was tantamount to a death warrant. They are little more than public butcher shops. Westerners involved in serious auto accidents were usually air lifted immediately to Europe, fresh injuries and all.

There is a saying in Africa: For a headache, take aspirin; for anything else, take UTA (the French West African airline).

The Princess was justified in being upset. I had begun to take her even disposition and gentle temperament for granted. My greatest fear, that she would crack under the pressures of relative deprivation, was proving unfounded. She was a gutsy woman. The tougher it became, the more she seemed to relish the experience. Perhaps she was my type, after all.

A group of Germans had pulled in next to us in a Land Rover with a large red cross on the door. They laid around all day in their hammocks drinking African beer and listening to music by The Doors.

I struck up a conversation with one of them. They were on their way to Algeria after driving through most of West Africa. I suggested we were considering going on to Senegal.

He rolled his eyes in disgust. "That is not a good idea. You will have to go through Mali," he said in a thick German accent. "They are the robbers of West Africa. Watch out for the police.

Make sure your lights work — your papers are in order. Prepare to pay them. The road from Bamako to Senegal is the worst in West Africa."

"What about Abidjan, Ivory Coast?"

"It is very expensive and full of thieves. Forget it. Go to Togo. Lomé is the Pearl of West Africa. You will like it."

During our initial planning, Lomé, had been a possible destination, along with the Ivory Coast and Senegal. They were in different directions, however: Senegal was due west; Lomé, to the south; Abidjan, southwest. After my conversation with our German neighbor I began to tilt toward Lomé. It had one of the lowest costs of living in West Africa and did not require a visa of Americans.

Lomé also appealed because we had already crossed so many climatic zones the idea of ending up in the tropics seemed appropriate: From sea to shining sea; from North African sand to tropical mud. The idea had symmetry.

We needn't make a decision until we reached Ouagadougou, 325 miles further west. At that point we would have to choose — south or west.

I turned back around to find two Africans carefully inspecting the MOG.

Campgrounds provided a great deal of privacy, but not enough. Several times each day Nigérines would wander through buying whatever was available from the campers. Mostly, they wanted auto parts, tools, jerry cans and electronics. Usually I said no, but I had just replaced my two front tires with new spares we had carried across the Sahara and was interested in selling off the worst, along with several other items we didn't need.

The way to indicate you have something to sell is to display it next to your car and then sit back and relax. It was like baiting your hook and falling asleep on the river bank with the line attached to your big toe. It didn't take long to get a nibble. Within a few minutes two or three fellows wandered up to inspect the merchandise.

"What do you want?" I asked the two eyeing the MOG.

"What do you have for sale?" I showed them a tarp, an

THE GREAT OIL SPILL

extra tire and some tools.

One man was interested in a pick and shovel set I had bought for the desert but had never used.

"Thirty dollars," I told him.

"I can buy these made in Nigeria for fifteen," he replied.

"These are German," I countered. "They are better than Nigeria's."

"So what?" he retorted, irritably. "In Germany everything is too expensive. You paid too much." He made it clear he wouldn't be suckered the way I was. He pushed money into my hands. I counted $15.

"They will cost me $30 to replace," I said, giving it back.

He shoved the money at me again. I shoved it back. He was getting mad. Everytime I said no, he got madder.

"What's the matter with you?" he complained.

"Not enough money," I said.

"You no good businessman," he snorted, and walked away.

I didn't sell anything else that day or in the future. There was a considerable gap between what Africans could afford to pay and an item's replacement value. The African who had walked away had probably offered top price for the pick and shovel by his standards. And he was right. Anything we had bought in Germany was over-priced, even by American standards.

What he didn't understand was that we were both suffering from the effects of a weak dollar. Two or three years earlier the money he offered would have been worth twenty-five percent more. At that moment, though, he didn't give a hoot about international currency fluctuations. For his money, I was still a lousy businessman.

Snapshot

DO I HAVE A DEAL FOR YOU!

"I have some clothes to sell," I announced to the bartender. "Know anyone who might be interested?"

He looked me over and asked what kind of clothes.

"American sportswear," I answered, thinking that would certainly get his attention. "Jeans, T-shirts, sweatshirts, really hip stuff from the States. I'll be over at my truck tonight before dinner."

I had brought a stack of old clothes expressly for the purpose of resale, feeling certain I could make a killing. I had heard of jeans being sold in Russia for five times their original price. American pop culture was our biggest export and I planned to cash in on faded blue jeans, red bandanas, sweatshirts with logos of the Dallas Cowboys and Kansas City Chiefs and an assortment of T-shirts emblazoned with various restaurant names. My favorite shirt was chartreuse with a large black artichoke in the center, a gift of the California Artichoke Board.

In return, I planned to pump the money right back into the local economy by purchasing a fine piece of African artwork. In anticipation, I had leafed through several art books before leaving home to train my eye to the fine points of museum-quality art. I could picture the piece in my mind: simple, elegant, unmistakably exotic.

From the day I had set foot in Africa, I had been casing out each town as a prospective site for my clothing sale. The population would require the proper balance of youth, a little disposable income and a fine taste in used clothing. I had thought this combination would be easy to find. Wrong.

SNAPSHOT: DO I HAVE A DEAL FOR YOU!

Most North Africans dressed in traditional robes and had no use for Western clothing, trendy as it might be. In West Africa, people were begging for water and food. So much for disposable income.

I was getting desperate. Staefan and I were reaching the end of our trip. We would be leaving Burkina Faso in a day or two heading into Togo, the last country on our itinerary. I still had a duffel bag full of old clothes and had yet to purchase my art piece. Both time and art were running short.

I would have to settle for whatever audience was at hand. I did a capsule analysis of our campground, Camping Ouaga in Ouagadougou, Burkina Faso. There were palm frond zeriba huts, pet monkeys tied to trees, a bar, restaurant and WC, even though it was just a hole in the floor. The campground was above average by African standards and a decent site for my clothing sale, though I'd have to cut prices a bit.

The time was now. The bartender would be my advertisement. One word to him would be the equivalent of twenty minutes on prime time TV. Since I had been a good customer during our stay, he knew where the truck was and would be able to lead others there.

I returned to the MOG to plan my sale. I laid out my treasures in neat stacks on our camp table and sat back in anticipation mentally calculating my profits. I could picture the African carving on my wall.

I heard voices. A crowd was approaching. The bartender had done his job. There were about ten males, young boys to middle-aged men, walking my way. I stood behind the camp table thinking through my sales pitch in French and smiled as they gathered around.

These were serious shoppers. They began to plow through the stacks, pulling out pieces that caught their eyes. Just as I had predicted, they were going wild over this stuff, although I noticed no one had picked up my chartreuse artichoke shirt. But everything else? They loved it! Each person had several items in their hands. There was not much left. I should have brought more.

"How much?" one man asked holding up a pair of my

blue jeans.

"Three thousand CFA," I told him ($10).

"For these?" he exclaimed hoarsely. "They have holes in them; they're frayed at the ends. Look!"

"That's the style in America," I replied. "They're perfect."

"I don't want jeans with holes," he replied and dumped them back on the table.

A boy held up another pair of jeans, pointing to a rip in the seams. "What is this?"

"That's the style," I explained in earnest. "In America, you'd be very cool."

He made a face and laid them back on the pile. This was not going well.

"How much for this T-shirt?" another asked.

"Fifteen hundred CFA," I said ($5).

He let out a laugh and dropped them on the table.

"We do not have much money," one of them told me. "You have to give us a price we can afford."

I held up one of the T-shirts. "How much will you give me?"

"Three hundred," the kid said ($1).

"What?" I almost shouted. "Three hundred? No way. One thousand ($3.35)."

"Okay, if you throw in the jeans and a bandana."

"I can't give you all that," I countered. "You're trying to rob me."

The crowd began to mutter. They laid the clothes back down on the table and began to drift off.

"Wait!" I was desperate for a sale. "OK, I'll take 1,000."

The kid smiled and handed over some faded bills, slipped on the T-shirt, tied a red bandana around his neck, tucked the jeans under his arm and walked away.

The next man in line picked up a T-shirt, pair of jeans and a bandana and handed me 1,000 CFA.

"Wait a minute," I said, pushing the money away. "That was just for the first sale."

"You gave him a good price. I want a good price too," he demanded.

"Alright, alright." The next one wanted to buy the T-shirt I had on.

"No, no, this is my favorite. It's not for sale," I laughed and pointed to the stack of polyester and cotton T-shirts on the table.

"I don't want those. I like yours. Make me a deal," he persisted.

I sold him the all-cotton shirt off my back for 100 CFA (35¢), promising to bring it to him later.

The others crowded around scooping up clothes and pushing money at me. I was hauling it in as fast as I could. When the table was empty of everything — everything, that is, except the chartreuse artichoke shirt — the crowd disappeared.

I gathered up all the 100 CFA notes and wandered over to the bar, an assortment of tables and chairs spread beneath a canopy of fragrant frangipani trees. I ordered two large African beers for me and Staefan while I proceeded to calculate my profits. The kid who brought the beers had a wide smile on his face. He was wearing one of my Dallas Cowboys T-shirts.

In less than fifteen minutes, Staefan and I drank my profit.

17

ANOTHER PARK, ANOTHER DOLLAR

We left Niamey around noon on a leisurely hundred mile drive to the *Parcs Nationaux du W*, or the W National Park, so named because it is built around a W-shaped bend in the Nigér River.

The park actually straddles three countries — Nigér, Benin and Burkina Faso — and was reputedly one of the best places in West Africa to view game. There had been a conspicuous absence of anything wild on our trip outside of the weather and a few abandoned camels. My hopes were high.

Arriving shortly after noon, we went immediately to the lodge at park headquarters to inquire about facilities. I explained to the clerk we wished to camp somewhere for the night, take an early morning drive through the park and exit into Burkina Faso.

He shook his head. "You cannot camp," he said. "We have no place to camp."

"Couldn't we park somewhere under a tree?"

"No. No. If we let you camp then you would not rent the rooms."

He certainly had a point. A sterile bungalow with two single beds and a simple, but clean bathroom, was $65 a night, steep for what was offered, although the setting was spectacular — on the rim of an impressive gorge. There was a swimming pool, too, but it had an abandoned appearance, algae green with floating leaves.

ANOTHER PARK, ANOTHER DOLLAR

My impression was that none of the bungalows was rented, which would account for their no camping policy, although the manager insisted they were "near capacity."

The bungalow's relatively high price illustrates one of the enigmas of West Africa. In arguably the poorest region of the world you have to be near wealthy to enjoy only a modest living. One could make the reasonable assumption, based on the dire poverty of the region, that a small room at a game lodge could be had for about $15 a night. After all, labor is cheap, or should be, and demand is not great.

That's not how it works. It is precisely the extreme poverty of the masses that makes living so expensive.

There are two economies in West Africa: The local one of subsistence living, like what we had experienced on the steps of the SCORE supermarket, and the international economy for ex-patriots, tourists, and the few well-heeled Africans who could afford to pay for an imported Western-style of living. The gap between the two is as enormous as between a water buffalo and a Boeing 747. Since there is no middle class in these countries, no middle ground between extreme wealth and poverty, there are no middle class services.

The locals work menial jobs, are paid pennies a day, buy their cigarettes individually from a stall, and may rent a hut in the slums for $3 a month. The Ex-Pat is attached to an embassy, an international business or relief agency, is paid in francs, marks or dollars, buys his cigarettes by the carton and pays astronomical rents — one or two thousand dollars a month or more — for a Western-style home in a restricted suburb.

Capital is scarce, therefore expensive, and since there is no manufacturing base virtually all goods are imported, with the possible exceptions of a few staples, and maybe beer and cigarettes. Most consumer goods come through France, even if they're from Germany or Japan, and arrive air freight. The French always get their cut before the African governments slap on the hefty fifty to one hundred percent duties needed to raise revenue.

In West Africa, if you don't go first class, you go no class.

"Where can we camp?" I asked the clerk. The Princess and I had finished our short tour of the modest facilities and were eager to get situated.

He pointed in the direction we had come. About fifty kilometers back, he told us, in a town we had come through.

I pulled out my Michelin map and pointed to a road. "In the morning we want to drive this road through the park into Burkina Faso."

He shook his head. "The road is no good. It has been cut."

Before the park was established a tourist could drive through the area and exit into either Burkina Faso or Benin. With the park, the roads were severed forcing visitors to enter each country's share of the park and pay separate admissions. It was a tri-national park in name only. If we were going to see anything of the park, we had to do it that afternoon.

At the entrance was a list of prices: Admission: $12.50 each; Guide Service, $6/half day, $10/full day. I felt as if we were buying admission to the Jungleland Theme Park at Disneyland.

We were also required to leave our passports with the park warden, an obvious attempt to thwart a one-way trip. It would be easy, once down the road, to tell the guide to take a hike and then continue overland into Burkina Faso.

We were introduced to our mandatory guide, an elderly man with few teeth dressed in khaki pants and shirt, who remained nameless. We wanted to hire him for half-a-day, I explained, and then pressed him as to what constituted a half day. Was it six hours, four, or less?

He smiled and talked in circles, although he did manage to make clear the published price was only suggested. Most tourists, he explained, gave him more.

We set out with our guide sitting on top of the MOG, his feet dangling through the turret in the Princess' face, which meant there was no way she could take pictures. We followed well worn tracks through a rolling terrain of low scrub trees and thick undergrowth. Occasionally, our guide would pound on top of the cab (a signal for me to stop) point into the brush and jabber.

ANOTHER PARK, ANOTHER DOLLAR

"What is it? the Princess would ask.

"An elephant," he would say.

"Where?"

"There! Over there."

"Where?"

We would strain to see through the thick brush. Only if the animal moved could we find it, and even then, our sighting was limited to a hind quarter, or the top of a back. We were always too far away and it was forbidden to leave the road. We would drive on.

Every few minutes he would pound the top and I would stop.

"Over there," he would say. "A gazelle." Or a waterbuck, or a bird.

After an hour-and-a-half of driving around our guide announced we were going back. It was too hot, he told us, and he had a headache. When we reached the park entrance, he immediately wanted to know what we would pay him.

"Two thousand CFA," I told him. ($7) It should have been half that according to the published schedule.

He shoved the money in his pocket. "What will you give me as a gift? Americans always give me gifts. The French never do," he added, increasing the pressure.

I looked at the Princess in amazement. The sheer audacity, of this little guy. Already we were paying him double, which I thought more than generous. I coughed up a pack of cigarettes. Sometimes it was easier to give in than to justify why there would be no gift.

As we headed away from the park, it became painfully clear we had been fleeced again.

Like most services in this part of the world, the game park had not been structured for the benefit of guests, but solely for the purpose of vacuuming as much money from the unsuspecting in as short a time as possible.

We had seen so little I wondered if the park actually contained animals? I fancied that as we had set out on our excursion, the warden had dispatched word to a dozen kids crouched in the brush, who held up life-sized cutouts of animals just close enough to be seen, but far enough away so we couldn't tell the difference. The guide would dutifully point them out with much fanfare, and quickly move on to the next predetermined point in our structured itinerary.

Those who have encountered the grassy plains of East Africa with their magnificent herds are bound to be disappointed. Our experience lent credibility to the saying that one goes to East Africa for the animals, West Africa for the people.

It was late in the afternoon when we set off from the park. I wanted to get across the border into Burkina Faso before dark. A few minutes later we passed the same control point at a Y in the road we had passed earlier that morning. Since we had checked in with the guard once, I was prepared to drive on through, but he jumped out of his hut and flagged us down.

We spent the next half-hour lounging about as he entered the same information into his ledger that he had earlier that day. Only this time there was a twist.

"Where are you going, *chef*?" he asked, all smiles. I had given him cigarettes earlier. Now we were friends, *chef* being an endearing word for 'boss-man.'

"To Burkina Faso."

"Oh, well. Since that is the case there is a 2500 CFA ($9) departure tax. You can pay it here and go straight through, or if you prefer, you could return to Niamey and use the main road, in which case there will be no tax. It's up to you."

The departure tax was obviously something he was enforcing for his own benefit. If we paid the tax, we would get an exit stamp and immediately depart for the border, which was three miles away. If we didn't, it was back to Niamey, which was nearly one hundred. Gasoline alone would cost us three times the tax, not to mention lost time. This guy had a great racket going.

I laid the tax on the table. It disappeared into the folds of his tunic. I thought of asking for a receipt, but that was pointless.

He handed us our passports, smiled and wished us long life

ANOTHER PARK, ANOTHER DOLLAR

and a pleasant trip. Ten minutes later, at the border, another policeman with narrow eyes and a dirty look searched the MOG from top to bottom, looking in places others had not bothered. Most searches seemed more an attempt to satisfy curiosity than anything else. This guy was different. He was looking for something. Finally, he raised the barrier and waived us through.

"What do you think he wanted?" I asked the Princess. She shrugged.

The only thing I could imagine was guns. If we had been carrying a gun and that guard had found it, we would've been in hot water.

In these parts only three types of people carry guns — the military or police, and mercenaries. Since we obviously weren't either of the former, there was only one option left. At the least, it would probably have meant expulsion; at the most, interrogation, jail and then expulsion. Those who suggest taking a gun to Africa (outside of sanctioned hunting expeditions) are foolish romantics.

A gun would not have protected us against our real enemies — malaria, cholera, typhoid, and insane African drivers. The best defense of any traveler in these parts was common sense, good humor and a bar of soap.

The Burkinabé border station was only a few hundred meters down the road from the surly-faced guard who had checked us out of Nigér. I was expecting the same kind of reception, or worse.

Two weeks before we had left home, there had been a coup attempt in this small, land-locked country that was still referred to on our Michelin map as Upper Volta. Such attempts always send waves of paranoia through officialdom resulting in increased scrutiny by security police.

I was pleasantly surprised. The Burkinabé official was full of good humor as he practiced his English while filling out the forms.

"How much did you pay for your car?" he asked.

"Five thousand dollars." I lied suspecting the only reason he would ask was to hit us with a tax based on the vehicle's value.

He translated the dollars into CFA on a small calculator and entered a figure on the forms.

"It is worth 5 million CFA here (about $18,000). But, of course, you can't sell it. Too bad," he chuckled.

It was too bad. We were beginning to think of just such a possibility. Eighteen thousand would have covered most of our costs.

The transit form he handed us had 'Sale Forbidden' stamped across the face in red ink. It was too bad, indeed.

We spent the night parked behind a police station in the small town of Kantchari. It had been dark for several hours when we finally stopped. We had been driving on some pretty awful back roads and were exhausted. By lantern the Princess fixed a dinner of hot soup and we went to bed immediately.

The next morning I was awakened early by loud engine noises. I peeked through the small window in the sleeping cab. A large bus had stopped a few feet away. All the passengers were lined up next to the bus in military formation.

The policeman, who had given us permission to park behind his station, was walking down the line checking identification papers. When he had finished, he barked an order and the passengers broke rank and scattered to the small food stalls set up around the station and along the road.

Every African country I am familiar with requires its citizens to carry a national identity card. These cards are usually small folders about the size of a passport. Inside is a picture of the bearer, information about birth, occupation, maybe something about educational level, and the names of parents and where they were born. This card must be produced upon demand. Failure to have one will lead to jail.

Africans express great surprise when they learn that Americans do not have and are not required to carry an identity card.

"You do not have an identity card?" they would ask in astonishment.

"That's right," I would confirm.

"How does the government know you are a citizen? How do the police know who you are?" they would ask in confusion.

"That's exactly the point," I would counter. "We don't want the government to know who we are. We don't want the

ANOTHER PARK, ANOTHER DOLLAR

police to know too much."

It was totally beyond their experience.

Of course, I fudged a bit. I finessed the role of a driver's license as an ID, and our Social Security cards, which already serve as our national identity card considering everyone over the age of one must have a number.

By happenstance, we had spent the night alongside the main highway linking Niamey with Ouagadougou. The police station was a major checkpoint for those coming into or leaving Burkina Faso.

We climbed out of the MOG right into the thick of the crowd. Privacy in Africa, as we had discovered, is measured in brief moments, although as we prepared our breakfast of hot tea, bread and fruit, the Burkinabé kept a respectful distance even as they eyed us. It was a touch of politeness we much appreciated.

The general mood of the Burkinabé people was quite pleasant. They seemed a happy-go-lucky group, more open and congenial than the Nigériennes. Although the security checks still occurred with frequency, they lacked the intensity of those in Nigér.

The further we pushed into Burkina Faso, the more I relaxed even to the point of driving through or around road barriers unless a policemen was standing directly in the way, something I would not have done earlier.

The terrain was still flat, dry and dusty although there were signs of cultivation everywhere. Small clusters of round, thatch-covered mud huts were set among the fields. Herds of white cattle, their ribs prominently displayed, ranged along the road tended by kids in rags. They always waved as we passed.

Giant baobob trees dotted the landscape. The natives considered the trees sacred. We had been warned not to molest the trees as they were often the home to wild bees. A European development worker, we had been told, had accidentally leaned against a baobob tree. The vibration of his touch had aroused the bees inside.

They swarmed out and stung him to death.

18

SIGN PAINTERS AND FOREIGN AID

Throughout Nigér and into Burkina Faso there were frequent large signs along the roadside announcing various development projects funded by a host of international agencies: UNESCO, the United Nations Development Program (UNDP), the World Health Organization (WHO), CARE, Save the Children and the United States Agency for International Development (USAID) among others.

'This is the site of . . .' the sign would begin, followed by the name of the project, which ran the gamut from experimental farms, irrigation projects, health and sanitation projects and clinics, to livestock demonstrations and schools. All were proudly announced along with the name and sometimes the flag of the sponsoring country: Germany, the Netherlands, Switzerland, France, Japan, the United States, and a half dozen others.

It was great public relations, assuming the locals could read, which most couldn't, but I saw few indications that anything was actually being accomplished. Along with the billboards, we passed numerous official vehicles, everything from new Toyota 4 X 4s to Mercedes with the logos of their agencies painted on the doors.

It made me wonder about the millions of dollars in aid that were being pumped into these countries each year and what had become of it.

In 1988, for instance, the United States alone dumped about $43 million into Nigér, $22 million into Burkina Faso and another $34 million into Mali. This was in addition to the $130

SIGN PAINTERS AND FOREIGN AID

million the United States has contributed to regional development programs, such as the African Development Fund.

The United Nations has contributed additional millions through UNESCO, UNICEF, WHO, FAO, World Bank and related agencies, and so have other nations.

Where had it all gone?

The only obvious signs of development work were the signs themselves announcing the developments. I concluded that a third of the foreign aid went to sign painters, another third was spent on roads so officials would have something smooth to drive on with their foreign-aid-purchased Toyotas while they drove about the country inspecting the work of the sign painters, and the last third ended up in the Swiss bank accounts of the presidents and senior officials of each country. Not directly, of course. That would be too obvious.

Official dollars that come in the front door displace dollars that leak out the back door. Aid dollars spent on rural health, for example, indirectly relieves the government of having to spend as much, or any, of its own money on these programs. Between massive corruption and the genuine lack of concern these governments display toward their own people, millions evaporate.

As a prime example, the President of Zaire, Mobutu Sese Seko, has a personal fortune estimated in the billions, easily the equivalent of all the aid pumped into his country in the last decade. In contrast, Zaire has one of the highest infant mortality rates in the world.

Seko's not the only African leader to fleece his country. It's common practice. The President of Cameroon spends a great deal of time at his villa in France, which he travels to in his personal Boeing 727.

A UN official told me of his experience trying to obtain permission from the Minister of Agriculture of a West African country to establish an agricultural development project. The minister wouldn't sign off on the project until funding for a trip for his family to Paris and a new car for his wife was included in the proposal.

When I pressed the official why he didn't withdraw the

Much of the vibrancy of black Africa lies in its children, and they are everywhere.

proposal and refuse the funding, he replied he was under terrific pressure from his own bureaucracy to spend his agency's money and that if he couldn't initiate projects the agency would replace him with someone who could.

None of this will change, of course. There is a worldwide bureaucracy set up around aid distribution. Stop foreign aid and thousands of bureaucrats would be disemboweled.

The pure cynicism with which aid is dispensed is best captured in this little poem given to me by an aid official:

> Excuse me friends, I must catch my jet.
> I'm off to join the Development Set;
> My bags are packed and I've had all my shots,
> I have traveller's checks and pills for the trots.
>
> The Development Set is bright and noble,
> Our thoughts are deep and our vision global.
> Although we move in the better classes,
> Our thoughts are always with the masses.

SIGN PAINTERS AND FOREIGN AID

In Sheraton Hotels in scattered nations
We damn multinational corporations.
Injustice seems easy to protest
In such seething hotbeds of social rest.

We discuss malnutrition over steaks
And plan hunger talks over coffee breaks.
Whether Asian floods or African drought,
We face each issue with an open mouth.

We bring in consultants whose circumlocution
Raises difficulties for every solution,
Thus guaranteeing continued good eating
By showing the need for another meeting.

Consultants, it's said, believe it no crime
To borrow your watch to tell you the time.
The expenses, however, are justified
When one thinks of the jobs they might later provide.

The language of the Development Set
Stretches the English alphabet;
We use swell words like "epigenetic,"
"Micro," "macro" and "logarithmetic."

It pleasures us to be so esoteric
It's so intellectually atmospheric!
And though establishments may be unmoved,
Our vocabularies are much improved.

When the talk gets deep and you're feeling dumb
You can keep your shame to a minimum;
To show that you, too, are intelligent
Smugly ask, "Is it really development?"

Or say, "That's fine in practice but don't you see:
It doesn't work out in theory!"

A few may find this incomprehensible,
But most will admire you as deep and sensible.

Development Set homes are extremely chic,
Full of carvings, curios and draped in batik.
Eye-level photographs subtly assure
That your host is at home with the great and the poor.

Enough of these verses — on with the mission!
Our task is as broad as the human condition.
Just pray God the biblical promise is true,
The poor ye shall always have with you.

The Minister of Agriculture's family went to Paris and his wife got her new car.

Ouagadougou was a pleasant city of broad, tree-lined avenues with a few tall buildings and lots of bicycles and motor bikes. It was small enough we could be dropped by taxi in the center of the city and cover most of it by foot.

I had been impressed with Burkina Faso (Upper Volta before 1984) since crossing the border. It's one of the smaller countries in West Africa, being geographically about the size of Colorado with a population of seven million.

While French control came in 1896, it was not established as a country until 1947. Similar to its neighbor, Nigér, Burkina Faso achieved independence in 1960, but remains heavily dependent on French and international aid.

Burkina Faso is another one of those Sahalian countries that has been heavily affected by lack of rain. Each year thousands of workers migrate south to work in the more fertile countries along the coast. Still, annual per capita income is only $150, while literacy is around eight percent and life expectancy is forty-two years. Burkina Faso remains firmly entrenched in that select club of the five poorest countries in the world.

But that's the down side.

With our entry into Burkina Faso, our immersion into black West Africa and into the African's *joie de vie,* had begun. Here

SIGN PAINTERS AND FOREIGN AID

were a people living at barely subsistence level surrounded by economic and political instability, ravaged by droughts and high rates of infant mortality, who seemed to grasp happiness from the jaws of constant and pervasive tragedy.

These are a people who love music, who dress in outlandish colors, who press the flesh, are full of chatter, laughter and good will and who are always eager to hustle a deal.

After only a few days in this enigmatic country, I was forced to contemplate the paradox of a seemingly happy people living under such wretched conditions.

Part of their secret, I now believe, was in not knowing they were poor. It is relative deprivation that counts. When everyone exists at the same level, when Western TV isn't peppering society with messages of insecurity and discontent, happiness can be found even though it may be tough finding food.

The other part of the secret is that Africans truly enjoy people. Families and friends — often one and the same in villages comprised of extended families — are the riches of life. All life is built around the family and its needs. Activity comes to a sudden halt for a friend. Nothing is more important than being in the company of another; of sharing mutual joys and sorrows.

An African told me: "I was in Montreal to study. Everyone does their business, does their friendship, over the phone. It was horrible. You can't see who you are talking to. How can you be with someone you can't see? I like it better here. When I have business I go to see the person. We spend time together. That is how life should be."

The Princess and I were still intent on discovering if we were lucky enough to have received mail. I was also interested to determine if our reception in Niamey by the official American community would be repeated here, or if our earlier experience had been a fluke.

We found the United States Cultural Center and walked into the lobby.

"What do you want?" we were asked guardedly by a local seated behind a desk.

I asked to speak to one of the United States Information

228   THE LION IN THE MOON

Service officers. In a few minutes a woman emerged from an inner office. She had a look of uncertainty on her face, as though she couldn't conceive of why anyone would want to talk with her.

"Our mission is to serve the information needs of the Burkinabé people," she explained, with looks that suggested she might get fired if she were seen talking to us. "I'm not sure what services we might provide you."

After asking about mail and getting a negative response, I asked if it might be possible to get a sandwich at the American Recreation Center.

She seemed doubtful. "I think they only allow members, but you can try."

We thanked her and departed. On the way out I picked up a mimeographed newsletter laying on the corner of a desk. It's audience was the Burkinabé who drop by the cultural center to use the library, study English or apply for the handful of scholarships available to study in the United States.

One article caught my eye:

Why do Americans act like that? Visiting the United States? Great! But be prepared: The values Americans live by may seem strange to you. As a result you may find their actions confusing, even unbelievable! In an effort to help you understand the Americans with whom you will be relating, here are some thought-provoking generalizations about TIME AND ITS CONTROL. Time is of utmost importance to most Americans. It is something to be *on, filled, saved, used, spent, wasted, lost, gained, planned, given* and even *killed*. Americans are more concerned with getting things accomplished on time than they are with developing interpersonal relations. Their lives seem controlled by the little machines they wear on their wrists, cutting their discussions off abruptly to make their next appointment on time. This philosophy has enabled Americans to be extremely productive, and productivity is

SIGN PAINTERS AND FOREIGN AID

highly valued in their country.

It was a subtle reminder that in spite of what we are led to believe by our politicians and media, America is not the center of the universe and Americans are as confusing to other peoples as they are to us.

We found the American Recreation Center about two blocks away. It featured a snack bar, tennis courts, swimming pool and general recreation facilities available to Americans living in the country.

At one time, earlier in the century, these centers would have been British or French. Those days are gone. In most every Third World country, the United States has taken up the slack, even if the American community numbered only a dozen or two.

We wandered in the door. The thought of a hamburger and coke, which normally had little appeal, made my mouth water. The building was deserted. From a back office an American woman approached.

"May I help?" she asked, in a tone that suggested the opposite. She had the appearance of a housewife.

"We were driving through Ouaga on our way south and we were told it might be possible to get a hamburger here," I said.

"I'm sorry, but you were misinformed. You can only be allowed in the Center if you are here on official government business, are a member or the guests of a member."

"None of the above apply, I'm afraid," I answered with disappointment. "We were just hoping we could order a hamburger, that's all. Sounds like the rules are pretty strict."

"Yes, the rules are strictly enforced."

Outside, I commented to the Princess that the thought had obviously never occurred to the woman that we could have been her guests. We decided we were better off avoiding the official American community from now on.

19

ART AND DEVELOPMENT

The Princess and I spent two pleasant afternoons in Ouagadougou's newly constructed central market. It was an imposing multi-storied, open air, concrete building that covered most of a city block. The lower floors were devoted to hundreds of small fruit and vegetable stalls while the upper floors were restricted to arts and crafts. It was by far the most vibrant market we had seen.

One young shopkeeper cornered us in his open stall. The Princess picked out a woven basket and six ornately decorated gourd spoons and asked the price. He responded with something outrageous and became upset when she offered him only a fraction of what he asked. We haggled a few moments but he was not about to compromise. Reluctantly, we left his shop and roamed the floor to compare prices. He followed.

Each time we stopped he was at her elbow watching closely as she negotiated for an item. When she found similar items in a competitor's stall and concluded a price substantially below what the young man had asked, he became furious.

"I have wasted my day on you," he hissed in my ear. There was anger in his eyes. For a flash I thought he might attack me.

I pulled myself up to my six foot two frame, smiled disarmingly (I hoped), and said: "You haven't wasted anything. You are a businessman. Sometimes you sell something; sometimes you don't."

Several long moments of silence slipped by. He wasn't sure how to respond. His anger suddenly turned to astonishment,

ART AND DEVELOPMENT   231

then laughter. He slapped my hand in the traditional handshake.

"Yes, you are right," he chirped. "I am a businessman. I win some. I lose some."

We parted amicably, but not necessarily the best of friends, our purchases tucked under our arms.

Down the road we entered the small clapboard shop of Hadji, a Muslim Nigériene mask seller. He was an older, dignified gentleman with a deeply wrinkled face dressed in a fine white cloth robe that swept the ground.

I carefully surveyed the masks he had on display. Having established a small collection from my stay in Cameroon, I was eager to add to it.

I spied a large, dust-coated wooden slab under the table and dragged it out. It was a Mossi sun mask, about two inches thick and three feet in diameter, very similar in design to an Aztec sun tablet.

"How much?" I asked.

Hadji immediately went into his, 'you've picked the one piece that I have reserved for my daughter on her wedding' routine, and quoted an astronomical price in the several hundreds of dollars.

I laughed and shook my head.

"This is an antique Mossi mask," he said. "Very few left. Very rare. Hard to find."

"It is only hard to find," I kidded him, "because it was buried under your table."

A hint of amusement crossed his eyes suggesting the upcoming bargaining session would be a delightful experience.

I countered with a price twenty percent of his. His eyes lit up even more and he chuckled aloud as he shook his head. "Not possible. There are masks like this in museums."

"If this were that valuable it would be in a museum, too," I responded.

He laughed some more. "What is your best price?"

I increased my offer by ten percent. He dropped his by twenty. The negotiations had reached a temporary plateau. We shifted topics and spent the next few minutes discussing unrelated subjects. He wanted to know where we were from, where we were going and why we were in Burkina Faso. I asked questions about his family.

"This is an expensive mask," he announced, finally returning to the subject that occupied both our interests. "I cannot let you have it for nothing."

"It is expensive only because it is so large I will have to build another room to put it in," I countered.

He chuckled again and stroked his beard. "Best price?"

I increased my offer by five percent. He came down another twenty. We bartered on for another half-hour. Finally, we were inches apart and split the difference.

I had bought an original Mossi tribal mask for about one-third his asking price. It may not have been museum quality, but they're not a dime-a-dozen, either.

While an assistant wrapped it in a piece of old burlap, Hadji laughed and patted me on the arm. "I like you," he said. "You do not just offer a price. You make conversation. That is why you get a good price."

Later on I learned Hadji was a dealer of some reputation. He had masks in his personal collection worth tens of thousands of dollars. Collectors from Europe regularly flew into Ouaga with their sophisticated carbon-dating equipment to buy from him. In the end, Hadji sold me the mask not for the money but for the repartee.

As we walked away from the Nigériene's small shop with its dusty clutter of folk art, I pondered some of the differences between art in Africa and at home.

By and large, African art is crudely conceived in a style art critics would probably call primitive, but I think of as simplicity. Themes often center on life itself: copulation, pregnancy, birth, nursing, puberty, old age and death. African art depicts all these events and does so with unabashed fervor.

Statues of men are shown complete with penises, sometimes erect; women have enlarged breasts, children are often depicted nursing. African women spend a great portion of their lives bearing children, and their children may suckle until their

ART AND DEVELOPMENT

third or fourth birthday. I have observed women offering a breast to four-and-five-year-olds to keep them from crying; thus, its primacy in art.

African art gushes from the spiritual core of these people, from their natural exuberance for life and their need to express themselves. With the possible exception of national dance troupes, which are often government fabrications for political purposes, or government co-ops set up to produce art for tourists, neither the creator nor the creation are identified with government.

With the African context in mind, I questioned whether so much of our own art, funded so heavily by the government, was truly 'art?'

It strikes me that government and art do not coexist in a natural state. Isn't art, after all, a way of forcing the viewer to reconsider the old in a new way? Governments, on the other hand, are preoccupied with viewing the new in an old way. The two are incompatible – an oxymoron.

On our fourth morning in Ouaga we packed the rear of the MOG with Burkinabé woven baskets and small works of art we had collected and headed for Togo. We had passed the turnoff on our way into the city and now had to retrace our route about seventy-five miles due east against strong headwinds before we could turn south.

Passing through the same, monotonous dry brown landscape with its clusters of primitive mud huts, small livestock pens and hordes of children, I wondered if there were such a concept in these people's minds as 'progress?' Do these people expect that anything different will happen in their lifetime?

It's a thorny, circular problem. Expectations lead to change. Change, in turn, leads to progress. And progress, if it proves desirable, validates the original set of expectations.

In American society, 'expectation/change/progress' is a unified theme associated with a better tomorrow. We expect 'change/progress' to cure our social, political and economic ills. What we can change (and we believe we can change anything, if we try) we can improve; therefore, the more change the

234   THE LION IN THE MOON

better — so the theory goes.

Change is such a powerful idea, so deeply rooted in our national psyche that many of us worship change as an end in itself.

But what about the average African? Does he, or she, even consider progress desirable? Is change to be embraced or feared?

When life is static for generations, as it has been — and still is— in much of Africa, the absence of change becomes a virtue. Does that mean expectations of a better life are absent? Turned around, if a better life never happens, should one bother having expectations that it will? This is at the heart of fatalism, the 'underground' religion of Africa.

Having said this, small seeds of change have been planted in Africa through development workers, tourism, television, education and the trickle of consumer goods. These seeds have rooted creating an embryonic but rising tide of expectations among many young Africans.

They flock to the cities in search of opportunities only to find slums, more disease and disillusionment. Across Africa the young are increasingly demanding change and these demands have turned many societies into volatile powder kegs.

It was an easy drive to the border marred only by an increase in security checks. At one point we were stopped four times within a three-mile stretch, first by the local police, then by the district police, then customs and finally, as the border was within sight, by a national *gendarme*.

It seemed a rivalry was in progress. Each official asked the same questions, each searched the MOG, each entered the same data in their ledgers, and each stamped our documents, as if the other agencies didn't exist or were not to be trusted.

The *gendarme* was the most efficient. After scrutinizing our documents in detail, he asked for a receipt for some tax, which I had never heard of. When I shrugged my shoulders, he asked us to accompany him to his office, a one room hut with a crooked flag pole in front. Inside was a wood table and chair and a cot in a corner. There was no electricity. The windows and doors were wide open for light.

Referring frequently to our documents, he quickly filled

ART AND DEVELOPMENT

out a form, which he handed to me to sign. I read it through. It was a citation. I was being fined $16. At the bottom was written: Refused to pay road tax.

"I haven't refused to pay anything," I told him. "We've never been asked to pay. This is the first time." Maybe some of the police barriers I had circumvented had been taxing stations.

"How do I know that you didn't refuse?" he asked. "You have passed ten tax stations since Nigér. You could not pay only by refusing."

Was he kidding? It seemed an implausible situation. How many tourists would refuse to pay a tax in an African country when they were vulnerable to a policeman's whims?

Resignedly, I signed the citation and stuck a copy in the pocket of my dusty shirt as a souvenir. At least it was legitimate. Some consolation.

I caught sight of the *gendarme* watching us drive off in my rearview mirror and quickly averted my eyes to the road ahead. Eye contact with the police most anywhere in Africa is usually a mistake, even when they can't see you. It's an invitation to be stopped, as if eye contact implies you have something to hide.

As most police are on foot, there is little they can do if you pretend ignorance of their presence. Make the mistake of eye contact, however, let them know that you know they are there, and you deserve the consequences — blowing whistles, waving arms, dancing feet as the police magically spring from the curb to block your way.

Then the interrogation begins: "Where are you going? Where are you coming from? What is in the truck? Didn't you see the white line you crossed? It is illegal to cross that line. You have broken the law. Passport, Visa, Insurance, Registration, Driver's License. Do you know the consequences of breaking the law?"

Invariably, I knew the consequences — profuse apologies followed by a hundred explanations and a few dollars discretely tucked into your passport you deliver to his outstretched hand.

Eye contact can be a dangerous and expensive habit.

Snapshot

VICTIM OF CIRCUMSTANCE

"In the region of the Unknown, Africa is the Absolute."

As I stood in a hot, tin-roofed mud hut just miles from the Togo border, Victor Hugo's statement floated into my head. Two sinewy lizards raced across the wall and disappeared into a crack. The largest wasp I'd ever seen circled dangerously low overhead.

The African soldier did not seem to notice. Outfitted in tight military fatigues, slanted beret and dirty laced-up black boots, he was spending a long time reviewing my papers. By the authority invested in him, only he could say the word that would allow us to drive out of Burkina Faso and into the magical land of Togo.

"Dallas," he read aloud in a deep voice. He looked at me with a humorless expression. "You are the ones who shot Kennedy."

It was the last thing I expected, to be held accountable for the death of President Kennedy in West Africa in the '90s. To be sure, Kennedy was a hero here, as was Martin Luther King. There was hardly a city in black Africa that had not named a boulevard, bridge or park after each of the slain civil rights leaders. (Contrary to how he may be viewed at home, Kennedy is considered a civil rights leader in many parts of the world.)

He fingered my passport a moment longer, as if thinking what punishment would be appropriate for such a heinous crime as being from Dallas, Texas. He led us out into the blinding sun. "Unpack everything," he commanded, motioning to the MOG. "Everything."

SNAPSHOT: VICTIM OF CIRCUMSTANCE

Staefan and I exchanged looks of exasperation. We had nothing to hide, but we were exhausted from driving all morning and sweating in the midday heat.

Staefan opened the side and back compartments while I hauled out our duffel bags and dumped them onto the ground. Several guards rummaged through our belongings. Another climbed inside the MOG to poke through our sleeping bags, peel back the mattresses, and probe every possible hiding place. They didn't find what they were looking for.

Frustrated, the first soldier did not know how to proceed. Surely there must be some way to punish these people from Dallas, he seemed to be thinking. Staefan and I had picked all our belongings from the dirt and stashed them in the MOG as quickly as possible. We didn't want to give them any more time to think.

"Show me the receipt for the 'somethingoranother' tax," he commanded.

"*Comment* ?" I asked, knowing we did not have any such receipt.

"The 'somethingoranother' tax, you must have paid it. I want to see the receipt," he said raising his voice.

Staefan reached into his pocket and pulled out a wad of papers collected from the African towns we had passed through. He would hold up a paper and the soldier would shake his head. When Staefan had gone through his stack, I tried to explain to the soldier we had never been asked to pay a 'somethingoranother' tax.

"Take off those dark glasses," he said suddenly, not paying attention to my excuses. "You don't see me wearing dark glasses, do you?"

Indeed, he was not. I removed mine, realizing the mirrored lenses only gave him back his own reflection, not a reflection of what I might be thinking. If he could read my eyes, he'd see I liked Kennedy, was Catholic, had visited Arlington Cemetery and the eternal flame, vacationed in Hyannisport, and had a mother whose idol was Jackie Kennedy before the O.

"You speak French. Come with me, Madame," he said.

238 THE LION IN THE MOON

I followed the soldier to the shade of a tree where he began filling out a form for us to sign. It stated we had refused to pay the 'somethingoranother' tax and had paid only under duress.

How would Jackie have handled this?

In a softer, whisper-like voice, I said: "Honestly, we have never, ever been asked to pay the 'somethingoranother' tax. If only we had been asked."

"You could have refused to pay," he responded, unmoved.

Dare not pay? In an African country where a border guard's whim might land us in jail, or worse? It was too hot for such a futile argument.

I jettisoned my Jackie solution. Staefan signed a form admitting that he had, indeed, deliberately and with malice of forethought avoided paying the 'somethingoranother' tax. We hoped nothing worse would come of it down the road.

Satisfied he had found some indiscretion he could rectify, the soldier blessed us with the magic word *passé*. I climbed back into the MOG, grateful for small favors.

We had been harassed, searched, hassled and detained over an hour all because in Dallas almost thirty years earlier, Jack Kennedy had been shot.

20

TO GO TO TOGO

Togo, with 3.5 million people, is a sliver of a country, sixty miles wide and 350 miles north/south, or about the size and shape of a slice of Gouda cheese. One major all-weather highway runs down the spine of the country. Stray thirty miles to the left or right and you are in another country.

It is such a slight piece of real estate by African standards, a bit smaller than West Virginia with twice the population, that it seems ironic to be called a country at all. Historically, Togo was a major source of slaves. Germany took control of the region in 1884 and France and England assumed administration under a United Nations mandate following the Second World War.

At the time of independence in 1960, the French section became Togo while the British part was combined with Ghana — formerly the Gold Coast — which England had colonized for 113 years. Coffee and cocoa are the chief crops and life expectancy remains under fifty years.

The formalities of entering Togo were minimal. Since a visa was not required of Americans, the border officials checked registration and insurance and stamped us into the country.

Almost immediately we were hit with a barrage of security checks. It was unexpected. I had heard such glowing reports about Togo that I assumed these obstacles were history. I had forgotten that Togo was still part of black Africa with its own form of paranoia. The checks were beginning to make me paranoid, too.

We were barely ten miles inside the country when we

240   THE LION IN THE MOON

encountered our first barrier.

The policeman lifted himself off the bench where he had been laying under a tree, put on his hat and with great effort to overcome his excessive weight and built-in inertia, walked up a slight incline to the road where we waited.

Instinctively, I removed my dark glasses. They arouse great suspicion as they are considered a trademark of European colonialism. African police are uncomfortable if they can't see your eyes.

"*Passeport, s'il vous plait.*"

I handed it out the window. By this time it was so full of official stamps that the policeman couldn't locate what he was looking for. Many of these people are illiterate. They could recognize the stamps of their own government and read dates, but otherwise seemed at a loss. I helped him find the right page.

"Where you go?"

"Lomé," I responded. He thought about it a moment.

"Where you come from?"

"Burkina Faso."

He thought some more conveying an air of boredom, or maybe his mind wasn't working after his nap.

"Tourist?" I nodded.

He rattled something in rapid French and pointed to the back of the truck.

"*No parle Francais,*" I responded in fractured French. "*Parle Anglaise. Americain.*"

This seemed to confuse him for a moment. "Why you no speak French?" he asked in broken English. A suspicious look entered his eyes.

I shrugged. "*Americain,*" I repeated.

He thought for a long moment, nodded again and handed back my passport. He didn't ask for the Princess'. "I see in back of *camion,*" he said, flatly.

I opened the rear door where we kept our food. "*Cuisine,*" I explained. "*For le camping.*"

He began to poke through our stuff asking questions in halting English. I explained patiently. He glanced at my pants with all the pockets down the legs.

Open-air African markets are a kaleidoscope of colors, exuberance and raw energy.

"*Pantalons de la militaire?*"

"*No, pantalons de la piste* (of the bush)," I joked.

"*Militaire*," he repeated with a scowl. "What gift you have for me?"

"What would you like?"

He spied the five plastic water containers and picked up one that was empty. "This. What is this?"

"For water." He arched a brow with interest.

"Would you like it?" We were across the desert and water was no longer a problem.

"If you give it to me I will take it," he replied, blandly. A classic response.

I gave it to him. With the flip of a wrist, he motioned we were free to go.

A pen here, a cigarette there, a water bottle or two, a shirt, a pair of pants, some film, slowly but surely, as we moved from country to country, crossing boundaries, through endless police checks, we were being relieved of our excess wealth. The

242 THE LION IN THE MOON

frustration was not only the constant requests for gifts, but the very repetitiveness of the checks.

The Princess had kept score. Except for border formalities, we were not stopped in Algeria at all. When we entered black Africa, though, it all changed. We were stopped ten times in Nigér, twelve times in Burkina Faso, and we would be detained twelve times in Togo, or once every thirty miles!

In hindsight, it seems unbelievable. Imagine crossing the State of Pennsylvania, or Oregon, and being stopped every thirty miles for security checks. One of the great freedoms we enjoy is unhindered mobility.

Always, my first response to the absurdity of all the security was to rail at the bureaucratic stupidity of the same dull people asking the same dull questions. But I knew there was a method to this madness.

Black African governments are totalitarian and frail. There is no way to express dissent; no free elections. A leader's claim to legitimacy hangs by a thread. Power is wrenched and passed from one set of bloody hands to another. Today's president is tomorrow's meat. Watch everyone, trust no one.

Tight internal security requires dividing the country into cells, each with its own security system. Everything that moves in or out of the cell is checked. Others check on the checkers. It breeds paranoia but enables the president to sleep a few hours each night and stay in power a few years longer than he might.

Internal security aside, we were often stopped out of sheer boredom. We were a novelty. They hadn't seen a rig like ours. When they discovered we were Americans, their curiosity was heightened. Often, the people doing the checking hadn't the faintest idea what they were looking for. They just wanted to look. In the process they might extract a gift or two.

In Diapoang, the first town south of the Burkinabé border, we pulled into a roadside café for a beer to cut the heat. In moments, we were surrounded by friendly Togolaise eager for conversation. They had been cutting the heat all day judging by the tables of empty beer bottles.

One of the friendliest was a third grade school teacher. He

TO GO TO TOGO 243

had trained in Abidjan (Ivory Coast) in Commercial Representation, as he called it, but couldn't find a job. So he had become a teacher and was now saddled with thirty students, he told us, twenty-eight boys and two girls. The girls were there only because their families were wealthy.

Midway through the conversation a robust woman with a great smile appeared bearing a glass plate of spicy African fettuccine. This was his sister, the teacher explained. "I have asked her to fix you something special." It smelled wonderful and was devoured in seconds.

"Togo is the best," our friend crowed as he sipped on yet another beer. His eyes were glassy. "In Abidjan they stick a knife in you and take what is yours. In Ghana (the country bordering Togo on the west) the people are poor. In Benin (to the east) the people are not happy with their government. They are sad. Here, it is best. Here, people are happy."

After a couple of weeks in Togo, I concluded he was probably right. It did seem a happy, relatively prosperous country.

We resumed our trek south. The terrain began to change. The dry, unforgiving soil of Nigér and Burkina Faso that had effectively checked population growth was gone. The land turned rich and rolling and took on the look of intense agriculture. In several fields small tractors cultivated with steel discs. With the lushness, however, came the people. They multiplied rapidly becoming thicker than the mosquitos.

Three or four small village compounds appeared every mile. People milled in the fields. Long lines of brightly dressed women, some bare-breasted, walked the sides of the road with large clay urns or cloth-covered bundles balanced on their heads. Dozens gathered about each community well engaging in social discourse as they waited their turn to draw water—the equivalent of the office coffee pot.

I could understand the Pope's fascination with black Africa and why he travels there often. Millions have yet to be won over to the white man's religion. By focusing on the dark continent, not only could His Holiness stem the southern drift of Islam, but could bolster the sagging ranks of world Catholicism

244   THE LION IN THE MOON

as thousands slip from his grasp in the United States and Latin America to competing denominations. In Central America alone Catholicism has declined ten percent in the last twenty years. Converting Africans to Catholicism means tapping into the world's most prolific baby machine. How long will the Pope stay white?

It is a phenomenal experience to walk through an African village market; to be submerged in the dynamics of African life; surrounded by a sea of black faces punctuated by flashing white teeth — a sea that ripples and swells like an onrushing ocean tide as the crowd surges and sways.

Everywhere, there are the vibrant colors of African cloth; the cackle of live chickens and the grunts of pigs and cows. And always, drifting across the crowd are the constant and conflicting harangues of vendors out to attract your attention.

And the children are everywhere. They ooze from under tables, clog the narrow aisles and reach out as you pass. They follow in twos and threes and sometimes in packs. They touch you (are you black under your white skin?) and giggle, their bright eyes full of mischief and hope. It was rare to see a woman without a baby on her back and several children under five at her heels..

African countries must maintain spectacular rates of economic growth to offset their exploding populations. Most don't and in spite of massive foreign aid, life declines, steadily but surely. Children, literally, are eating Africa's future.

A few miles south of the happy cafe at Diapoang was the *Parc National de la Kéran*. The main highway dissected the park on a north-south axis. The school teacher had told us we might see elephants. We were hoping he was right. The countryside, though not yet jungle, offered greater promise than the dry scrub brush of *Parc W*.

A large sign announced the park boundary. All vehicles must stop. I pulled to the side of the road before a barricade, turned off the engine and entered the game warden's one room office. He sat behind a little table, fingering the ubiquitous ledger. On the wall next to his elbow was a school house clock.

TO GO TO TOGO   245

It was necessary for us to sign in with the warden and receive a pass to transit the park.

After entering our names into his ledger, the warden announced: "Photo permits are ten dollars. The permit means you can stop and take all the pictures you want."

"What if I don't buy a permit?" I asked.

"You are not allowed to take pictures. You can only drive straight through the park and must not stop. You must still pay a small transit fee, but you must drive straight through. You cannot stop. You cannot take pictures." He had made his point. The idea was to buy a permit.

The transit fee was $2. It all struck me as another scam. If the animals were within sight of the road, we could see them anyway, permit or not. We didn't need pictures. If they weren't, why bother with a permit?

"We just want to drive straight through," I said. The warden's face showed visible disappointment. Then came the hook.

He would give us a form on which he had entered the time we left his office at the park entrance. We had to travel at exactly 50 KPH (35 MPH). It would take us exactly one hour to reach the next check point where the time we arrived would be noted.

From that point we would have exactly thirty minutes to reach the final check point at the park exit. We had to arrive at each check point exactly on time. Arriving early meant we sped. Arriving late implied we had stopped to take pictures. Either way, we would be fined.

"If you buy the permit you can drive as you like. You will not be timed. Now that you understand the rules, would you like a photo permit?" the warden asked one more time.

I shook my head no.

He shrugged and entered the time on our form. We were off to the races.

I now faced certain logistical problems. The MOG's speedometer was still broken from the Saharan sand storm, so I had no way of knowing our speed. The alternative was to time ourselves, but the Princess had traded her watch away in Arlit and I

246   THE LION IN THE MOON

didn't own one. All that remained was instinct.

We were six minutes early at the first check point. The new warden stared at our paper and drummed his fingers on the table, unsure what to do.

"Is this your first time in the park?" he asked in French.

"We are going to Lomé," I responded in English. "It's a beautiful day outside and a wonderful time of year to be driving through Togo."

Obviously, we weren't communicating. The warden was stymied. Finally, he wrote the time we arrived on the sheet, and the time we would leave and stamped it.

We climbed back into the MOG, started the engine and waited for one of the assistants to raise the barrier. It was almost up when he noticed the sheep skull I had tied to a pole on the side of the truck. The barrier came down. Quickly, a small group gathered and began, in great animation, to debate the skull. They were considering if it were antelope.

The warden came out of his office. "Where did you get that?" he demanded.

"From Algeria," I said. "I found it in the desert, under a thorn tree."

He looked at it carefully, undecided. Another man checked it out, then started to laugh. "*C'est mouton*" he announced. "*C'est mouton.*" All the men began to laugh. I did too, sort of.

"You had better put that skull inside the truck until you leave the park," the warden admonished. "Not everyone can tell an antelope from a sheep." I stowed it under my seat and the barrier was raised. A close call.

We arrived at the second and final check point within one minute of our appointed time, and were stamped out. In our hour and a half drive through a beautiful and fertile game park we had seen a few interesting birds and in the distance, a small herd of antelope.

I had seen more wild game in the grasslands of Wyoming.

Snapshot

CP'S VILLAGE

The pale moon was rising through the twisted branches of the sacred baobob tree when we arrived at CP's village.

Staefan and I had met CP, a Peace Corpsman, at Restaurant Le Château, a favorite hangout of American volunteers in central Togo. The restaurant had good, inexpensive Western food and clean toilets — both a rarity. Staefan had mentioned we were looking for a place to camp.

"Come with me to my village," CP had suggested. "It's only a few miles east. You can camp in the field next to my house. The kids will love your truck."

He rode ahead on his little Suzuki motor bike weaving in and out of the hordes of people who seemed unmindful they were clogging a road. All Peace Corps volunteers were given small motor bikes for transportation. This luxury was soon to stop, CP told me, due to the high number of injuries resulting from accidents.

We drove slowly and carefully trying to keep CP in sight, yet mindful of the thin path he had created through the thick crowd. An accident here would be a disaster.

The people of CP's village, somehow sensing they were about to be invaded, lined up to greet us. There were at least twenty silhouetted against the darkening red sky. Tall and narrow as Giacometti sculptures, their almost-naked bodies were coated with a fine earthen powder.

We parked in an open corn field between groupings of round mud huts with pointed thatched roofs. Immediately, we

A family compound in CP's village, typical of how most families live in rural West Africa.

were engulfed by a quiet circle of admiring children who watched every detail of our movements.

CP lived in a compound with an extended African family. Protected by a high wall, the compound linked several rooms around a small inner courtyard. There were many of these compounds within a short walking distance of each other. Across a two-acre open field would be another, then a field, and beyond that another compound, and so it went hopscotch fashion across Togo. These were not so much villages as the African equivalent of high density suburbia.

Pushing open a wood gate, CP led us into a hardened earth courtyard with a massive mango tree growing in the center. Its oval-shaped leaves played softly in the night air. It had grown quite dark in the fifteen minutes since our arrival; night comes quickly and without warning in the tropics.

CP flicked on a flashlight and guided us through his quarters, part of a washed pink house trimmed with faded blue

SNAPSHOT: CP'S VILLAGE

shutters. Inside were several small rooms with bare plaster walls. The family he was living with was wealthy by village standards, CP explained. They had concrete floors.

He lived in only two of the several rooms that had been made available: One was a sitting room with two vinyl chairs and a card table; the other was for sleeping. His bed was a floor pad covered with several layers of blankets. Mosquito netting hung in the doorways.

A young boy magically appeared with a kerosene lantern. As he swung it about, the dim light threw animated shadows on the walls.

"You're welcome to use my shower," CP offered, as he set the lantern on the card table.

"That would be wonderful." I couldn't believe such a luxury existed. I followed him into the courtyard with great anticipation. Across the way was a door of weathered wood boards. CP unlatched it and stepped aside.

The shower was a small cubical lit by a single white candle set in its own drippings on a small table. In the center of the cement floor was a tin pail next to an open drain, which diverted water through the back wall into the field. I strained in the dim light to find the showerhead. There was none.

"I rigged this up when I got here," CP explained proudly. "You use that cup," he added, pointing to a tin drinking cup next to the candle.

He called out and a small boy came running, the same one who had appeared with the kerosene lantern.

"Tell him when you are ready and he will fetch water from the well," CP instructed.

The youngster smiled widely showing his white teeth as if to say, at your service, Madame. Would he stay with me? I wondered. I hadn't expected this to be a community affair.

I studied the closet-sized room thinking through the process of an African shower. My little friend would run to the well and carry back a ten-gallon pail of water on his head. I would undress by candlelight, careful not to extinguish the flame, and shower by throwing cups of cold water over my head. After I

250 THE LION IN THE MOON

soaped I would rinse with more cupfuls of cold water. I was too tired to tackle this.

"Thanks, CP," I mumbled. "I think I'll wait for morning. Right now I'm starved."

I gathered food supplies and cooking utensils from the MOG and prepared dinner on the card table in the courtyard by the glow of a butane lantern. It would be a simple meal of fried potatoes and tuna, bread and hot tea.

Insects circled the lantern. Some were huge, the size of small bats. Large winged ants dropped from the mango tree above to sizzle in the hot olive oil of the frying pan. I carefully flicked them into the dirt before slicing the potatoes into the pan. Since entering the tropics insects had become part of life.

CP's 'man,' who did odd jobs for him, was a few feet away ironing on a table covered with a cloth. A kerosene lamp hung from a branch above his head. He would pull shirts and pants from a wicker basket on the ground and carefully lay them across the table. When he was satisfied, he would fan the hot coals inside the ancient iron until they glowed. Just when they had lost their fiery intensity, he would pass the iron many times over the cotton garments, pressing out the wrinkles.

I wondered absently if CP were the only one who wore ironed clothes, or for that matter, if his were the only clothes worth ironing?

"Where are you from?" the ironer asked me politely in French.

"Texas," I told him, knowing he had probably never heard of it.

"You look like you are from Paris," he smiled.

"I went to school in Paris, for a year."

He laughed, happy to be partially right. "I knew you were from Paris. I could tell."

I did have my hair cut in a very chic, asymmetrical style that could have been the work of a Parisian coiffeur. He wanted to know about Paris and New York. "They must be the most wonderful cities in the world," he said wistfully.

How could I describe such places to a young African who

SNAPSHOT: CP'S VILLAGE

most likely had been born, would live and die within this very compound.

"They are magic cities of tall buildings, bright lights, and many, many people," I said "Everybody who lives in Togo could fit in just one small part of Paris."

He seemed impressed but I knew he still didn't understand. He most likely had no idea how many people even lived in Togo.

After dinner, CP and I sat in the courtyard beneath a blanket of bright stars, lounging in chairs pulled from his living room. We talked about the darkness of African nights and his life in Togo.

CP struck me as an anomaly. He was young — in his early twenties — with short, curly blond hair and a patrician, Ivy League air. He was not the type I would have expected to find in the Peace Corps, let alone, Africa. He talked around his personal story, focusing instead on pleasantries of his two years in Togo. He would be leaving for home soon. There was melancholy in his voice as he reminisced.

"What will you do at home?" I asked.

He shrugged slightly. "Graduate school, I guess. I thought of staying on here but two years is probably plenty."

"What will you miss?"

He thought for a moment. "The children."

Behind us came a chorus of whispers and soft giggles. About twenty feet away a half dozen children had climbed on top of the wall and were watching us with unrestrained joviality. They were virtually indistinguishable from the blackness of night.

"Sing the song I taught you for Babs," CP called to them in French.

More whispering and giggling. Finally, the soft refrain: "You are my sunshine, my only sunshine. You make me happy when skies are blue . . . "

It was the only English they knew and they sang it for us perfectly, over and over and over until they finally broke into laughter and disappeared over the wall.

I awoke in the early morning to the scent of wood fires sending their first wisps of smoke into the sky. I peeked out the window of our sleeping compartment. Goats and chickens rummaged for food in the tired looking corn field next to the MOG. Two boys were squatting in the tall weeds doing their toilet. A line of chattering young girls, each balancing a large tin pail on her head, was headed downhill to the community well to draw water. They wove past the little boys without blinking an eye.

I lay back in my bunk. Another morning in Africa.

21

UNANSWERED QUESTIONS

I couldn't figure out what had happened to the jungle.

I was still partly captivated by the stereotype of Africa being a vast ocean of intractable vines, crocodiles and swinging monkeys. It was a difficult idea to shake. We were now within shouting distance of the Gulf of Guinea and still no jungle. All the signs of the tropics were there. The heat had become thicker and my sticky body suggested heavy humidity. The trees had turned into forests; the plants were tropical, thick, with broad leaves. Groves of banana trees appeared, along with papaya and palms. Interspersed were fields of pineapples and plantations of cacao trees mixed with low coffee bushes. But where was that jungle?

Actually, it wasn't that great a mystery. It used to be everywhere. The bluish-white haze that lay against the green knobby hills on the horizon was what remained. The jungle was going up in smoke. What was left was being slashed and burned clearing the way for more fields and more people. The destruction of the ecosystem was not just a problem of the Amazon.

At Kara, a third of the way down the spine of Togo, we stopped for lunch and ended up staying two days.

Kara was a pleasant, highlands town of about 30,000, with cool nights and relatively few mosquitos. The president of Togo, Gnassingbe Eyadema, hailed from these parts and had invested considerable money into the region building a new brewery and radio station, and encouraged tourism.

A fancy hotel with a modern, crystal clear pool dominated

Staefan indulges in a gourd of palm wine at a roadside 'wine tasting room.' The wine had the look and taste of warm, rancid coconut milk.

a hill. We paid a small fee and spent a luxurious afternoon swimming and laying about, talking to a few Europeans and Peace Corps volunteers.

One volunteer, a woman in her early twenties from Indianapolis, was near the end of her two-year stay. Her impending departure produced conflicting emotions.

"It will be wonderful to get home," she commented, as she gazed wistfully across the railing at a street peddler who had been eyeing us for some time. "But then I know I will miss Togo. The people are wonderful and it is one of the best places in Africa for a volunteer."

Togo, in fact, was such a popular place among volunteers that many vacationed here from other West African countries and an association of ex-Togo Corps people had sprung up in the United States. One of their activities was to sponsor an annual Christmas charter flight back to Lomé, a rare tribute to any African country.

UNANSWERED QUESTIONS

"Did you know that sixty percent of the volunteers in Togo have electricity and running water!" she stated. "That's very high by African standards."

"What did you do here?" I inquired.

"Most of us are 'pragmatic engineers.'" She smiled at the euphemism. "We're involved in practical projects, like making simple concrete stoves for cooking. The women here cook by setting a pot on three rocks and building a fire under it. But that's very inefficient. Most of the heat escapes out the sides. So we make small stoves with concrete sides and a metal grate on top — sort of a concrete box. We make them and hand them out, and show others how to make them. It's no big deal."

"Do they work?"

"Work fine. Use less wood, hotter fire — the women think they're great. They'd come back and tell us how much money they'd saved on wood and how much quicker food cooked."

She stopped for a moment searching for words. "But it's so frustrating. If we make the stoves for them, the women will use them. But we can't get the women to make them for themselves, even when they know our stoves are better."

"What's wrong?"

She shrugged. "I wish I knew. No motivation. It doesn't seem to matter. If we give it to them, fine. If we don't, they do without."

Another volunteer nodded his head and joined in. "These people are funny," he added. "You don't know how to motivate them. They pretty much do what they want at their own pace. Sometimes, something gets done."

I asked him what he did.

"I'm a bookkeeper for some co-ops that the government has set up."

"Have you had training as an accountant?"

"No." He shook his head. "It's pretty simple, really. Basic math. There are three of us doing the same job for five co-ops. It only takes a few hours a week. Actually, one of us could handle all five. The toughest part is working with the Togolaise heads of the co-ops. The bureaucracy here is awful. The simplest things are sent to the highest levels. Nobody will make a decision.

Nothing happens until the top man signs it off. We spend a lot of time hanging around and waiting, and fighting the bureaucracy.

"A lot of it's political," he went on. "Sometimes the government people want us to do something special for a certain village because they want to favor one tribe over another. We'll tell them no. What we do for one we do for all. That really blows their minds. These government people aren't used to being told no."

"If you're over-staffed why doesn't the Peace Corps reassign some of you?" I asked.

"Where? As far as I can figure out, this whole country's over-staffed. Togo is a big deal to the Peace Corps. It was the first African country to accept the Corps and relations with the United States are pretty good, so the Corps dumps a lot of volunteers in here. Politics, I guess."

By mid-afternoon of the next day we had dropped from the higher, cool plateau down to the coastal plain. The humidity was heavy; so was the intense heat. It had been so long coming. Now, there was no relief. There was no question we were in the tropics. I thought briefly of returning to Kara simply so we could breathe.

As we approached the northern outskirts of Lomé, I could smell the salty air of the gulf. After thousands of miles of desert I was excited about the ocean. I dreamed of spending at least two days submerged. It would take that long to heal the cracks in my dry skin.

Our goal was Ramatou Plâge, a campground on the beach five miles east of the city. It had been recommended in a guide book. After an hour of mindless wandering through a labyrinth of unmarked streets, we found the right road and soon were positioning the MOG on a low bluff at the edge of the beach.

A stiff southerly breeze blew off the water right through our sleeping cabin providing not only air conditioning but relief from the mosquitos. On those few nights when the breeze was flat we cooked in our bunks and fell asleep to the high pitched whine of mosquitoes massing for the kill.

The beach was our frontyard. Some years before, a paved road had paralleled the beach about fifty yards out. Angry seas

UNANSWERED QUESTIONS

had churned over the road breaking it into a reef and forming, in the process, a perfect swimming lagoon. It was now the most popular swimming spot in Lomé.

On the far side of the reef lay the rusting carcass of an old cargo ship that had been washed onto the rocks many years earlier. It swayed ever so gently before the incessant pounding of the waves.

This would be our home for the next week while we tackled the two major problems of our return: Finding the most inexpensive way back to Paris and doing something with the MOG — sell it or ship it. Neither had been prearranged, so we set aside the mornings for the tasks while the early afternoons were devoted to combing the vibrant outdoor markets for the unusual.

Late afternoons were for swimming. After a light supper we would sit on the bluff to watch the sun burn itself out. The moonlit waves rolled onto the beach in a rhythmic, hypnotic cadence.

Africa is not only a continent of contrasts — desert and tropics, poverty and wealth, white and black, sand and mud — but of enigmas as well. The most enduring impression was the upbeat happiness of people living a fragile existence, deprived of virtually all the material comforts we consider necessities, including health care and social security.

They are a vulnerable people surrounded by reminders of their own paper-thin mortality — the crippled, the hungry, the diseased and disfigured. Funerals are a constant of village life. A woman must have eight children to insure that four, hopefully five, will live; a forty-five year old man discovers that few of his childhood friends are still alive.

Yet, smiles came quickly to their faces, laughter to their lips. They are eager to be friends, to touch and to share. They lead unpretentious lives, with a child-like innocence, full of vigor and lust for life.

Many of us think of Africa as a primitive continent and Africans as primitive peoples. The label is usually pejorative. After two months submerged in the African experience I began to question the whole concept of 'primitive.'

The dictionary defines primitive as original or primary, or

that characterized in an early stage of development. The issue is not whether Africans, by this definition, are primitive — by most standards they do lead a primary existence — but whether they deserve the label of primitive as applied in its more popular definition — ignorant, savage, inferior.

For example, it is not unusual to see groups of bare-breasted African women, colorful skirts about their waists, walking the side of the road. Much of the world would consider this primitive (backward?) behavior. Many African governments, in fact, discourage tourists taking pictures of such women because of sensitivity to being labeled primitive by an outside, unsympathetic world.

If bare breasts are a sign of primitiveness, how then do we separate this behavior from that of millions of European women who flock to the Mediterranean beaches to spend the day in a near naked state? Are these women also primitive? Are we talking about primitive behavior, or uninhibited behavior? If the lack of inhibitions can be construed as primitive, then many European women share the same tribal traits as their African sisters.

Perhaps it is that European women at the beach, or African women at home, share a common root — a sense of being grounded, of knowing who they are, of having confidence in their own identity and the strength of their culture. With this kind of strength there is less inhibition, more willingness to be human, more tolerance for primitive, uninhibited behavior.

On the other hand, and this is the enigma, economically, technically, politically, in so many ways, African societies are primitive in that they have failed to evolve.

For the last 1500 miles through a good portion of West Africa, through two of the five poorest countries on earth, through near Stone Age existence of mud huts, scrape-and-scratch agriculture, flies, mosquitos, cholera, malaria, typhoid, and diseases you can't pronounce, with people wallowing in their own filth and life without change, a single question kept buzzing through my mind: What happened in Africa (or what failed to happen) that a whole continent of people failed to develop with the rest of the world. What is missing?

Why, for instance, was it the Europeans who colonized

UNANSWERED QUESTIONS

Africa and not the other way around? Why did the Arabs cross the great desert to buy and transport slaves northward and not the other way around? Why did manufactured goods flow south and not north? Why did African civilization, for all purposes, cease to evolve after the tribe? Why did these people fall so far behind? Certainly, at one point, it was a game of equals.

Black Africa has been pretty much a stagnant, savage and primitive place for most of recorded history. Anthropologists, no doubt, will point out exceptions, where at some point in history a certain tribe in a certain part of the continent was advanced for its time, but then lost its edge.

Five hundred years ago, for instance, the Mossi of Burkina Faso had developed a social structure with ministers and a court system, music, art and philosophy, and ruled considerable land before succumbing to invasions from the north.

Development is always relative to its surroundings, however. While the Mossi were undoubtedly advanced for Africa, they still lagged societies elsewhere in the world, and when their time came, they were easily toppled. Even today, there are few bright lights in darkest Africa.

The tribe was the basic unit and still is. There are over two thousand tribes, each with its own language or dialect, customs and traditions. They killed each other off, sold each other into slavery (within Africa first, then to the Arabs, and later to the Europeans, who exported the slaves to the New World) and committed such random acts of savagery that early European explorers were dumbfounded.

Stanley (of Livingstone fame) writes of entering one village in East Africa where the village chief was so eager to impress the explorer with his hospitality that he ordered ten men to step forward and kneel. One by one he cut off their heads — sort of a welcome wagon. Then they all sat down for dinner. Accounts by other explorers are just as vivid.

The modern African country is essentially a collection of tribes. The European colonizers, almost at whim, carved up the continent into random nations, often throwing hostile tribes together, sometimes splitting tribes, but rarely with any thought to future self-governance. The result has been a great deal of instability with coups, dictatorships and more coups.

On the other hand, what if the colonizers had not come? What would Africa look like today if the Africans had arranged their own borders? No telling, but chances are the continent might be even more unstable and fractured than it is. If tribal boundaries had been followed, for instance, there might not be fifty-two countries, but five hundred, a thousand, or more.

While post-colonial nationhood has restored pride to the Africans, for many, if not most countries, it has also led to economic disaster. Tribal politics, gross economic mismanagement and the ascendancy of military thugs disguised as leaders have resulted in many of these countries being worse off now than they were under their colonial masters.

Africans will rarely discuss this. They prefer, instead, to focus on colonialism as a convenient and saleable excuse for their inability to progress economically.

True, colonization, by and large, was not good for Africa. The colonizers destroyed much of what they found including the egos and self-esteem of the Africans themselves. They decapitated tribes, shuffled boundaries creating artificial nations, swapped lands for political purposes, looted natural resources and gave not a damn for the consequences.

But in the process, nations were created, slavery was abolished and a skeletal infrastructure of agriculture, roads, railroads, education and administration was established. The French provided West Africa with a firm financial base and in East Africa the British left behind a rational basis for civil service and the habit of afternoon tea, if that's considered a plus.

Perhaps the single most important legacy of the colonizers was the unifying of hundreds of tribes with a single language. Africa today is divided primarily between French and English speaking regions. For the first time in the history of the continent Africans can communicate with each other.

The other issue Africans and those of African descent raise in defense of under-achievement is slavery. This subject is no less than a political minefield, one which is best left to dema-

UNANSWERED QUESTIONS

gogues. It's important to realize, however, that slavery was a deeply rooted institution in the African fabric long before the outside world became involved. While the Arabs exploited slavery and the Europeans created the broader market, the Europeans were also responsible for ending it, in a few cases long before even some African tribes were willing.

Still, the question remains, and continues to haunt: What failed to happen in Africa, beyond colonialism and slavery that accounts for a whole continent failing to develop past the tribal stage? This is a question for which I have found few answers. Indeed, few answers are available from any source that are satisfying.

Snapshot

FUFU AND
THE MARLBORO MAN

The African sitting to my right was staring at me.

"What is the matter, did you not wash your hands?" he asked intently eyeing my slow movements.

I was tepidly pulling very fine shreds of meat off the bone and dipping them in the red sauce. I was eating rat, after all, and it was a new experience.

I nodded at him that yes, I had washed. Bouga had helped me, pouring the cup of cool water through my hands while I held them over a small bowl. We were all sitting at a communal wood table with benches pulled up to either side. The room was a concrete cell with bars over the three openings that let in a faint breeze.

I had wanted to try something typical of the region.

"Show us where you like to eat," I had flippantly said to Bouga, our guide and mentor for our short stay in Kpalimé, a large village in the central highlands of Togo. "Order your favorite, for all of us."

He took me at my word.

Bouga, a tall, slender teenager with a handsome face, always dressed in coordinated colors of red, white and blue. His white polo shirt was inscribed with the Marlboro logo and a red belt with the words Marlboro, Marlboro, Marlboro encircled his waist.

Bouga was the local Marlboro man, he announced with some pride. His job was to spread the gospel according to Marlboro. In

SNAPSHOT: FUFU AND THE MARLBORO MAN 263

the meantime, he would be pleased to be our guide.

He led us, taking several shortcuts through creeks and behind houses, to a small building in the square of the bus station.

"My favorite restaurant," he announced.

It looked busy enough. At the entrance, three women stood around a giant wood mortar pounding a white, glutinous substance with long poles. Each would pound in sequence so as not to interfere with the others. THUMP, THUMP, THUMP. The heavy poles would strike the bottom of the mortar in a cadence as they laughed and chattered among themselves. THUMP, THUMP, THUMP. Their pounding would go on for hours.

They were making fufu, a fermented bread-like dough derived from boiled cassava root, a staple of these people. Every meal included fufu, just as most European meals included bread. The rhythmic thumping of the fufu women rippled throughout the villages of the region.

Bouga had brought me a small plastic bowl with a mound of fufu he had just pulled from the trough. Two other bowls contained meat chunks still on the bone and a red dipping sauce. Now we were ready to eat, our host declared.

As my mind was devising strategies for circumventing the meal, I felt a tap on my arm. A small boy with bright eyes was selling nail polish. He tried to shove a bottle into my hand. The polish was sparkling pink, made in China. I shook my head no and returned to the meal. Staefan was way ahead of me.

The African next to me, noticing my timidity, demonstrated the correct way to eat fufu. He tore off a large chunk from the mound in his own bowl, pushed a generous portion of stringy meat into the center, dunked it into the sauce, and shoved it into his mouth.

The meat was rat, not the rat of Charles Dickens lore, but African rat, a rodent the size of a ground hog that the villagers snared in the jungle undergrowth. It had a greasy, wild game taste with stringy meat that, along with chicken, was a favorite of these people. It was not one of mine. A rat, after all, is a rat.

I could have ordered chicken hot off the grill. Just outside, a woman was barbecuing several birds on a wire grill stretched

264   THE LION IN THE MOON

over an oil barrel. The cook sprinkled the chicken with salt, pepper and Maggi seasoning. Grilled onions and tomatos came as a side dish. Next to the chickens were skewers of grilled, curried mystery meat, maybe goat or even dog.

No chicken for me, thank you. I wanted to eat native.

I smiled faintly and nodded. My instructor watched as I made more of an effort. I broke off a second, slightly larger piece of fufu, pushed some meat into the center, dipped it into the sauce and gingerly edged the morsel into my mouth. He smiled his approval.

A young boy in the corner was selling Cokes. I nodded slightly in his direction. He thrust a life-saving Coke into my hand. I quickly took a large gulp. It was lukewarm, as usual; the greasy taste of rat lingered.

Earlier that morning we had slipped into a small dining establishment near our African hotel — no camping in this village — for breakfast and coffee. It was a tin shack with a beaded curtain separating the interior from the street. Three or four wood tables with an odd assortment of chairs surrounded a small open kitchen. The faded blue walls were streaked with smoke and grease.

It was very Californian, I kept telling myself, with the exposed kitchen and the cook holding center stage. The flies brought me back to reality.

The waitress had hauled over a blackboard bigger than herself so we could easily read the simple menu: *puli puli* (chicken with a hot red sauce), a couple of local dishes, omelettes, bread and coffee. Staefan and I ordered the omelettes with bread and coffee.

Others drifted into the open room and paused, eyeing us with indecision before selecting a table across the way. Whether they were being polite and allowing us privacy, allowing themselves privacy, or simply thought us bad medicine this early in the morning, I will never know. We did have a table of four to ourselves, a rarity in an African restaurant from what I had observed.

On the counter was a two-burner countertop stove sur-

SNAPSHOT: FUFU AND THE MARLBORO MAN   265

rounded by a stack of eggs. Two blackened omelette pans, a toaster oven, and salt and pepper were the cook's only tools.

The young woman brought us instant Nescafé, two cups of hot water with sugar on the side and a small can of condensed milk. Our cups had handles. The other customers, all natives of the village, were drinking their beverage from bowls. I thought at first she had run out of bowls. But, no, there were more stacked on a side counter. Handled cups were her way of accommodating us.

Other small food stalls dotted the village. Each was concerned with a speciality. One woman sold bowls of lemon grass drink. Another had a covered pot of stewed chicken with okra and groundnuts (peanuts). Others sold grilled plaintain. One woman specialized in black eyed peas.

Each woman presided over her table as a priestess at mass. She would ritually prepare her dish and watch as her client ate. When the meal was consumed, she would rinse the dirty service with a swipe of her hand in a bucket of water at her feet. The bowl was placed back on the table, ready for the next customer.

After a lengthy afternoon stroll through the coffee and cacao plantations that bordered Kpalimé, we set out in pursuit of a more Western dinner. We had not gone far when Staefan pointed to a poster of a 'superburger' hanging on the outside of one restaurant. It was a gorgeous vision. A juicy, thick beef patty, a crisp lettuce wedge, red tomato slices and thick chunks of onion were piled on a steaming bun. The burger was several layers tall and irresistible.

"This is for me," Staefan announced and disappeared through the doorway.

I was much too skeptical to fall for this. I decided to sit down anyway, to see what would happen.

At my elbow was a tap, tap, tap. The little boy with bright eyes was holding up the bottle of Chinese sparkling nail polish. He wanted to paint my nails, he told me. I smiled and shook my head, no.

After a twenty-minute wait, the superburger arrived: a very small bun in the center of a very large plate. Staefan's face fell. I

266 THE LION IN THE MOON

was sipping a Flag beer trying not to look too superior, just happy to be there.

Staefan removed the top bun and yes, there was a patty, he discovered, of very thin, gray looking matter. Possibly it was beef. There was nothing else — no wedge of lettuce, no thick chunks of onion, no slices of juicy tomatoes. He stared at it awhile, before liberally dousing it with salt and pepper. It was gone in three bites. Fufu, I decided, did have its merits.

The Marlboro man was waiting outside. Being white made it difficult for us to hide in black Africa. It wasn't that we didn't relish his company. It was that once you hired a guide, he was yours for life. While Bouga was helpful in orienting us to Kpalimé, we did want to explore by ourselves.

Often during our two-day stay, we found it necessary to retreat to our hotel room under the pretext of a nap only to carefully exit through a side door. Within an hour or two, however, there he was.

"I've finally found you," he would exclaim, fearing he would be fired for shirking his duty.

The hamburger had been a disaster. Staefan insisted on real food. With Bouga in the lead we set out in search of the perfect meal.

"This way," he commanded, assuming his proper role as official guide, setting off at a brisk pace. Soon we were there, a more substantial restaurant than what we had encountered so far.

"This one is for tourists," Bouga announced, leading us through the door. I sensed the Marlboro man was also savoring a decent meal.

Brightly painted murals of dancing African women covered the walls of the bar; the courtyard walls were covered with primitive village scenes. We found a shady table under a thatched roof. Looking up, I noticed the thatch was made of beer caps.

The waitress eventually shuffled our way. She was a large, woman with a long skirt of bright African fabric and hair bound in a kerchief. We ordered two beers in the largest size bottle available. Bouga ordered a Coke. When she returned with the beer, I asked for a glass.

SNAPSHOT: FUFU AND THE MARLBORO MAN

"No more glasses," she said matter of factly.

"How are the hamburgers?" Staefan asked.

"They're very flat," she responded and shuffled off.

Meanwhile, our private party had been expanding. There were now six of us crowded around the table including our little friend with the Chinese polish. He kept his eye on me the whole time. Like moths to a flame, wherever we sat, young Africans appeared out of nowhere to attach themselves to us.

Staefan and I tackled our strong, quart-sized bottles of African beer and settled in for the wait. Time slipped by. We ordered more beer. In the distance, our waitress shuffled towards us with our food. I had forgotten we had ordered.

She set before me an omelette with tomatoes and onions served on a floral plate that could have belonged to my grandmother; Staefan had *bifteck* and salad. As always, there were round slices from French baguettes. I was so hungry I didn't look up until I had consumed every morsel. The food was wonderful.

As soon as we had finished, our new African friends rejoined us at the table. They had politely left during our meal to sit a short distance away, all except for the small boy with the polish and Bouga, our *gardien* and life-long friend. The little boy moved closer and set the tiny bottle beside my plate.

By now I had finished two quarts of Flag beer and was feeling very neighborly. I looked into the little boy's bright eyes and paid a substantial amount for the bottle of Made in China pink sparkling nail polish.

Snapshot

THE CURSE

"Madame!" a young voice shouted. "Would you like to take my photo?"

She was a teenage girl with hips wrapped in bright green and black African cloth and an almost white Western T-shirt. I couldn't believe I had heard correctly. I had been wandering for some time through the open-air stalls of the market looking for just such an opportunity.

"Do you want me to take your picture?" I asked, uncertain if indeed that is what she wished.

"*Oui, prenez mon photo,*" she replied with a wide smile.

As I raised my camera she struck a pose, bending over to scoop grain from a woven basket at her feet. I took several photos as she changed positions, pleased I had finally found a willing subject who even smiled into the lens.

Some of the women in the next stall grumbled and covered their faces when they heard the shutter click. A buzz arose among them and I heard an older woman with deeply wrinkled coal-black skin accuse me in French of "stealing" photos. She was not happy and mumbled something at me, which I did not understand. The glare in her eyes was evident, however. It was a cursing look.

It hadn't been easy photographing people in Africa. They were among the shiest subjects I had ever encountered, partly due to their nature, partly to their belief that a photo might rob them of their soul. The mere act of raising my camera was enough to send them scurrying in the opposite direction. Occa-

SNAPSHOT: THE CURSE 269

sionally, a merchant might allow photographs of her stand (without her) in exchange for a gift of money, but usually I encountered stern glares, shaking fists or verbal abuse.

Being a travel and food writer, the exotic people and rambling markets of West Africa were so enticing I was compelled to obtain photos at any price. Out of self-defense, I would sling my camera around my neck, the lens poking through my jacket, and surreptitiously click the shutter at random as I turned in various directions. It was a nifty trick, I thought, although I couldn't be sure of the framing.

Finally, in this young girl I had a willing subject — too willing, it turned out. She kept posing and I kept shooting. I had taken nearly a roll but she pressed for more.

"One more. Take another," she would insist, assuming yet another pose.

Not wanting to appear ungrateful, I would oblige with just one more, and then another. It was feast or famine.

"I am out of film," I finally told her. "The camera is empty." That brought a look of uncertainty to her face. I wondered if she understood that a camera could be empty?

I thanked her and started to walk on.

"You will bring me a photo?" she asked.

I tried to explain this was not an instantaneous process. The film would have to be developed and I would be gone by then. She did not seem to understand.

"If I am not here, you can bring it to my mother. She has a stall upstairs," the girl replied, pointing to the large, two-story enclosed market a few hundred feet away.

I did not know how I would possibly recognize her mother. The girl assured me I would. More likely, she would tell her mother to watch for the white woman with a camera.

Once more, I tried to explain the film would not be developed until later, maybe a month or two. It was futile. She insisted I bring her a photo. I finally agreed, thinking I could return with our Polaroid camera and satisfy her instantly.

"*N'oubliez-pas*," she shouted after me. "I will be waiting!"

With a final thank you, I scurried into the covered concrete

The beginning of the curse:
She begged me to take her picture.

market and up the stairs to the second floor. I still needed more market shots. Maybe a change of venue would help, though it was hard to be inconspicuous in a crowd of blacks.

From the second floor, I discovered I could shoot the

SNAPSHOT: THE CURSE

271

entire outdoor market through small windows in the concrete wall without detection. Or so I thought. After several shots, a woman appeared from nowhere and demanded money because I was standing in her allotted space.

At first I thought she was joking, but as she persisted in a louder and louder voice, I realized she was very serious. A crowd was gathering. I pretended not to speak a word of French and thanked her profusely in English for allowing me to trespass into her space. The crowd was more curious than hostile. Sensing my discomfort, they began to laugh as the woman became more insistent I pay her. I smiled broadly and nodded my head deeply in thanks, retreating toward the stairs. It was better in the open market, I concluded.

I walked through the thick crowd looking for Staefan, growing dizzy from the masses of people and hot sun. He popped out from behind a stall and grabbed my camera, excited about some chickens he had seen in the market. "Good luck," I yelled after him as I sat down in the shade, exhausted.

Twenty minutes later, he emerged from the throbbing market.

"It's murder in there," he groaned. "I nearly got clobbered. Let's get out of here."

We threaded our way through the crowded streets back to the MOG. I thought of the Polaroid, but the girl in the market was so far away. It would take half-an-hour to walk back and find her. The cool seat of the MOG felt good. A cold drink would feel even better. "Let's go," I said to Staefan, dismissing my promise.

The next day we arrived in the port city of Lomé, the capital of Togo and the termination of our trip. We set up camp on the beach a few miles outside the city.

The night heat was suffocating. I climbed into my bunk with the waves crashing just beyond. We had left both doors of the MOG wide open in an attempt to keep cool. The mosquitoes arrived in due time to practice their own form of sadism. I didn't know whether it was better to enjoy the night breeze at the risk of malaria or die of heat stroke in a sealed container.

My fate was decided for me. About midnight I became

violently ill. My body was on fire. I broke out in a cold sweat and spent the rest of the night and early morning hours crouched outside the MOG.

I had been cursed. It was the only explanation. There was nothing wrong with Staefan. The old woman at the market had cursed me for stealing pictures. In my quest for obtaining photographs, I had shown no respect for their privacy nor their spiritual beliefs. The deed was done, however, and now I was being punished. I had never been so sick. I knew I was going to die.

By ten the next morning, however, I was still alive; just barely, I concluded. My only hope for a quick recovery was to return to the market and apologize to that old woman, if I could find her, and deliver that photo to the young girl who had so willingly posed for me. Please, I pleaded with Staefan. He thought I was crazy.

The curse intensified. A violent storm blew in from the Atlantic washing away most of my favorite beach, toppling palm trees, and cutting off electricity. The campground was a muddy disaster. Staefan rented a zeriba hut so I could die in a real bed. I was grateful but weak in my diminished state of suffering.

After three days, time enough to reflect on what a dastardly person I was, I woke up and was well. The old woman had lifted the curse when she sensed I had learned my lesson.

22

WORLD CLASS SCAMS

We moved ahead with our plans to depart.

Travel agencies were not good sources for information on inexpensive flights to Europe. Most airlines had their own offices and each quoted a different fare. Aeroflot, the Russian airline, traditionally the least expensive and that favored by students on the bum, only flew from neighboring Ghana and Benin. Since finding respectability by joining IATA (the International Air Transport Association), Aeroflot's fares had increased considerably and still required transit via Moscow.

Another possibility was Nigerian Airways, which has the reputation of being the worst airline in Africa. When we entered their office, a large sign on the wall greeted us: "Nigerian Airways is not responsible for checked luggage." We left immediately.

Flying Nigerian Airways also meant transiting Lagos, which many consider the worst airport in the world. Stories of the Lagos Airport are legion and include everything from extortion by customs agents to women being raped in the transit lounge.

We checked out Ghana Airways, an airline with a better reputation. They were linked with British Airways, flew new DC-10s to London, Paris and Dusseldorf and offered attractive fares. The downside was they flew to Paris only once a week, every Thursday, and landed several hours after our Thursday morning departure from Paris to Dallas.

We finally stumbled across an attractive fare that combined an Air Afrique flight from Lomé to Abidjan, and Iberia from Abidjan to Madrid leaving several days for a leisurely train trip to

274 THE LION IN THE MOON

Paris through the Basque Country of Spain. We made reservations for a flight departing in five days.

On the way back to the MOG, we accumulated a following of money changers, spry fellows who danced about waving rolls of bills enticing us with outlandish exchange rates.

Based on the French franc, the pure CFA exchange rate for a dollar was 285. I had obtained 282 from an American money changer who lived in Togo, and the banks offered 280. The changers offered 300. Since there was no black market to speak of, it had to be a scam. But what kind?

I had been the victim of many successful scams over the years, having lost money in a variety of places including Kenya, Tanzania, Greece and Taiwan. I figured I knew all the tricks and was curious if I could spot this scheme as it developed. I wanted nothing to happen, however, until we had reached the security of the MOG. Thieves work on confusion. Once in the MOG, with a wall to my back and limited access, I could more easily control the exchange.

Two of the most popular scams I've encountered are the bait and switch, and the bait and clip. In the first, the money you think you are buying is switched for something worthless, like newspaper. In the second, you receive money, but only a fraction of what was promised. Both happen so fast by the time you realize you have been taken the culprits have long melted into the crowds.

Bait and switch works this way: You are surrounded by a group of sharks, three to five, who play on your greed by offering exceptionally high exchange rates, often twenty-five percent more than the legal rate. They are friendly and disarming.

"How much do you want to change, *chef?*" one of the sharks will ask.

"Fifty dollars," you respond. Dreaming of the killing you are about to make, you would like to change more, but caution prevails.

"Why not a hundred?" the shark responds. His friends join in with encouragement waving rolls of bills in your face. Their attitude suggests they are big time dealers and $50 is not worth

WORLD CLASS SCAMS

275

their effort.

This is the first tip off. A legitimate money changer — and there are many who are content to operate on a two or three point margin — will accept whatever you offer. A shark will induce you to double or triple the figure. He isn't after a profit, after all, but the kill.

"OK," you respond. "I'll go for a hundred."

"Let's see the money," one of the sharks says. He has counted out the equivalent in local currency and flashes it in your face.

You pull five twenty dollar bills out of your pocket. The shark takes the money and quickly sticks it into an envelope, all the while glancing about quickly as if he's nervous. This makes you nervous so you begin to look about, too, and lose your concentration. At the same time, one of his buddies slips the local currency into an envelope and seals it. This all happens simultaneously and within seconds.

When that voice in the back of your mind begins to question the envelopes, and why all the secrecy, you suddenly realize something is very wrong. In desperation you lunge for the envelope that contains your money, except now there are two envelopes and you're not sure which is yours.

At the instant you reach out, one of the sharks yells, "POLICE!" and everything comes unglued. The guy holding your money says something like, "The police, we've got to get the hell out of here," and starts to run. In the process, he throws down your envelope as if it's too hot to handle. In moments, the group has scattered. You're left standing alone. There are no police.

Confused, you pick up the envelope, tear it open and a wad of newspaper bills falls to the ground. Around you a few people snicker but avert their eyes when you look up. Never once did you detect the switching of envelopes.

The second scam, the bait and clip, was the one the Princess and I were about to experience.

We were sitting in the MOG with both side doors open. There were three sharks on my side, two on hers, trying to

276 THE LION IN THE MOON

squeeze into the door openings. Their shoulders were at the level of my lap. We had the strategic advantage of commanding the high ground.

"How much do you want to change?" one asked.

"What's the rate?" I responded.

"Three hundred," one said. "If you change one hundred, I give three hundred and ten."

I agreed to one hundred. He counted out a roll of CFA and held it out.

"Where is your money?" he asked.

"I want to see your money first," I said. I took his money and counted it. "Only 29,000 here. You owe me 2,000 more."

The man gave me a startled look. The sharks jabbered among themselves and produced the difference. I counted it again and held a few of the bills to the light checking on the water marks. Satisfied, I handed the bills to the Princess to count. When she finished, a shark on her side nonchalantly said:

"I need to give you some 5,000 notes. Too many small ones. I need the small money." He took the money from the Princess. This is when the switch would take place, after we had already decided the money was authentic and complete.

All of this was happening in a sea of confusion. The sharks were pushing and shoving, talking at once and waving their arms in the air. When the man retrieved the money, he shuffled some bills and wrapped the whole thing in a 5,000 note and held it out with the demand that it was time for me to turn over my money.

I reached across the Princess' lap and took the roll. "Just a moment," I said. "I want to count it again."

That set off a maelstrom of protest and confusion. One man shouted at me to produce my money. Another yelled I had already counted it three times. A third was climbing into the cab trying to grab the money from my hand. I twitched and turned and kept counting.

The sharks were climbing in both doors waving their hands in my face trying to interrupt my count. One man was practically sitting in my lap. I was so busy dodging their clutching

WORLD CLASS SCAMS

hands I finally gave up and handed the money back but not before I had determined there was not more than fifty dollars worth of CFA in the roll.

I started the engine.

"What about the money?" one of the sharks yelled as we drove off.

There are other scams that do not involve changing money. One that was exercised on me in East Africa some years ago involved refugees. I was approached by a nice looking young man on the streets of Nairobi asking if I were an American. When I responded positively, he lapsed into a long explanation of how he had relatives in New York City and he was dying to meet Americans to learn more about them.

"Could you spare a few moments for a cup of coffee?" he asked politely.

Not wanting to be too ugly of an American, I consented and followed him to a small coffee bar where we sat in a circular booth. Shortly after we ordered two of this friends appeared. They sat and ordered coffee. At this point I was boxed into the booth.

With the arrival of his friends, the conversation changed. They were both refugees from Uganda and were on their way to Tanzania to a boarding school but had run out of money and could go no further. Could I please help them?

They then plunged into a long explanation of how miserable life was in Uganda, how they could not go home, but how they couldn't stay in Kenya, either, because the police will pick them up and deport them back to Uganda where they will be put in prison for being politically active. They went on and on playing heavily on my sense of guilt about being white and having everything while they were black and had nothing. What help could I provide?

This was obviously a set up, or maybe it wasn't so obvious, as it had undoubtedly worked before. I asked how much help they needed and was told one hundred dollars would do very nicely, thank you. The request was followed by another heavy dose of guilt.

They did make me feel guilty and they did make me squirm. My greatest concern, however, at that point was how to extricate myself from the booth.

"I will be glad to help," I finally told them, "but I will need some proof of your identity and need. Do you have passports?"

"That is not possible," one of them said. "We are refugees. That's why the police will pick us up, because we have no papers."

I thought about that a moment. "At least I will need some proof that you are going to school and someone to vouch for your identity. Do you have a letter from the boarding school in Tanzania?"

"Yes, of course," they all nodded.

"Who will vouch that you are refugees?"

"My father," the first man said, the one who had gotten me into this.

We agreed to meet the next day at the same coffee bar. We all shook hands and parted. As the three walked away the waiter handed me the bill for the coffees. It was a small price for a bit of entertainment. I did not meet them the next day or see them again.

Several years later I read a small newspaper article about a similar scam being successfully pulled on an American journalist. He lost one hundred fifty dollars.

I felt a little smug.

Snapshot

VISITING A VOODOO PHARMACY

Our guide was riding on my lap in the front seat of the MOG.

"À gauche," or "À droit," he would command pointing a stubby finger out the window this way or that.

He was young — not more than twelve — and dressed in floppy sandals, a dark pair of worn shorts, and a dirty khaki shirt.

Kokou (every child born on a Wednesday in his tribe was called Kokou) was one of a horde of aggressive, street-smart kids we were constantly attracting. They offered us their services as guide, guardian of the MOG or general gopher. Usually we said no. But Kokou was different. With an engaging smile and a disarming line of chatter, we decided he might be of use after all.

"We want to go to the fetish market," I instructed our guide. "Can you take us there?"

Kokou's black face broke into a broad smile. "Of course. It is near here. We must go in your truck."

He directed us farther and farther out of the modern city of Lomé down potholed dirt roads and past miles of shantytowns. It had been raining and the road had been churned into a sea of axle-deep mud. Staefan drove most of the way in four-wheel drive.

"How far is it?" Staefan kept asking, to which Kokou would reply, "Not far, very near, keep going."

Finally we arrived at what was a horrific display of animal parts.

Wood tables and stalls were piled with skulls, bones and

The voodoo pharmacy offers a cure for most every disease.

unidentifiable objects. There were birds' beaks, lion and jaguar heads, alligator jaws and whole dried porcupines. Dogs' heads, obviously severed with a machete, were piled high. They still retained their fur and bulging eyes and their mouths were stretched back to show all their teeth. There were snakes as well, some long and coiled, others had only their heads remaining.

Long horsetails hung from a pole, slowly blowing in the wind; tortoise shells three feet wide were propped up against a shack; and stretched animal skins dried in the sun. I peeked into a woven basket and saw two live baby owls, their orange eyes blinking to purple, cowering in a corner. What were these for? To cure bad eyesight? They wouldn't live long. I was not liking this at all.

If you were a believer in voodoo, this was your pharmacy. There was something here to cure everything, if you had the faith.

An older man took us in tow. "Voodoo became popular," he explained, "because of the lack of hospitals. Since there were no doctors, the Africans invented the medicine man."

SNAPSHOT: VISITING A VOODOO PHARMACY 281

This is how it works: If you have an illness, you visit your family 'doctor.' He will read your horoscope, diagnose your problem and give you a prescription, which you take to the voodoo pharmacy – the fetish market. The prescription is not for a Western drug like Valium or Darvon, but for native medicine, like warthog teeth, bird's tail and dog's eyes.

To remedy a speech impediment, for example, the doctor might include a piece of parrot's beak in the patient's prescription. After the fetish market pharmacist fills the prescription, the ingredients are returned to the doctor who then prepares a secret concoction with the ground parrot's beak. When the patient drinks the medicine (or has it injected or applied topically) the doctor reinforces the healing process with secret incantations.

A doctor's reputation and standing in the community, as is generally true anywhere, depends upon his ability to cure his patients. The more he cures, the more word gets around and the more patients he attracts.

If the patient isn't cured it could be due to a number of factors: the patient lacked sufficient faith, the parrot's beak wasn't of sufficient strength, it was from the wrong variety of parrot, or the beak had lost its potency. In response, the doctor would vary the prescription until the patient was cured.

I was not willing to risk my life to find out if voodoo worked. Besides, I really didn't have any illnesses to complain of, not after seeing those piles of sacrificial animals.

I could use some good luck, however. Surely that would be safe.

Our older guide led us to a small hut where we carefully stepped over a cowrie shell into the office of Clement Avounzounton, *'explicateur des forces vodous Africains.'* Clement was the son of the village voodoo chief.

He was sitting in the corner in the dark. As my eyes adjusted to the blackness, I noticed he was about my age, or younger. He was seated on a small stool next to a large, carved wood head with large eyes and mouth. The hut was filled with masks and statues. Above our heads hung bunches of dried herbs. Staefan and I sat on a low wood bench across from him and waited.

Clement asked us, individually, for our names. As we repeated them, he rang a crude bell and chanted something to the statue. As if knowing exactly what we needed, he placed a fetish in each of our left hands.

"This is a telephone fetish," announced our guide, who also served as our interpreter. Clement spoke only the native dialect.

It was a cute, miniature figure of a man wrapped in cord with a small chisel-like piece of stick, the 'receiver,' hanging by a string. The instructions for its use were very specific:

"Hold the figure in your left hand with the receiver in the right," Clement instructed through the interpreter. "Whisper into the figure's mouth where you are traveling. Ask for protection, then push the receiver into the figure's mouth. Carry it with you and you will be protected against all accidents."

Apparently, Togo's President Eyedama was carrying one of these telephone fetishes when his plane crashed several years earlier. Eyedama emerged unscathed, while others died (presumably, according to our guide, because they were not carrying their fetishes). If it worked for the president, our guide suggested, it would certainly work for us.

Our voodoo master continued: "This is a personal fetish to protect you against poison by food or drink."

It was a small leather pouch ornamented with two cowrie shells at the end of a cord. Cowrie shells were the ancient form of money in Africa and are now used as rich ornamentation. Inside each pouch was a melange of various dried herbs from the branches above our heads. I could not make out what they were in the dark.

Clement put a necklace over each of our heads as he explained their power. People were often being poisoned and this would protect us. "You do not have to be afraid of any food," he added.

He seemed pretty sure of himself. I guessed food poisoning was a major problem in the tropics where refrigeration was

SNAPSHOT: VISITING A VOODOO PHARMACY 283

nonexistent. This seemed a little medieval to me, but if it would work on a bad oyster I was all for it.

A funny feeling crept over me. My body began to relax. I felt content and unusually happy. I wondered if Staefan felt the same. I glanced his way but couldn't tell in the low light. What would account for this feeling? Burning incense or something more devilish? I detected nothing. But something was going on. We continued.

The next fetish was a beautiful ebony seed, shiny black and smooth, a little larger than a silver dollar. But no, this was not a fetish.

"The ebony seed is very powerful in itself," Clement told us. "It is for memory and intelligence. Put it under your pillow when you sleep. On waking, take the seed in your left hand and rub it across the forehead, from right to left, three times. Rub it once down the middle of the forehead, from top to bottom. Then return it to under the pillow."

Clement asked if we were married. Just as I was about to shake my head no, Staefan nodded his head yes. Clement placed a small fetish of two twigs bound to a larger one in my left palm and placed Staefan's hand over mine.

"This fetish is man and woman bound together, united, with only death able to separate them," we were told.

Joan of Arc bound at the stake, I thought to myself.

He continued the bell ringing and chanting and the interpreter told us this was to ensure a good marriage: no divorce.

"Rub the fetish with your fragrance," I was instructed, "then rub it in your palm and whisper the name of your spouse three times." I am to carry it with me always.

I was still floating on some high and enjoying myself immensely.

Clement handed Staefan a stick. I couldn't wait to hear this story. Our interpreter began:

"This is an aphrodisiac for men," he said. "Peel back the bark and it will emit a fragrance. Cut the stick into small pieces, soak them in water for forty-eight hours. Drink a little of the liquid about six in the evening and it will give you 'the force.' It

284 THE LION IN THE MOON

will recharge the batteries," our guide explained further, just in case we didn't understand. This, I thought, is the best one yet. Staefan seemed unimpressed.

The interpreter, sensing disbelief, swore to Staefan it worked "very, very well." He looked to me for support. I told him Staefan didn't need it. He interpreted this to Clement and they both laughed, elbowing each other. They put the stick aside.

Clement handed me a doll, but not a soft doll to stick pins in and hurt other people. This doll was about seven inches tall and crudely carved from a stick of wood, dressed in body-hugging burlap grossly stitched onto her body and bejeweled in seeds and cowrie shells. Her hair, which once belonged to a horse, was nailed onto her forehead.

I thought the doll unique. She was supposed to bring me good fortune and luck.

The last fetish looked like a snowman with two white feathers stuck in his head. This was to protect the home from evil spirits. When I leave the house, I am to light a cigarette and put it in the snowman's mouth. When I protested I did not smoke, Clement suggested incense would work just as well.

The pile of fetishes had grown quite large. It suddenly occurred to me these were not gifts. Sure enough, the inter-preter asked us which of these fetishes we wanted. I already knew I wanted all of mine.

Staefan, who had kept his head, asked, "How much?"

"For a small price, a very small price," the intrepreter answered.

Clement proceeded to bless my pile of fetishes and me, ringing the bell again and chanting in front of the big head. I am asked to repeat, "I take this in my hand," then was told to touch the floor three times. I was beginning to feel a little silly. He does the same with Staefan.

With great solemnity, Clement announced the price, "12,000 CFA," as if it were divinely sent.

Staefan handed his pile of fetishes back. "That's almost $40," he told me.

"No, no," they protested. "You can't give back good luck.

SNAPSHOT: VISITING A VOODOO PHARMACY

285

Your spirit is in the fetishes. They are only good for you. They will not work for anybody else. If you do no take them we will have to destroy them."

Staefan capitulated and agreed to keep several of the fetishes and paid 5,000 CFA, about twenty dollars.

"It's not good to dispute too much over it," our interpreter explained, taking the money. "They are small, but very powerful."

After we touched the floor again, we walked out into the bright light and back to the MOG. I was coming down from either a real or perceived high. Staefan said he felt nothing. I looked at the crude fetishes in my lap and felt as if I had just played a game of 'Simon Says.' Didn't I just touch the floor when I was told and wasn't I conned into spending $20 for a pile of wood, or did I really believe these things would work?

That night my voodoo doll slept in my sleeping bag. I wore the poison necklace at all times, put the phone fetish in my backpack and slipped the stone under my pillow, though I was careful not to let anyone see me cross my head with it in the mornings.

When we left Lomé a few days later on our return to Paris, the security guard at the airport pulled my voodoo doll from her resting place in the top of the knapsack and demanded, "What is that?"

I explained it was for good luck. He twisted his face, incredulously shook his head, and put her back where he found her. I looked at her again on the plane and realized how crude she was. But I didn't care what others thought. After all, she had my spirits in her, not theirs.

One day, several weeks later, I could not find the marriage fetish. It was gone. I looked through everything — in boxes, behind the desk, behind books in the shelves. It was nowhere.

I had rubbed it with fragrance, as I had been instructed, whispered Staefan's name in it and carried it with me. But we were not married. Somehow, that stone face in Clement's tiny hut in Togo knew we had lied and had called the fetish back. My spirits were escaping back to Africa.

23

GOODBYE WITH REGRETS

We returned from a lengthy taxi excursion to Lomé to find a man sitting beside the MOG waiting for us.

He had been there all day, he explained. He was an agent for a plantation owner from Ghana who wanted to buy our truck. Was it for sale?

I affirmed it was, for the right price. Now that our plane reservations were set the next hurdle was disposing of the MOG. If this man were serious it would save shipping the truck home.

After some discussion we reached an agreement on the price including the agent's commission. He would go to Ghana — it was only ten miles to the border — wrap up the sale and return in two days. In the meantime, could I loan him a little money for bus fare to the border? It could be subtracted from his commission, of course. Reluctantly, I gave him a couple of bucks.

The next day I made arrangements with a Togolaise shipper to transport the MOG to Houston. I had little confidence it would be sold, even though the agent reappeared to assure me the sale was certain. The plantation owner was gathering the money. What did I prefer, dollars, francs or CFA?

In Africa, nothing is certain.

A common ploy in the used car business, particularly when it involves foreigners, is for an African buyer to agree upon a price very near that which the seller is asking. In the meantime, the buyer learns the seller's time table, travel plans, the last day the transaction can be consummated and if other offers are pending.

GOODBYE WITH REGRETS

Believing the sale certain, the seller, typically, relaxes and refuses other possible offers. At the appointed time the buyer shows up with a long face and an even longer explanation. He still wants the car, but due to events beyond his control (medical bills or the bank wouldn't loan the money) he cannot offer the full price. He is terribly sorry.

What is the seller to do? He is flying to Europe the next morning. There is no time to negotiate with someone else. Either he sells the car, abandons it, or cancels his flight and begins the process again. Often the car is sacrificed for fifty or sixty cents on the dollar. I was determined not to fall into this trap.

Our few remaining days drifted by to the sound of pounding surf and a stiff unrelenting ocean breeze. The morning we were to leave I arose early to watch the sun rise over the ocean, my last in Africa. After breakfast I began the task of cleaning out our kitchen segregating what was partially used or unusable from what we could take home.

I set a cardboard box in the sand and began to toss — a bag of shriveled vegetables, one used bar of soap, several potatoes with mold, an unopened three-pound summer sausage we had brought from Dallas, which was now showing signs of internal stress, a half jar of peanut butter — all went into the box at my feet.

Immediately, several of the Togolaise who worked at the camp surrounded the box in a mad, almost desperate scramble for our rejects. The wilted veggies, moldy potatoes and rancid sausage would be someone's dinner.

I was stunned. The laughter that filled these people never betrayed their plight. Happiness and material well being are not necessarily bedfellows.

Word spread quickly we were leaving. The crowd grew. What did we want to sell? I remembered our experience in Niamey. I couldn't hope to sell anything for replacement cost; it was above their means. An $18 butane lamp went for ten; $5 water jugs for a dollar; T-shirts for a dollar each; small items like pens, we gave away. Soon the MOG was bare.

All the while I had my eyes open for Lawson and his sister, Heléne. She had approached us on the beach a few days earlier

THE LION IN THE MOON

offering to tailor African shirts for us.

"I know what Americans like," she announced. "*Les chemises* must be big." We placed an order for two shirts. The next day she showed up with swatches of material for us to choose what we liked.

"Could she make a dozen shirts?" I asked.

"Of course," she replied. "We make shirts for people in France."

"I need them in five days."

"No problem. I will deliver them the day before you leave."

That evening her younger brother, Lawson, showed up. He wanted to check on this scheme and to collect some money. He would need capital to buy the material, he told us. I gave him an advance.

"I will deliver the shirts here on the morning you leave," he stated, delaying the time table by twenty-four hours. "If something happens and that is impossible, I will deliver them to the airport."

The MOG had been cleaned out. We were packed and still no Lawson. Our flight left at two that afternoon. There was still hope he would meet us at the airport.

The buyer for the MOG hadn't shown up either. No surprise there.

At noon we delivered the truck to the freight agent and took a taxi to the airport. I was wearing nylon sunglasses with fluorescent pink temples. The cab driver lusted after them. When we reached the airport I paid him and tossed the glasses into the front seat as a tip. He giggled delight and drove off with a smile so wide it cracked his face.

We checked our luggage and stalled in front of immigration. Once we entered the maze of procedures we would never see Lawson even if he appeared. We waited until the last minute. No Lawson.

The Air Afrique flight to Abidjan was plush. Classical music was piped through the cabin. I sat back, breathed deeply and opened the complimentary bottle of French Bordeaux. The shadowy coastline of West Africa slipped beneath the wing. I

GOODBYE WITH REGRETS

closed my eyes. The Princess and I were in the lap of luxury but my thoughts were miles away in the dunes of the Sahara. Would I ever see them again?

It had been a phenomenal trip. The Princess had been a wonderful companion. She had handled even the most trying of circumstances with poise and humor. My fears of a few months earlier, that she might crack under the strain, or worse, that our styles would prove hopelessly at odds, had proved unfounded. She was a jewel.

Several weeks later, a small bundle arrived at the post office in Santa Fe. In it were twelve shirts and a penned note:

Dear Staefan and Babs: I could not meet you at the airport. The shirts were not ready. It was God's will.

Snapshot

THE LION IN THE MOON

I didn't realize then that we were living the adventure. After all, as Emerson wrote, "No one suspects the days to be gods."

We traveled across vast Saharan sands by day, broke bread with whatever interesting stranger we might meet, and slept with the stars above us not knowing what tomorrow might bring.

We shared *puli puli* beneath a fat yellow moon, sipped *pression* in village bars while playing *woaley* with the locals, and finally sunk our toes in the sapphire waters of the Bay of Benin where dark-skinned tropical girls gathered at our feet like docile sea lions, stroking our skin and begging us to buy pineapple and coconuts from baskets that had been balanced on their heads. Living the exotic daily, it became the norm and ordinary.

"Nothing prepares you for Africa," Staefan had told me months ago in Dallas. "Nothing."

I thought he was overplaying the scene. The Fulbright scholar who had lived in Cameroon for a year was stretching out a melodramatic carpet onto which the young ingenue was to dutifully set foot, thus embarking on her first real adventure.

Yet my decision to disappear into a Third World country with a blue-eyed stranger had been entirely visceral. There was, if not a *coup de foudre*, an immediate symbiosis between us. Staefan would turn out to be the adventurer I had imagined, but with a sensitive soul and quick wit that surprised and captivated me. Two months wandering in Africa was an acid test of any relationship, and he had passed with flying colors. I need not

SNAPSHOT: THE LION IN THE MOON 291

have feared; we had remained friends.

"You must have romantic notions of Africa, everyone does," he persisted. "You'll be disappointed." But I wasn't. When I told him later that I didn't think I would like it as much as I did, he asked me, "Then why did you come?"

Why was I drawn to Africa and why is it I cannot get her out of my mind?

In my dreams, I fall back into her cool black arms. The Sahara surrounds me with her cloak of silence, my naked body brushes against her silken sand dunes and I am lulled to sleep beneath a twinkling sky, the constellations now familiar friends.

My mind wanders back to the mysterious oases where life is hidden behind walls and veils and the wailing call to prayer is as lonely and hypnotic as the howling of a coyote in the New Mexican desert. I remember the mix of childlike innocence and wisdom in the people and long to return to their simpler, albeit difficult, way of life.

Two months spent wandering Africa had freed my soul and the life of a nomad had crept oh-so-easily into my blood. Standing in the blazing moonlight of the desert, I felt rescued from the quicksand of a former existence.

It was the mirage of the mysterious Arab cloaked in black who had saved me.

Disrupting my dreams in the Sahara, he forced me to face my fears of the unknown that, once confronted, dissolved like sand sliding through my fingers.

I examined my life and saw I could cut a path of my own choosing, just as we had made our own tracks across the desert. It was as simple an epiphany as that, yet it would eventually change the way I chose to live my life. When I had finally accepted the magnitude of his message, the Arab in black disappeared from my dreams.

How could I leave this passionate, unpredictable life of *La Bonne Nomad* to return to what Henry Miller described as "the air-conditioned nightmare" back home where man and nature are so completely divorced from each other? And how does one jump off the boring treadmill to nowhere and into a life of passion?

THE LION IN THE MOON

In Ouagadougou one evening there was a crowd parading through the dusty streets. They were making lots of noise, banging tin pans, playing drums and shouting, anything that would make a racket. I ran out into the street to watch but could not figure out what they were doing.

An old man was leaning against a wall. "They are chasing out the lion," he explained.

"A lion!" I exclaimed, fearfully looking out into the darkness.

"No, no," he laughed, pointing toward the night sky. "The lion is in the moon."

I looked up and sure enough, there he was. A full white globe with a golden lion's face creeping across it. The longer the noise continued, the less of the lion's face I could see. It was working. They were indeed chasing him away.

"The lion is bad," explained the old man. "You have to chase him away."

Back home in Dallas, the lion of my monotonous existence reappeared at my door. I am sure the Arab in black sent him as a reminder to follow my passion. It was time to make some noise and chase the lion from my moon.

Within months I would quit my job, move to the New Mexican desert, marry my adventurer and carve a new direction for my career.

Postscript

As this book goes to press the environment along our route has become considerably more unstable. Muslim fundamentalism is on the rise in Algeria posing a threat to Western tourists; political instability in Nigér and Burkina Faso make travel an uncertain proposition and pro-democracy forces are battling it out with the government in the streets of Lomé, Togo.

Those who wish to follow our route through the Sahara, however, need only wait a year or two for the next cyle of passivity. Keep in mind that turbulence in Africa is nothing new. In some respects it is the only constant.

Or, as the French might say, the more Africa changes, the more it stays the same.

The trick to adventure travel is to carefully consider the odds and then go anyway.

If you have doubts about any country, you might call the State Department's Citizen's Emergency Center Hotline at (202) 647-5225. But remember, these people are paid to be conservative.

S&B

Babs was born in Texas in 1956. She attended Chatham Hall preparatory and graduated from Hollins College of Virginia in 1978 with degrees in Art History and French. Shortly thereafter, she returned to Paris, France, to work in the showroom of designer Louis Feraud and to attend *L'Academie du Vin*. She has devoted the last ten years to writing about her favorites: food, wine and travel, for newspapers and national magazines. She currently writes and lives in the shadow of the Ortiz Mountains south of Santa Fe with her husband, Staefan.

Staefan was born in Oregon in 1943, moved to Hawaii at age seven, traveled the Orient after high school and minutes after graduating from Stanford, boarded a Greyhound bus for the east coast with fifty dollars in his pocket and never looked back. To date he has passed through nearly seventy-five countries and lived in several including Taiwan, Libya and Cameroon, where he was a Fulbright Lecturer in mass media. Along the way, he received a doctorate from the University of Texas and has taught at several universities. He is the father of three grown boys and currently resides in Santa Fe with his charming princess.

THE LION IN THE MOON

For additional copies of *The Lion in the Moon,* telephone TOLL-FREE 1-800-356-9315 or FAX TOLL FREE 1-800-242-0036, Master Card/VISA accepted.

To order *The Lion in the Moon* directly from the publisher, send your check or money order for $19.95 plus $3.50 shipping and handling ($23.45 postpaid) to: Rainbow Books, Inc., Order Dept. 1-T, P. O. Box 430, Highland City, FL 33846-0430.

For QUANTITY PURCHASES, telephone Rainbow Books, Inc., (813) 648-4420 or write to Rainbow Books, Inc., P. O. Box 430, Highland City, FL 33846-0430.